Choice-Free Rationality

Choice-Free Rationality
A Positive Theory of Political Behavior

Robert Grafstein

Ann Arbor

THE UNIVERSITY OF MICHIGAN PRESS

Copyright © by the University of Michigan 1999
All rights reserved
Published in the United States of America by
The University of Michigan Press
Manufactured in the United States of America
♾ Printed on acid-free paper

2002   2001   2000   1999   4   3   2   1

A CIP catalog record for this book is available from the British Library.

Library of Congress Cataloging-in-Publication Data

Grafstein, Robert, 1948–
    Choice-free rationality : a positive theory of political behavior
  / Robert Grafstein.
       p.   cm.
    Includes bibliographical references and index.
    ISBN 0-472-11054-3 (alk. paper)
    1. Rational choice theory.   I. Title.
  HM495.G73   1999
  301′.01—dc21   99-36970
                                                          CIP

To Joan, Michael, and Stephanie

Contents

Figures

Preface

Rational choice theorists have a lot of explaining to do. Among the important patterns of behavior that have resisted a satisfactory rational choice analysis are turnout in mass democratic elections; the uncoerced provision of public goods generally; the importance of ethnic identity in political mobilization; certain varieties of altruism; retaliation and other retrospective behavior; the struggle by putatively rational leaders and citizens alike—sometimes successful and sometimes unsuccessful—to resist temptation in favor of long-term rewards; and the apparently irrational phenomenon of framing effects, including the impact on elections of the way issues are ideologically described. This book addresses these problems using formal and informal models reflecting Richard Jeffrey's (1983) definition of rationality as the maximization of expected utility conditional on the act of the agent.

In an uncertain world, rational agents cannot simply maximize the utility associated with the outcomes of interest to them. They must factor in the likelihood that those outcomes will occur. According to the standard definition of rationality, which characterizes individuals as maximizing their expected utility, a rational agent recognizes this uncertainty by multiplying each outcome's utility by the probability his action will bring it about. According to Jeffrey's alternative hypothesis, which characterizes individuals as maximizing their *conditional* expected utility, a rational agent multiplies each outcome's utility by its probability given her action.

At first sight, the difference between the two formulations may seem innocuous, even obscure. Nevertheless I show through formal and informal examples that Jeffrey's innovation dramatically improves rational choice theory's ability to explain important political and social phenomena. To take one example that will prove crucial later, conditional expected utility maximization can explain turnout in mass elections. Mass turnout has been an embarrassing, even notorious, puzzle for the standard approach. The gain in explanatory power, then, is impressive. Faced with the phenomena listed previously, by contrast, expected utility theory finds itself alternately contorted to fit the ad hoc demands of the problem or simply stymied.

If relatively small technical changes generate such large empirical gains, it is reasonable to ask, why is expected utility theory dominant? One reason is that the applications outlined in the preceding have not been fully developed until now. Another more important answer is that advocates of the standard theory deny that conditional expected utility maximization is rational. In fact, some argue, it constitutes almost willful self-delusion. Conditional expected utility maximizers are alleged to mistake statistical relations between their actions and outcomes for the causal relations that determine the real impact of their decisions. They thereby inflate their estimate of the true consequences of their acts, which they may then undertake despite the negligible impact these acts really have. Anyone who votes instrumentally in a mass election in order to maximize conditional expected utility is alleged to be guilty of this mistake. For conditional expected utility maximizers are willing to vote even though they stand a very small chance of altering the outcome. Genuinely rational agents, by contrast, avoid this trap by assessing only what their actions are likely to cause. True, every election year millions seem to defy this analysis, whereas conditional expected utility theory is apparently able to explain their behavior. But the explanation, say critics, is illusory. Conditional expected utility theory has, in Bertrand Russell's phrase, all the advantages of theft over honest toil.

To its challengers, conditional expected utility maximization is a fallacy parading as a decision theory. Yet, I shall argue, this customary dismissal misses the point, unfortunately a very important point. When the logic of conditional expected utility theory is followed to the end, which I believe even its proponents have not done, the issue of causation begins to look like a red herring. What actually distinguishes the two versions of utility theory is their treatment of those particular reputedly causal forces, choice and free will. Conditional expected utility theory's deviation from expected utility theory reflects a profound disagreement over the role of human choice in scientific explanation.

As we shall see, for their criticisms to make sense, expected utility theorists must believe that each rational agent freely chooses and determines his actions. Since he determines the act he winds up choosing, it cannot possibly help him decide what to do, even when it conveys otherwise important information about the behavior of other decision makers, be they voters, fellow members of an ethnic group, or simply individuals with whom he shares an interest in bowling. Because he is metaphysically free, an expected utility maximizer can ignore important statistical truths characterizing his own behavior's relation to the behavior of other individuals. Standing outside the statistical association between his choices and the acts of others, he can choose how best to exploit the causal impact of his acts without regard for their statistical implications.

In short, however scientific its aspirations, expected utility theory ultimately appeals to free choice itself as an explanatory variable. It maintains its plausibility by exempting agents from the statistical relations in which their behavior is embedded. But it can do so only by paying what I regard as inappropriate homage to the prescientific glory of human beings acting as free agents. Thus standard rational choice theory is metaphysical in the pejorative sense of the term.

Conditional expected utility theorists recognize no such detached vantage point for the decision maker. A conditional expected utility maximizer directly conditions on her acts because the information they convey is as valid for her as it is for anyone else. A concrete individual embedded in a concrete social and political environment, she is not free to transcend the implications of her behavior. To conditional expected utility theory, then, human actors are fully part of the world in which they act.

Perhaps a brief elaboration of the voting example will help. Suppose we are observing someone at the start of an election in a closely contested race. Our vantage point is essentially hers: we do not yet know what she will do, nor do we know what other potential voters will do. We do know, however, that the supporters of her favorite candidate are remarkably homogeneous and that she is as representative of those supporters as representative supporters get. Her actions, then, are good indicators of the behavior of others in her group. In particular, if we learn that she will vote we will be more inclined to predict the success of her candidate even though her own contribution to the total vote is minor. Put another way, if we chart the possible worlds in which she votes and her favored candidate wins and the possible worlds in which she abstains and her candidate wins, we find a substantial and positive difference in their relative likelihood. Of course, there is a fact of the matter as to what world she is in; however no one at the time of her decision has this information.

Conditional expected utility theory treats this decision maker as rational when, given the information she has, her behavior places her in those possible worlds having a higher chance of being favorable to her. Other things being equal, rational individuals are more likely to be successful. Expected utility theory, on the other hand, ultimately suggests that the observable probabilities of her success do not determine what decision is really rational for her. Somehow she is free to consider her own vote's contribution to the candidate without considering what we as observers see and factor into our calculations about her vote, namely, the likelihood of alternative levels of aggregate support associated with her alternative choices. She is not constrained by the stochastic facts governing her situation. Conditional expected utility theorists find such an assumption about her freedom bizarre.

To some, I realize, this brief defense of the conditional expected utility approach will look like a desperate philosophical diversion. Yet the shoe is really on the other foot: due to the metaphysical baggage they introduce into their analysis, expected utility theorists ignore legitimate and, in many ways, formally cleaner solutions to empirical problems in political science. Instead, they insist on the power of the agent to transcend statistically relevant features of his own behavior. In allowing this, these theorists accord the agent a power called free will whose existence would necessitate a fundamental revision of those sciences currently providing our inventory of the universe's forces. This is an odd denouement for an approach priding itself on being the hardest of hardheaded social science.

The main object of this book, again, is to confront certain unresolved empirical problems in social science based on a systematic application of conditional expected utility theory. The first chapter develops and defends the theory in relatively abstract terms. The second through fourth chapters defend it in a more scientifically direct way, by applying it respectively to ethnic identity and mobilization, ideology, and altruism and intertemporal choice. The fifth chapter focuses on policy analysis and methodological debates in econometrics. It shows how microquestions about the role of free will in rational decision making reappear as much larger questions concerning the normative role of rational choice theory, a role that assumes that the recipients of rational advice are free to take it. We will concentrate on the prospects for useful macroeconomic policy analysis. The fifth chapter also addresses the analysis of cooperation as a foundation for parliamentary institutions. Using these illustrations, this chapter shows how solutions to quandaries arising independently of conditional expected utility theory nonetheless are informed by and reinforce its assumptions. Finally, the concluding chapter addresses some of the findings of experimental psychology most troubling to rational choice theory. In all, we shall see that the notion of choice-free rationality has a number of important empirical ramifications.

In developing the idea of choice-free rationality I have had help from a number of individuals, including anonymous referees for various publications. The onymous commentators on earlier written and oral versions of what became parts of this book include Scott Ainsworth, William Bianco, James Coleman, Shrikant Dash, David Freeman, John Freeman, George Graham, Kevin Hoover, Richard Jeffrey, William Keech, George Klosko, George Krause, Kristen Monroe, Michael Munger, Joe Oppenheimer, Giovanni Sartori, Karol Sołtan, and Christopher Wlezien. As for any remaining errors, I have only myself to blame. Munger generously volunteered an advance copy of his and Melvin Hinich's then forthcoming book on ideology. To conclude with a final expression of gratitude, my family continues to test my dismissal of the prescientific glory of humanity.

Introduction

The temptation to anthropomorphize is, fortunately, at a historic low. Rain, sunshine, lightning, and tornadoes are no longer attributed to purposeful gods and spirits lurking behind or inside these ordinary physical phenomena. Science has succeeded in removing choice and free will from nearly all the machinery of the universe. In the future, cognitive psychology, allied with computer science, may complete this mission where anthropomorphizing first started, in our heads. When this happens, it will be unreasonable to anthropomorphize even human beings.

In the meantime, science must proceed despite its uncertainty about how much of anthropomorphism will ultimately survive. This book rests on the assumption that, given the history of science, anthropomorphism is a bad bet and therefore it constitutes a mistake even in the study of politics, humanity's apparently most self-conscious form of purposeful and controlled social interaction. Human behavior is behavior. It is the immediate consequence of what goes on inside the brain, not an expression of a special will or free choice executed by a distinct entity, a human self, that happens to have a brain. Politics, similarly, is not the expression of a hidden spiritual world lodged somewhere within human actors.

The agent traditionally conceived—the agent who appears in standard rational choice theory and, in particular, expected utility theory—not only believes and desires but as a decision maker is the source of his beliefs and desires. He is the source, a careful examination of the standard theory will show, because he is assumed to have the special capacity to cause himself to believe, prefer, deliberate, decide, and act. Hence when the individual's behavior is explained in terms of *his* beliefs and desires, this pronoun marks a distinct cause of what the organism embodying those psychological states does. The subject somehow acts on both its biological inheritance and its environment.

Political science is better off without positing this free-willed subject. Here I propose to avoid it by populating political models with individuals who maximize their conditional expected utility. There are other, considerably more ambitious strategies—an approach rooted in biology comes to mind—but the rational choice alternative is much less speculative. Ultimately, of course, the proof of the conditional expected utility hypothesis is in its applications, a number of which will be presented in this book. Yet a full defense also requires us to recognize its more profound and controversial ramifications. For as I noted in the preface, critics of this approach charge that these applications suborn irrationality. In focusing on the outcomes their acts statistically portend and not what they cause, the criticism goes, maximizers of conditional expected utility are being fooled in various ways avoided by successful students of introductory statistics. This criticism is my main reason for briefly delving in chapter 1 into the philosophical ramifications of rationality. It is only at this level that one can see the deep and, I think, important motivation for models assuming conditional expected utility maximization.

I

Although we will be exploring the definition of conditional expected utility maximization at length, in brief an agent who is rational according to this definition acts in such a way that her expected utility, conditional on her act, is as large as it can be. This means that the utility associated with each of the outcomes consistent with her acting a particular way is multiplied by its probability of occurring given the act. The conditional expected utility of an act, in turn, is the sum of each of these outcome-times-probability multiplications. The rational agent's act is the one associated with the highest such sum. Formally, given a set of actions $\{A_1, A_2, \ldots, A_k, \ldots, A_n\}$ the rational act A_k is the one for which $\sum_j U(O_j)\text{prob}(O_j \mid A_k)$ is maximized, where $\text{prob}(O_j \mid A_k)$ is the probability of outcome j conditional on action A_k.

Consider the important case of voting in mass elections. In deciding whether to vote, a conditional expected utility maximizer will compare the likelihood of a victory for her preferred candidate given her own participation with the likelihood of a victory given her abstention. When there is statistical dependence between the agent's decision and the decisions of others, we will see, this probability difference multiplied by the net utility of victory can be sufficiently large to motivate the agent to vote even though voting is costly.

Thus suppose that Sally Smith's preferred candidate in a presidential election will lose unless he receives a majority of the vote and that, in her mind, his election is worth $20,000 compared to his opponent's $10,000. For the purpose of this example, we will say that, given Smith's decision to vote, the probability her candidate wins—the probability that at least 50 percent of the voting public plus 1 votes for him—is .55 and the probability he loses is .45. Given her decision to abstain, by contrast, the probability her candidate wins reduces to .51 and his complementary probability of losing increases to .49. Not that Smith's single vote changes the probabilities so dramatically. Rather, given certain racial, ethnic, or gender characteristics she shares with others, her own decision to vote or abstain provides additional information about the likelihood other supporters of her candidate will do the same. This, after all, is the kind of calculation made by virtually any quantitative voting study. Now if Sally Smith acts by maximizing her conditional expected utility, she chooses between the two possible acts—voting and abstaining—according to the following rule (equating money with utility to simplify the example). First, for voting, multiply the conditional probability of her candidate's winning given her vote by the utility she gains from his election (i.e., .55 × 20,000) and to that term add the conditional probability of her candidate's losing multiplied by the utility his loss represents (i.e., .45 × 10,000): .55 × 20,000 + .45 × 10,000 = 15,500. This is the conditional expected utility of voting. Second, similarly calculate the conditional expected utility of abstaining: .51 × 20,000 + .49 × 10,000 = 15,100. Therefore, Sally votes so long as the increase in conditional expected utility associated with voting (15,500 − 15,100 = 400) exceeds the cost of voting, that is, so long as the cost is less than $400. This is not a particularly difficult standard to meet. In all likelihood, Sally Smith votes.

According to the standard definition of rationality, most notably associated with Leonard Savage (1972), agents maximize their expected utility unconditionally. Formally, agents choose the action maximizing $\sum_j U(O_j)\mathrm{prob}(O_j)$, where j indexes the possible outcomes O_j of the agent's action. An agent, on this view, is not concerned with the conditional probability of outcomes since (1) his acts occur against a background of possible states of the world that are defined to be causally independent of his acts and (2) he knows what outcomes his acts would produce in each of those possible states. It is easy to see that the standard analysis of the voter's decision to participate (e.g., Downs 1957) satisfies both these requirements. First, it assumes that since no individual affects how others vote, the aggregate vote produced by all others is independent of his own. Second, it assumes that for each possible aggregate a voter can determine what difference to the outcome, if any, his own participation would make.

Although each combination of action and state determines a unique action, Downsians still worry about the agent's expectations because the agent is uncertain about which state of the world obtains. Participation in mass elections is largely anonymous, so a voter can only guess about what other potential voters are doing. These guesses constitute the agent's beliefs about the likelihood that her vote will produce a victory for her preferred candidate or deny victory to an opponent. On the standard view, then, the agent's expectation reflects the likelihood that his act will cause or produce particular outcomes associated with different amounts of utility. In the case of mass elections, the likelihood of causing a difference in the outcome of the election is judged to be much too small to motivate an instrumentally rational voter to participate.

To see how this conclusion is reached using our numerical example, let us convert Sally Smith into an expected utility maximizer. Since she is now interested in the causal impact of her acts, the political outcomes of interest to her are no longer winning and losing per se but the case in which she causes her candidate to win and the two cases in which she does not (her candidate wins without her and her candidate loses without her). The first outcome occurs only when Smith's vote breaks what would have been a tie between the candidates; otherwise, one of the latter two outcomes obtains. Thus Smith proceeds by first calculating the expected utility of voting: $[(\frac{1}{2})10^{-8} \times 20,000] + [.51(1 - (\frac{1}{2})10^{-8}) \times 20,000] + [.49(1 - (\frac{1}{2})10^{-8}) \times 10,000]$ where, abstracting from the electoral college, $(\frac{1}{2})10^{-8}$ reflects a typical estimate of the probability of a tie in a U.S. election (e.g., Chamberlain and Rothschild 1981), and in calculating the next two terms I have used as approximations probabilities from the preceding example. In this simple case, a vote by Smith in the event of a tie causes her candidate to win with probability 1, so the chance her candidate will win because of her vote is simply the unconditional probability of a tie. When there is not a tie, her vote has no causal impact, so her expected utility depends solely on the unconditional probabilities that her candidate will or will not get sufficient votes on his own. Next, Smith calculates the expected utility of abstaining. The rub here is that the probability of her causing a victory when there is a tie is zero, so when there is a tie she receives $(\frac{1}{2})10^{-8} \times 10,000$, while the other probabilities and utilities do not change. Therefore, the net difference in expected utility between voting and abstaining equals the difference between the first terms of Smith's two calculations: $[(\frac{1}{2})10^{-8} \times 20,000] - [(\frac{1}{2})10^{-8} \times 10,000] = \$0.00005$. Since Sally Smith's cost of voting is likely to be greater than this negligible sum, she will not vote. If her calculation is representative, roughly 100,000,000 votes in each U.S. presidential election go unexplained on this standard analysis.[1]

The case of voting presents us with a striking contrast. Conditional expected utility theory is consistent with positive turnout from an instrumentally rational electorate; expected utility theory is not. In this respect, expected utility theory fails to come to terms with reality. Yet many rational choice theorists have resisted the empirically sounder approach. They are not being stubborn or capricious. They have important reasons for their resistance. The argument for conditional expected utility theory must be equal to their defense.

II

One natural reaction to the preceding brief for conditional expected utility theory is that the supporting analysis underestimates Sally Smith's resources. Suppose her inclination to vote does indeed suggest an increased probability that others will vote. Knowing of this increase and convinced that her actual decision has no causal impact on the decisions of others, why does she fail to exploit her renewed confidence in the large turnout for her candidate by abstaining after all? In chapter 1, I will have much more to say in reply to this objection. For now, notice the underlying assumption that by her free choice Smith can detach herself from her statistical circumstances by electing to back off her original decision, leaving in place, so to speak, the (statistical) facts linking her behavior and the turnout of others. Apparently, she is not embedded in the world described by the original factual characterization of these statistical dependencies. Rather, she is in an autonomous position to exploit them at will.

By appealing to freedom of this sort, some might claim, expected utility theorists retain for humanity a shred of the dignity and autonomy that are increasingly under attack in this overly scientific world. A more cynical interpretation might be that expected utility theorists are in massive denial. For in order to appreciate the full implications of the voting example, I suggest, we must begin to see the hypothesis of conditional expected utility maximization as part of the larger, long-term project of applying social science to the species responsible for social science. A part of the world scientists study, human beings should not be invested with special powers of intervention associated with something called *choice* or *free will*. As forces in their own right, these are foreign to our scientific understanding of how the rest of the world operates. Their explanatory credentials, such as they are, come from metaphysics and theology, not any working science. Subsequent chapters will demonstrate that within political science, in any case, conditional expected utility theory's rejection of the free-choice assumption has important and specific implications for the structure of rational choice theory and its explanations of political behavior.

If free choice were merely a fifth wheel, gratuitous yet harmless, it would not represent an onerous burden, notwithstanding its continuing vulnerability to Occam's razor. In fact, a case could be made that humanistic conceptions of politics confer moral benefits on society as a whole by providing honorable and venerable standards to live by. But Noble Lies are still lies. Political science does best without them because anthropomorphism impairs our political scientific theories and distorts the standards political scientists apply when deciding whether to accept certain kinds of explanation.

It does so, moreover, in ways that are subtle and therefore difficult to detect. Rational choice theory, for example, prides itself on being science's leading representative in the social sciences. I think this pride is basically justified. Yet anthropomorphism has taken its toll even here. Just consider rational choice theory's persistent problems already noted, including the notorious problem of explaining turnout in mass democratic elections. Faced with this and other puzzles, standard rational choice theory has in many respects inspired false solutions, underestimated legitimate solutions, and generated problems where none exist. The infamous Prisoner's Dilemma illustrates the first consequence. An appropriate model of this game, I will suggest in chapter 1, does not reduce each decision maker's physical participation in the game into an incidental feature of a purely mental calculation. I argue that an anthropomorphizing game theory does this, thereby misjudging the constraints the dilemma represents and, therefore, misjudging the ways individuals can avoid them.

The Prisoner's Dilemma also illustrates the second consequence. I will suggest a formal solution to some empirical realizations of the game based, paradoxically, on the fact that the decision maker *and* her decision making are, at the point of decision, unavoidably embedded in that dilemma. As in the case of turnout in elections, an anthropomorphizing game theory is inclined to dismiss this solution because decision makers modeled this way are not, by its lights, sufficiently detached from the game they are playing.

Turning to the third consequence, we will find other less well-known but captivating paradoxes that are generated by anthropomorphizing rational choice theory. The standard theory is particularly vulnerable to puzzles that arise when rational policymakers, faced with a rational public, seem to lose the possibility of choosing a policy at all. Fortunately, these puzzles vanish when basic questions about the nature of rational decision making are addressed.

Rational choice theory avoids these three consequences—false solutions, missed solutions, and artificial problems—when it avoids assigning choice itself—the free exercise of the subject's will—an explanatory role. It ought to avoid this if only to accept the ontological discipline of the natural sciences with which it must coexist. Supernatural solutions to particular social scientific problems may compliment humanity, but science cannot progress by flattery. To avoid conjuring up forces that other scientific disciplines neither recognize nor accommodate in their explanations, rational choice theory ought to be choice free.

Yet this book's primary interest, I should reemphasize, is not the connection between choice and rationality as a philosophical or conceptual issue. As interesting as this topic may be, I shall focus mainly on the choice-free principle as a basis for developing solutions to the outstanding problems in rational choice theory noted in the preface. Rationality as the maximization of conditional expected utility, I claim, is a useful tool for explaining important patterns of political behavior. Conditional expected utility maximization, in turn, is best understood in terms of the principle of choice-free rationality.

III

These considerations dictate the course of the book, whose first task is an examination and defense of the idea of choice-free rationality. Ultimately, this means showing that the formal technology associated with this form of rationality provides a useful instrument for predicting and explaining behavior. The main reason for preferring conditional expected utility maximization as a definition of rationality is thus pragmatic: it better answers the questions that need answering. One such question is indeed the puzzle of turnout. Initially, however, the case for choice-free rationality also means showing that the best defense of it implies a nonanthropomorphic conception of rational choice. Conditional expected utility theory conforms to the choice-free principle of rationality in a very deep and significant way.

The goal of chapter 1 therefore necessitates some delicate maneuvers, at least judged by the usual disciplinary markers. On the one hand, this chapter explicitly brings philosophical considerations to bear. On the other hand, the resulting analysis is designed to be a form of empirical political theory, not philosophy. It does not look to philosophy for solutions or outside inspiration. Rather, it uses behavioral implications to explicate and validate a particular version of rational choice theory. This calls for formal models, not philosophical role models.

It also calls for changing some of rational choice theory's basic assumptions. I have no interest in constructing new philosophical glosses on the old assumptions. The assumptions themselves must go, not just their interpretation. Nor am I interested in changing the standard theory's psychological vocabulary. The sole problem with the familiar psychological terminology is the false sense of intellectual security this familiarity encourages. In any case, short of inventing a new language to describe mechanisms just vaguely understood, the only serious option is to remain loyal to a language we all inherited. Rational choice theory needs a new structure, not a new dictionary.

From this perspective, the traditional notion of choice represents, for scientific purposes, not just a peculiar vocabulary but a damaging addition to the theory's belief-desire explanations: "The traditional picture of the human situation . . . has been one in which human beings are not simply networks of beliefs and desires but rather beings which *have* those beliefs and desires. The traditional view is that there is a core self which can look at, decide among, use and express itself by means of, such beliefs and desires" (Rorty 1989, 10). In the end, this traditional picture orients not only those traditional social thinkers and philosophers who celebrate humanity—the "oh no, they can't take that away from me" school—but also the formal, science-first rational choice theorists with whom they have often done battle.

So we need to distinguish the elimination of the choice-making subject from the elimination of the beliefs and desires with which the rational subject is usually associated. As Richard Rorty notes, an individual can be a network of beliefs and desires without becoming a supernatural entity that has them. Just because choice-free rationality declines to use choice as an explanatory variable does not mean it forfeits traditional psychology altogether. The taint of traditional metaphysics notwithstanding, the rational choice assumption is still the best means to understand politics, partly for reasons that are well known— its deductive apparatus and formal clarity to name two—and partly for reasons developed later.

The aim of chapter 1, then, is to initiate a fairly radical reorientation of rational choice theory's foundation without making major changes in its broader formal structure or terminology. I forgo the traditional notion of free choice but avoid a fully ascetic approach lacking even the terminology of choice itself. Those adopting the traditional standpoint are bound to be skeptical. They will tend to see conditional expected utility theory as abandoning rather than restructuring rational choice theory. Insofar as it displaces the self or knowing and willing subject as the cause of behavior, traditional modelers will argue, this theory fails to provide serious rational choice explanations.

Chapter 2 immediately harnesses the proposed definition of rationality to the explanation of certain types of political behavior associated with ethnic identity. Ethnicity is clearly an important topic in its own right. Two things make it especially relevant to our discussion. First, ethnic identity, as an especially potent form of group identity, also represents the intersection of forces influencing the individual's most personal sense of self and forces determining the social and political structure of society. Ethnicity, then, is at once a perfect example of the interaction of individual and society and, due to its highly personalized content, a standing challenge to a behaviorally oriented rational choice theory.

Second, the topic of ethnicity provides a useful launching pad for a more general consideration of the categorizations rational agents use to form their conditional expectations. Any two individuals, after all, are similar in some respects and different in others. In order to apply conditional expected utility theory, we need an account of why certain categorizations, such as ethnicity, are so important for individuals calculating the likely behavior of others. Psychologists critical of rational choice theory (e.g., Tversky and Kahneman 1987) have emphasized, moreover, that experimental subjects are highly sensitive to the way alternatives are characterized—the so-called framing effect— whereas expected utility theory requires individuals to be indifferent to these seemingly arbitrary differences of classification. Conditional expected utility theory's rationalization of ethnic classification, therefore, represents an important response to this widespread criticism. Class consciousness is also a potential influence on behavior. Chapter 2 uses conditional expected utility theory to explore the theoretical and empirical connection between class and ethnicity, a topic on which there has been considerable disagreement.

Chapter 3 further generalizes the analysis of categorization by examining ideology. Ideology is often associated with distorted thinking and the political manipulation of its adherents. For these reasons, ideologues represent a significant challenge to the rationality assumption. Yet ideology also denotes stable and conceptually integrated belief systems. In this respect, ironically, opinion survey data suggesting that the mass public is largely nonideological also present problems for the rationality assumption. Chapter 3 shows that this apparent paradox dissolves once we recognize that opinion formation takes place in a dynamic political-economic environment. This chapter, in particular, develops formal models, consistent with the ideological character of a rational public, explaining the apparent distortions in thinking induced by ideology, its manipulation by political elites, and the damning survey results that have put the coherence of the public's political beliefs in question.

Belief constitutes only one side of the rational choice coin; the other side is preference. Although rational choice theory usually assumes that preferences reflect the agent's self-interest, this is not an intrinsic feature of rationality, so long as self-interest is understood in the ordinary egoistic way. An agent can maximize the conditional expected utility of her children, her friends, unknown members of her religious group, spotted owls, or future generations. Expanding the agent's preferences to include these goals is not much of a technical challenge.

Still, preferences should not be imputed to individuals on a purely expedient, ad hoc basis unless those individuals are purely ad hoc in their dealings with the world. This is where the traditional self-interest assumption comes into its own. It has obvious and stable biological roots, and biology is an important influence on behavior, rational or irrational. Whatever the ultimate mix of altruistic and self-interested motives may be, survival without self-interest is an iffy proposition. Models of rational altruism (e.g., Becker 1976; Trivers 1971; Margolis 1984) understandably include a self-interest component. And some models, like Robert Frank's (1988), try to show how honesty, cooperation, retrospective calculation, and various emotions such as love, hatred, resentment of unfairness, and the desire for revenge can be explained exclusively in terms of the self-interest of the organism.

Chapter 4 demonstrates that the self-interested maximization of conditional expected utility addresses a number of the puzzles the altruism assumption and similar innovations are meant to solve. Conditional expected utility theory either obviates these modifications of the rationality postulate or fills in crucial gaps in the promising explanations these modifications motivate. It plays the same role with respect to leading accounts of what might be called internal altruism—the sacrifice of one's present benefits for one's long-term gains.

In sum, accounting for ethnic identity, the impact of ideology, and various forms of altruism is technically possible within conditional expected utility theory. It thereby meets a strategic challenge that threatens expected utility theory. Conditional expected utility theory, however, faces a tactical challenge of its own, since exhibiting its usefulness in a wide range of settings only intensifies the odd dilemma facing it. For whatever this theory's broader credentials, it is most likely to gain acceptance among rational choice theorists if it can prove its empirical worth by rationalizing the seemingly irrational. The resulting association with the irrational, however, threatens to undermine its status as a theory of rationality. Success arouses suspicions, while the alternative, failure, speaks for itself.

Chapter 5 is a final attempt to make readers comfortable with success. Rather than portraying conditional expected utility theory as an alternative to existing approaches, this chapter shows that the kind of thinking underlying the theory plays a role, although not by name, in recognized attempts to grapple with specific problems of social scientific explanation and political science. The chapter first examines the paradox of policy advice formally developed by Thomas Sargent and Neil Wallace (1981): while the rationality of policy advisors—their efficient linking of means and the policymaker's ends—seems an essential feature of good advice, the empirical assumption that the policymaker is rational seems to preclude a useful role for such advice. The reason, according to these two macroeconomists, is that the very rational choice model used to understand the impact of policymakers' decision making undermines their freedom to alter their behavior in light of normative advice from rational choice theorists. The problem of freedom, then, does not require a special philosophical training or sensibility. It arises within a rational choice analysis that recognizes the full consequences of its own logic. The logic of conditional expected utility theory, I argue, resolves this paradox.

This raises the question of what form of policy analysis, if any, conditional expected utility theory is capable of providing. As in the confrontation with expected utility theory, this question forces us to confront the notion of causation, in this case, a version called *Granger causality,* which is particularly important in policy analysis using time-series data. I show that controversies regarding this notion of causation already reflect key assumptions associated with conditional expected utility maximization. In short, the issue of causation is not just a microlevel topic in the debate between two versions of decision theory. It resurfaces in macrolevel battles over the possibility of policy advice and the proper way to conduct policy analysis.

Next, chapter 5 shows that George Tsebelis's (1990) comparative analysis of major European political systems likewise requires the intuitions of conditional expected utility maximization in order to survive basic game theoretic criticisms. In both of these cases, of course, skeptics may well respond that fallacious thinking is simply more widespread than is commonly thought. But the point of this chapter is not to rescue a case that the first four chapters somehow bungled. Rather, this chapter is a last-minute invitation to accept the proposed mode of thinking about rationality, with the assurance that others, unconsciously or not, have made contributions because in some sense they found it plausible. Not only does conditional expected utility theory work but, chapter 5 suggests, it is not even clear that our intuitions about the nature of proper theory and technique militate against it.

Chapter 6 does what final chapters often do. It summarizes and synthesizes the material preceding it. Nonetheless, while earlier chapters serve to distinguish conditional expected utility theory from expected utility theory, this chapter briefly shifts the focus by addressing certain core features of expected utility shared by most forms of rational choice theory. In some respects, these features can be defended outright. Yet there is a considerable body of experimental evidence against a number of expected utility theory's central assumptions. In this respect, the jury, at best, is still out.

Given the possibility of a negative verdict, chapter 6 explores the extent to which the fates of conditional expected utility theory and expected utility theory are entwined. We discover that conditional expected utility maximization is easily reconciled with many of the concerns that first prompted the development of a number of the alternatives to expected utility theory. Some of these approaches, for example, deny expected utility theory's assumption of consequentialism, which holds that only the consequences of a choice matter, not the path to them (see, e.g., Machina 1989). Consequentialism is not as restrictive an assumption for conditional expected utility theory since, as we have noted, conditional expected utility maximizers can learn from their own actions. Therefore, there is no reason to think that different behavioral histories will lead conditional expected utility maximizers to make identical current decisions, even when their current alternatives are formally equivalent. In conjunction with the analysis of intertemporal choice developed in chapter 4, this finding suggests that the conditional version of expected utility theory holds considerable promise in the face of otherwise disconcerting experimental findings.

CHAPTER 1

Rational Choice Inside Out

This book defines rationality as the maximization of conditional expected utility (hereafter, CEU) in place of the more standard definition of rationality as the maximization of expected utility (hereafter, EU). My aim in this chapter is to develop and justify this substitution. In what is easily the most philosophical part of the book, this chapter grapples with the fact that CEU theory ultimately views human beings as full-scale objects of scientific analysis, whereas EU theory must at least partially exempt them from that analysis. For EU theory, in particular, the distinction between the first-person perspective of the rational decision maker and the third-person perspective of the scientific observer is theoretically deep and fundamental. For CEU theory it is not. While the primary reason for substituting the assumption of CEU for EU maximization remains its power to account for behavior that EU theory finds difficult to explain, any attempt to motivate this substitution must confront more philosophical qualms.

The debate between EU and CEU theory is developed here as a debate *within* the rational choice camp. The diversity of *rationality*'s definitions is not always appreciated by those who stand outside this approach. Critics of the rationality assumption, for example, commonly complain about its tendency to straitjacket what in reality is the richness and complexity of human behavior. Rationality, they argue, is an arid and limited concept suitable, at most, to describing individuals with a lot of time on their hands facing very carefully delineated alternatives. Although the theory of rationality may be clear and tidy, these critics complain, individuals and their decisions are not. At best, rationality reflects one aspect or dimension of human behavior.

Yet the dirty secret of rational choice theory is that the opposite is true: "contemporary research shows us that the notion of rationality itself is ill defined" (Ordeshook 1990, 29). It covers a multitude of behavior and reasoning styles and can prescribe an enormous variety of responses to a given situation.

This deflationary judgment is not an opportunity for "I told you so's" from rational choice theory's perennial critics. As Peter Ordeshook suggests, our increasing recognition of the ambiguity and uncertainty surrounding the notion has emerged from a continuing confrontation between carefully articulated formal theories and carefully delineated empirical problems, not from a priori speculation about the rationality concept's limits. Given the generality of the critics' attacks, their skepticism can easily be mistaken for prescience and profundity (the fact that my great-grandfather said everything is relative does not make him an Einstein). I propose to use the current flux and uncertainty in rational choice theory for inspiration, not condemnation. Rationality's ambiguity is an opportunity, rooted in developments within rational choice theory itself, to consider whether the leading definition represents the best route to explanatory success in analyzing political phenomena.

Political scientists involved with formal theory will be most acutely aware of the refinements of rationality occurring within game theory, which is now the standard framework for analyzing rational political behavior. In this chapter, I focus primarily on rationality in decision theoretic contexts, that is, games individuals play against nature rather than against other human beings. This is not as great a simplification as it may seem. For one thing, human beings often figure in the descriptions of the various states of nature the decision maker is confronting. For another thing, the shift from EU to CEU theory can be motivated largely without recourse to the additional complications of game theory. Initially it makes sense to take advantage of the relative simplicity of the decision theoretic context.

Moreover, although the distinction between games and decisions is important, standard game theoretic results involve transforming infinite iterations of an "if he thinks that I think that he thinks . . . " calculus into a decision theoretic problem (e.g., Luce and Raiffa 1957, 63–64). If the handed-down game theoretic notion of rationality has problems, it is well to remember that the notion was first handed down from decision theory.

There is a final consideration in favor of decision theory. Many recent attempts to ground and refine game theoretic results look for solutions that are not simply states of affairs no player unilaterally wants to leave—the famous Nash equilibrium—but states of affairs players are rationally motivated to produce. These attempts often involve a return to game theory's decision theoretic foundations (see, e.g., Aumann 1987).

I

We begin by returning to the important and in many ways paradigmatic example of mass elections, which we will now discuss in a much more abstract and general way. Harry is deciding whether to vote in a two-candidate, majority-rule election in which ties are broken by a coin toss and there are an odd number of potential voters. His decision problem, as standardly formulated in the EU tradition of Anthony Downs (1957), is represented by figure 1 (cf. Ordeshook 1986, 11):

	S_1	S_2	S_3	S_4	S_5
Vote for θ	O_2	O_3	O_1	O_1	O_1
Vote for ψ	O_2	O_2	O_2	O_3	O_1
Abstain	O_5	O_5	O_6	O_4	O_4

Fig. 1.   Voting with EU

where S_1 denotes the state of affairs in which, not counting Harry's potential vote, candidate θ is more than one vote behind candidate ψ; S_2 represents an exact one vote deficit for candidate θ without Harry's vote; S_3 represents an equal number of votes without Harry's; S_4 represents a one vote margin for candidate θ without Harry's vote; and S_5 is the state of affairs in which candidate θ has more than a one vote margin without Harry's. Harry's alternative courses of action corresponding to A_1, A_2, and A_3 are, respectively, vote for candidate θ, vote for candidate ψ, and abstain.

Any combination of a state and an action uniquely determines an outcome, as for example when Harry's vote creates a tie (i.e., Vote for θ and S_2). In the interest of simplicity, however, I have equated certain outcomes when the distinctions among them are irrelevant to Harry's purposes. In particular, O_1 means θ wins and Harry votes; O_2 means candidate ψ wins and Harry votes; O_3 means a tie and Harry votes; O_4 means candidate θ wins and Harry abstains; O_5 means candidate ψ wins and Harry abstains; and O_6 means a tie and Harry abstains. The crucial point is that if Harry knows which state of affairs obtains, he knows the relevant outcome of each of his actions.

Knowing which state of affairs obtains is not important when Harry is indifferent between the candidates since under those circumstances and assuming a net positive cost of voting, $U(O_1) = U(O_2) = U(O_3) < U(O_4) = U(O_5) = U(O_6)$, where U is Harry's utility function over the six possible outcomes. In the language of decision theory, abstention strictly dominates participation, and Harry will abstain regardless of the vote totals. If, on the other hand, Harry prefers candidate θ to candidate ψ, knowing which state of affairs obtains is important. Voting for θ now weakly dominates voting for ψ, since $U(O_1) > U(O_3) > U(O_2)$. Yet abstention may still be rational even if the cost of voting is relatively small (so that $U(O_1) > U(O_6) > U(O_3) > U(O_5)$). It depends on Harry's estimate of the likelihood of the various states S_i. According to the standard analysis, he builds this uncertainty into his calculation using the rules of EU theory.

When Harry has a preference in the election and follows the standard analysis, he calculates EU based on the probability (denoted as prob) he attaches to each of the S_i. These probabilities reflect his beliefs, with prob = 1 meaning absolute certainty and prob = 0 meaning strict impossibility. Formally, as noted in the introduction, $EU(A_k)$ is calculated as $\sum_j U(O_j)\text{prob}(O_j)$, where j indexes the possible outcomes O_j of the agent's action k. To simplify the resulting calculation, we will make the usual assumption that the positive cost of voting enters Harry's utility function linearly: this sure cost is subtracted from the expected gain from voting. Finally, if in Harry's view there are different utilities associated with the candidates, we can normalize the utility of candidate θ's winning as 1, of candidate ψ's winning as 0, and the "relatively small" cost as c, $0 < c < 1$. Recalling that in the event of a tie each candidate wins with probability $\frac{1}{2}$, the expected utility voting for θ is given by

$$EU(\text{Vote for } \theta) = (\tfrac{1}{2})\text{prob}(S_2)(1 - c) + \text{prob}(S_3)(1 - c)$$
$$+ \text{prob}(S_4)(1 - c) + \text{prob}(S_5)(1 - c),$$

where again $\text{prob}(S_i)$ is the probability of S_i. Since voting for θ dominates voting for ψ, this action can be dropped from consideration. The term $EU(\text{Vote for } \theta)$ must be compared only to

$$EU(\text{Abstain}) = (\tfrac{1}{2})\text{prob}(S_3) + \text{prob}(S_4) + \text{prob}(S_5).$$

Harry votes if $EU(\text{Vote for } \theta) > EU(\text{Abstain})$. After some algebraic manipulation, this will be true when

$$\tfrac{1}{2}[\text{prob}(S_2) + \text{prob}(S_3)]/[(\tfrac{1}{2})\text{prob}(S_2) + \text{prob}(S_3) + \text{prob}(S_4)$$
$$+ \text{prob}(S_5)] > c. \tag{1.1}$$

Thus Harry's participation turns on his estimation of the proportion of the relevant probabilities represented by $\text{prob}(S_2) + \text{prob}(S_3)$, the probability that Harry's vote makes or breaks a tie. This probability, in turn, depends on his estimate of the turnout from the remainder of the electorate.

The calculation of this probability is by no means obvious. William Riker and Peter Ordeshook (1968) assume a known constant probability for each voter's participation and by ordinary binomial calculations conclude that the chance of Harry's making or breaking a tie is very small when the electorate is large. Under these circumstances, virtually any positive cost of voting will overwhelm the expected utility associated with candidate θ's winning so long as Harry perceives the matter more or less accurately. Gary Chamberlain and Michael Rothschild (1981) more realistically factor in Harry's uncertainty about this probability of participation. They also recognize that the distribution of the probability may vary with different groups, say, men and women. Nonetheless, their analysis leads to the same negative conclusion about Harry's own participation.

Indeed this conclusion held sway for about twenty-five years. Yet for all its support and rationalist trappings, Harry's negative calculation is questionable, in fact nearly self-contradictory. As John Ledyard (1984) observes, if Harry recognizes that the voters whose turnout he is estimating make parallel calculations about his turnout and the turnout of others, then they will not in fact vote. But then Harry's own abstention is unreasonable since when there is universal abstention his vote will be decisive (see also Downs 1957, 267). This recalculation suggests that it is rational for Harry to participate, yet it also forces Harry to recalculate the probability of participation from others.

The probability of participation, in short, must be endogenous to the model of participation. This turns the decision theoretic calculation into a substantially more complicated game theoretic calculation. The complication seems to be a small price to pay, however, since Ledyard shows using the EU maximization model that the resulting equilibrium turnout is positive when candidates adopt distinct positions.

Unfortunately, this positive turnout rapidly limits to zero as the size of electorate goes to infinity (Palfrey and Rosenthal 1985). True, an increasingly small turnout remains positive for all finite sized electorates. And to borrow Paul Samuelson's observation, epsilon ain't zero. But epsilon bears no relationship to participation rates in U.S. presidential elections, which are themselves comparatively low. Endogenizing probabilities, then, does not remove the original puzzle of turnout. In this chapter, therefore, I will continue to accept the simplification afforded by the decision theoretic framework, confident that we are giving EU theory a fair hearing. We return to game theoretic considerations in chapter 2. The immediate task is to present CEU theory's version of the same decision problem.

II

Sally is deciding whether to vote in a two-candidate, majority-rule election in which ties are broken by a coin toss and there are an odd number of potential voters. Her decision problem, formulated in a manner consistent with a CEU calculus, is represented by figure 2 (see Grafstein 1991):

	W_1	W_2	W_3
Vote for θ	O_1	O_2	O_3
Vote for ψ	O_1	O_2	O_3
Abstain	O_4	O_5	O_6

Fig. 2. Voting with CEU

where W_1 is the world or state in which candidate θ wins; W_2 is the world in which candidate ψ wins; and W_3 is the world in which there is a tie. The three possible actions are as before; likewise O_1 occurs when candidate θ wins and Sally votes; O_2 when candidate ψ wins and she votes; O_3 when there is a tie and she votes; O_4 when candidate θ wins and she abstains; O_5 when candidate ψ wins and she abstains; and O_6 when there is a tie and she abstains.

Abstention is once again the strictly dominant strategy when voting is costly and Sally equally values the candidates. When Sally prefers candidate θ, it turns out that voting for that candidate still dominates voting for the alternative. Yet this conclusion can no longer be derived by a direct comparison of outcomes since we have further simplified the analysis given for EU maximization by equating all states in which a given candidate wins (this simplification is one of the decided pragmatic advantages of CEU maximization; see Eells 1982).

The obvious recommendation to vote for candidate θ is rescued by re-introducing probability. When Sally maximizes her CEU, her decisions factor in the probability of each outcome conditional on the relevant act (here, voting for candidate θ versus voting for candidate ψ), with probabilities again understood to represent Sally's true but subjective beliefs. In the case of CEU maximization, Sally's own behavior figures in this calculation. One way it figures is obvious and uncontroversial. Since Sally's vote contributes to candidate θ's (resp. candidate ψ's) vote total, the probability that θ (resp. ψ) wins or ties is affected by Sally's decision, albeit in a very small way for large elections. Therefore, although the potential outcomes themselves are identical in a comparison of the two possible votes, the distribution of the conditional probabilities of their outcomes will differ. As a result, Sally will not want to disadvantage candidate θ by voting for ψ, thereby raising ψ's conditional probability of winning.

Sally, in short, will ignore voting for candidate ψ and instead limit her comparison to voting for θ versus abstaining. As noted in the introduction, Sally will maximize $\sum_j U(O_j) \text{prob}(O_j \mid A_k)$, where k indexes the agent's possible actions A_k and $\text{prob}(O_j \mid A_k)$ is the probability of outcome j conditional on action A_k. As a conditional expected utility maximizer, in other words, Sally chooses the action given which her expected utility is highest. Staying with the original normalization of utility—1 if candidate θ wins, 0 if candidate ψ wins, and c for the cost of voting—Sally votes if the CEU of voting, CEU(Vote for θ), is greater than the CEU of abstaining, CEU(Abstain). This is true when

$$\text{prob}(O_1 \mid \text{Vote for } \theta)(1 - c) + (\tfrac{1}{2})\text{prob}(O_3 \mid \text{Vote for } \theta)(1 - c)$$
$$> \text{prob}(O_4 \mid \text{Abstain}) + (\tfrac{1}{2})\text{prob}(O_6 \mid \text{Abstain}).$$

This inequality is equivalent to

$$[\text{prob}(O_1 \mid \text{Vote for } \theta) + (\tfrac{1}{2})\text{prob}(O_3 \mid \text{Vote for } \theta)$$
$$- (\text{prob}(O_4 \mid \text{Abstain})$$
$$+ (\tfrac{1}{2})\text{prob}(O_6 \mid \text{Abstain}))]/[\text{prob}(O_1 \mid \text{Vote for } \theta)$$
$$+ (\tfrac{1}{2})(\text{prob}(O_4 \mid \text{Abstain})] > c, \tag{1.2}$$

which represents Sally's implicit rule for deciding whether to vote or abstain.

In order to draw out expression (1.2)'s behavioral implications, we need to get some insight into the component probabilities. One point about them has already been noted. The probability that candidate θ wins or ties is increased by Sally's decision to contribute to candidate θ's vote total. While this negligible contribution is enough to motivate Sally into voting for candidate θ over ψ, it is not sufficient to motivate Sally to vote. CEU maximization, however, need not take the probability of votes from others as fixed and given. The states of nature CEU maximization recognizes—W_1, W_2, and W_3—reflect the decisions of others as well as Sally's own, and there is ample evidence that these decisions are statistically related: the probability distribution of the W_i, given Sally's decision, does not in general equal the unconditional probability distribution of those W_i. Independent of Sally's own potential contribution to candidate θ's vote total, her decision whether to vote can provide information about the decisions of others.

What cognitive psychologists call the Consensus Effect (e.g., Fiske and Taylor 1984, 82–83) has been well documented. Individuals use their own characteristics (which here I take to include behavior) as a basis for judging the characteristics of others. Most important, the Consensus Effect has been documented in experimental studies of voting (e.g., Quattrone and Tversky 1986, 1988). Voters use their own participation as useful indicators of the participation of others, although George Quattrone and Amos Tversky count this finding as evidence against the rationality hypothesis, which they equate with EU maximization. More generally, John Orbell, Alphons van de Kragt, and Robyn Dawes (1991, 123) observe, "One of the most replicated findings from social dilemma experimental research is of a strong positive correlation between expectations of others' cooperation and one's own cooperation," where the "expectations often occur *subsequent* to one's own choice." From the standpoint of EU theory, both the cooperative outcome and this motivation are problematic.

One reason for the diagnostic use of the vote is, presumably, a sense of statistical interdependence with others who have chosen the same course in a clear and structured institutional setting. When this dependence is uniform across the partisan spectrum, voting will widen the expected numerical difference between candidates but will not reverse an expected lead. Yet there may be greater statistical dependence between Sally and potential voters of

Sally's own political persuasion. In this case, voting can be instrumentally rational even in large electorates. The inequality in expression (1.2) will hold.

Following Chamberlain and Rothschild's (1981) lead, moreover, we should recognize that individual calculations of statistical dependence may be sensitive to shared racial, ethnic, gender, or class identity, to mention the empirically most prominent characteristics. This will be more fully explored in chapter 2, but for now let us assume that interactions with other types of voters, or even nonvoting members of those groups, have provided information about statistical dependencies with those types. When Harry meets Sally, for example, Sally may learn about the behavior of groups to which they both belong and, in the process, may come to see a statistical dependence between her own behavior and his, as well as that of others like him.

In sum, there is good reason to believe that the expected *difference* in turnout for the two candidates increases given the voter's own decision. If so, the CEU criterion for participation can be satisfied for all size electorates. The awkward Downsian result of zero turnout no longer holds nor, as we shall see, does the finding that turnout approaches zero as the size of the electorate increases. This is a significant plus for instrumental CEU versus EU maximization.[1] One version agrees with the behavioral evidence in elections and other public goods settings; the other does not. One version agrees with the vast body of experimental evidence described by Quattrone and Tversky (1986, 1988), Orbell, van de Kragt, and Dawes (1991), and Ostrom (1998). The other version does not.

III

CEU maximization can explain positive turnout in mass elections. It rationalizes turnout so long as maximizing CEU is rational. The latter claim is the controversial one. Those already convinced of the reasonableness of CEU theory can turn to chapter 2. For those not yet convinced, the remainder of this chapter is a defense of CEU maximization as a rule of rationality. It requires a more intimate inspection of the CEU approach adopted here, both in relation to EU theory and to other versions of CEU theory.

One feature of CEU maximization needs little defense. When an individual makes inferences about other individuals' behavior from her own, she is sensibly revising her beliefs based on evidence, admittedly a small bit of evidence. Although cognitive psychologists typically refer to the Consensus Effect as the False Consensus Effect, no obvious mistake is being made; indeed Robyn Dawes (1990) shows that the inference can be inductively rational in the Bayesian sense. What understandably is more controversial is the further view that a rational individual will act on inferences drawn from her own projected acts. To many, this seems to reflect nothing more exciting than wishful thinking or "self-deception" (Quattrone and Tversky 1986).

Downsian voters are supposedly rational because their EU is calculated in terms of the causal consequences of their acts: they focus on those states S_2 and S_3 in which they create or break a tie and thereby cause their candidate to win. In fact, it is this presumed association between rationality and causation that gives rise to the charge of wishful thinking, since advocates of the Downsian approach often assume that CEU maximizers are secretly just as interested in the causal consequences of their acts. On this reading, CEU maximizers misinterpret an increase in their CEU as an increase in their political efficacy. What brings them to the polls is thus one variant of the ancient confusion between causation and spurious correlation. "Individuals decide to vote because they believe, magically, that this will lead others like them to do the same" (Elster 1985a, 366). This is why the alternative view of rational decision making, reflected in the Downsian analysis of voting, is often called Causal Decision Theory.[2]

Magic, of course, has no place in rational decision making. For the same reasons, Causal Decision theorists add, expectations not reflecting genuine causal relations have no place in rational decision making. Only a "voodoo decision theory" (Skyrms 1996) would base decisions on spurious correlations. Yet while CEU maximizers do not deny the relevance of causation to their disagreement with Causal Decision theorists, its role in decision making is more delicate than is sometimes recognized. If CEU maximization rested on simple ignorance of the way the world works, it would scarcely be worth anyone's sustained attention.

To begin separating fact from fiction in this debate, it is useful to note that even Downsian voters are not as cleanly fixated on causal influence as might first appear. Again consider Sally, who believes there is a large statistical dependence between her own vote and the votes of other supporters of her preferred candidate. From the standpoint of CEU maximization, Sally's decision can be understood as a choice between two lotteries: (I), which Sally chooses by voting, and (II), which Sally chooses by abstaining. Here are some numbers for vividness. Sally believes that (I) is associated with a 95 percent chance of $1,000,000 and a 5 percent chance of $0 and costs a dollar and (II) is associated with a 5 percent chance of $1,000,000 and a 95 percent chance of $0 and is free.[3]

In exaggerated form, these two lotteries reflect the different expected utilities associated with voting and abstention when there is high statistical dependence, with the dollar representing the cost of voting. To preclude the most obvious causal connection in this example, let us assume that the actual payoff in each of the lotteries—$1,000,000 or $0—has been determined, so the reward for choosing (I) or (II) has already been established. In one sense, then, Sally is not facing a true lottery since there is no "objective" indeterminacy to the outcome. In more relevant and accurate terms, her choice can have no causal impact on the outcome of choosing (I) or (II). Rather, the probabilities reflect Sally's beliefs about the payoffs from (I) and (II) given her uncertainty about the outcome, which happens to be unknown to her.

Clearly, the CEU maximizer chooses (I). What about the EU maximizer and the Downsian voter in particular? As already noted, Downsian voters are not entitled to deny the statistical facts embodied in the problem. But they will ignore them: because Sally cannot cause the payoffs associated with (I) and (II), which are already fixed and determined, she apparently must disregard probabilities that do not reflect the likelihood of causing $1,000,000. These, I gather, are the "spurious" dependencies that beguile only CEU maximizers, since in this case there is *no* chance she will cause the lottery's better outcome to occur. Accordingly, Sally maximizes EU by choosing (II) in order to avoid the sure loss of the dollar.

Obviously, the causal influence requirement applied to this decision problem is too strong even for Downsians to stomach. One way to weaken it is to describe Sally not as being unable to cause the particular payoff from (I) and (II) but as "causing" the better subjective lottery to be chosen (cf. Lewis 1983). Specifically, in choosing (I) Sally is not causing it to be the case, with high probability, that $1,000,000 is the payoff she chooses. Rather, she is causing it to be the case that the lottery she chooses pays $1,000,000 with high probability (these refined distinctions are often required to unpack and rationalize an EU analysis). When causation is characterized this way, the probabilities associated with (I) and (II) once again become relevant to Sally's calculation.[4]

Arguably, this distinction concerning the causal analysis restores (I). Yet it should take a considerable toll on the Downsian's confidence. To see why, note the link between the rationalization of (I) and the original turnout puzzle. If in the real voting case Downsian voters follow the prescription of the previous lottery, they will be willing to incorporate any probabilities reflecting the fact that by voting they are activating a superior subjective lottery. The subjective lottery remains operative in this revised Downsian calculus even though it has been objectively resolved: although Sally does not know what other voters are doing, it is nonetheless true that each individual is or is not voting and is doing so without any causal input from Sally. If activating the subjective lottery in (I) is a sufficient basis for attributing a causal effect to Sally, then presumably a subjective lottery is also a sufficient basis for her decision whether to vote in actual elections, again, even when no individual voter has a causal or even magical impact on anyone else's turnout. Thus Downsian voters in this revised scheme are willing to activate the better subjective lottery when the lottery in reality no longer exists.

The artificial lottery example suggests that Downsian voters who calculate according to subjective lotteries should be guided by statistical dependencies among voters' behavior based, say, on shared ethnic or racial identity. Of course, Downsian critics of CEU maximization may protest that the subjective lottery they envision concerns only causal possibilities: creating or breaking a tie. But why now revert to the strict causal interpretation? Granted, the original Downsian interpretation of voting does not compel an interpretation consistent with CEU maximization. The original is also consistent with the strict accounting of uncertainty to states of affairs and the strict accounting of causal efficacy to the calculation of likely *outcomes*. But this strict accounting also implies the awkward recommendation to choose lottery (II).

Choosing (I), we have seen, reflects a different lesson. If Downsian voters probably will not cause their favored candidate to win, neither will they cause, in that sense, the $1,000,000 to be the outcome of lottery (I). Nevertheless, they should choose (I), and, given sufficient statistical dependence with other supporters of their favored candidate, they should vote. Both the decision to vote and the decision to abstain equally depend on distinct causal and subjective probability elements. Only the CEU maximizer, however, acts as though she views her own choice as providing useful information about the lottery she is activating. CEU maximizers may or may not believe that an individual's vote confers its own utility as a consumption benefit—à la Downs—but they do believe it confers its own information.

To repeat, both CEU and EU maximizers accept the use of information relevant to the determination of subjective probability. Both, for example, will be interested in data about turnout from other groups. Voters who maximize EU, however, draw the line when it comes to using the evidence of their own decisions as indicators of the value of their participation, dismissing this prospect as wishful thinking.

They portray this dismissal as the wise rejection of considerations not bearing on the agent's ability to influence the outcome, a rejection of the "voters' illusion" (Quattrone and Tversky 1986). As the preceding account of the vote choice shows, this objection is seriously overstated. The point of contention is not behavior's capacity to cause or activate a particular lottery or have a particular probabilistic effect. Both approaches can be understood in those terms. The real difference between the two versions of maximization lies in how they understand the relation between decision makers and their own behavior. In the case of CEU maximization, individuals use their behavior diagnostically, treating it as a useful fact like any other. In the case of EU maximization, the decision maker's own behavior is the exception. Information from behavior cannot enter the decision maker's calculus; information from other sources can.

CEU and EU maximizers do not differ over whether or what voters' actions cause. They differ over the significance rational actors implicitly attribute to their own causal behavior. The reasons for this disagreement are rather deep. As the next section shows, EU maximizers believe a special relation—*metaphysical* is not too strong a term—between themselves and their behavior precludes the diagnostic use of their behavior. CEU maximizers grant no such exemption. The probabilities on which they act are conditional on the actions themselves.

IV

Since the complaint that CEU theory disregards causation is a red herring, we shall focus instead on the theory's diagnostic use of behavior. There is one fairly straightforward rendition of the EU maximizer's objection to the diagnostic use of his own behavior. Since an EU maximizer sees his behavior as the product of his own rational deliberations, which incorporate all his information about his behavior's consequences, his behavior cannot provide additional useful information about its own utility. In advance of his deliberations, the EU maximizer may of course be influenced by information relevant to his decision. In the case of voting, for example, he will be interested in data about support for candidates among groups with historically different participation rates. But the EU maximizer does not see his own behavior as a source of such information. Since it is his behavior, after all, what could it tell him when his decision already reflects his relevant beliefs and preferences?

A CEU maximizer, on the other hand, sees her behavior as providing information on a par with other sources. It can be as informative as the behavior of other individuals, whose beliefs and preferences she may also know. If she can learn from the behavior of others, she can learn from her own. Its value as a source of information is not diminished because it is hers.

Consider the problem of predicting divorce. Commenting on what in their view is the self-fulfilling motivational role of irrational belief, Richard Nisbett and Lee Ross (1980, 271; see also Elster 1989a, 7) ponder the case of newlyweds who are aware of the 40 percent divorce rate in their society: "It is far from clear that a bride and a groom would be well advised to believe, on their wedding day, that the probability of their divorce is as high as .40." They would be better off being irrational, for if the couple has falsely optimistic beliefs, Nisbett and Ross suggest, they will be more likely to create a more viable marriage.

According to CEU theory, by contrast, the bride and groom would not be well advised to accept the .40 figure because to do so would be to confuse the unconditional probability that any randomly chosen couple will experience a divorce with the probability conditional on the evidence of their own feelings expressed through their behavior. Unconditional probabilities incorporate (technically, integrate over) the numerous circumstances that collectively produce a high divorce rate. Special circumstances, including wedding day behavior, can lead to a quite different conditional expectation. The couple's own

"irrationally" increased chance of staying married suggests that the two probabilities are different. An EU maximizer will certainly alter his divorce predictions for other couples based on additional evidence provided by their own
behavior. He ought to do the same for his own.

How should decision makers regard their own acts? Evidently, EU maximizers must regard them differently than they would anyone else's. CEU
maximizers disavow a special relationship with their own acts. Their behavior
is not only a useful indicator of the behavior of others. As the example of
divorce illustrates, it can be a useful predictor of the CEU maximizer's own
future behavior.

To see exactly how the distinction between first-person and third-person
perspectives functions for EU maximizers, imagine a set of Prisoner's
Dilemma games as shown in figure 3, where C (cooperate) and D (defect) are
alternative choices and the first number in each box indicates Player I's utility
from that outcome and the second number indicates Player II's utility.

Player II

		C	D
Player I	**C**	5,5	0,10
	D	10,0	3,3

Fig. 3.   Prisoner's Dilemma

The standard EU analysis recommends strategy D since this is the superior
alternative no matter what the other player does.

But let us introduce into this standard story a complication that will be
relevant to CEU maximizers. Specifically, we assume that based on their past
behavior in other settings, certain of the players who meet in these games can
ex ante be expected to exhibit a certain statistical interdependence in their
behavior. Not that players know one another. They are anonymous in the sense
that they are unable to develop strategies contingent on the history of previous
encounters with individual players. Yet each player knows the preferences of
the other and knows whether the other player is a CEU or an EU maximizer. To
CEU maximizers, then, the behavior of any EU maximizer will be statistically
independent of their own. EU maximizers always play D regardless of a CEU
maximizer's choice.

A CEU maximizer i, however, will also believe that when meeting another CEU maximizer j, and assuming sufficient statistical interdependence (in
this case, prob($A_{kj} \mid A_{ki}) \geq \frac{5}{6}$, $k = C,D$), the CEU of C will be greater than the
CEU of D. EU maximizers are therefore achieving three units of utility in each

of their encounters whereas CEU maximizers are achieving three units in their encounters with EU maximizers but are gaining more in their encounters with fellow CEU maximizers. So given these statistical dependencies, the CEU maximizer can be expected to do better than the EU maximizer. True, when a CEU maximizer faces an EU maximizer, who always chooses noncooperation, the behavior of the two is statistically independent, and therefore noncooperation is the dominant strategy for both. But EU maximizers would not cooperate even when facing those whose conditional probability of cooperation would increase accordingly.

While CEU maximizers prosper in this scenario, there are ways they can exploit their advantage further. Why should they interact with EU maximizers, for example, when they can continue searching for their more valuable CEU counterparts? If, in other words, interaction is nonrandom by virtue of signal detection or geographical propinquity, then provided the search costs are low enough CEU maximizers can limit their attention to their own, mutually productive kind. Ironically, Brian Skyrms (1996, 61), who we have seen is no fan of CEU maximization as a norm of rationality, finds it to be an essential element in the explanation of human and nonhuman cooperation: "The crucial step in modifying evolutionary game theory to take account of correlations is just to calculate expected fitness according to Jeffrey's *The Logic of Decision* rather than Savage's *The Foundation of Statistics*." "Correlation of interaction," he adds, "should continue to play a part, perhaps an even more important part, in the theory of cultural evolution. If so, then the special characteristics of correlation in evolutionary game theory may be important for understanding the evolution of social norms and social institutions."

EU theorists, of course, will not be impressed by these conclusions. As far as they are concerned, the relative advantage of CEU maximization in evolutionary situations shows only that in games in which rational strategies do not produce socially optimal results, mutually incompetent players may, by dumb luck (or the luck of the dumb), reward one another. EU theorists are not about to change their recommendations in light of this quirk. To them, the strategy of choosing D is, by simple logic, always better than the strategy of choosing C.

Yet here the "better" strategy produces worse results. To see why this discrepancy arises, note that to this point we have examined CEU and EU maximizers from the first-person perspective on the Prisoner's Dilemma, trying to discover what is rational by each player's lights. Turning to the third-person perspective, we now consider the position of the EU maximizer, heretofore a staunch noncooperator, who becomes an EU maximizing *observer* of the play of others. Where would this EU theorist place his bets?

Given the choice of betting on the relative success of either of the two kinds of player, this observer should, for reasons just given, bet on players maximizing CEU and bet against his EU maximizing counterpart (see, e.g.,

Harper 1985). No doubt he will rationalize this apparent inconsistency by citing his role as a third-person observer. Statistical dependencies matter to him as observer because he is now betting on the Prisoner's Dilemma equivalent of actuarial tables. His concern is not with his own rational choice in the game but with the expected outcomes for others playing the game. His first-person perspective as player, on the other hand, somehow renders his own behavior decisively different from the behavior he observes, even different than his own behavior as interpreted by an observer.

As a participant, an EU maximizer is supposed to rise above the statistical regularities in which both EU maximizers and observers know their acts are embedded. His decision making "screens off" the statistical dependencies with which it is otherwise enmeshed, in the sense that his own intervention in the behavior process negates these statistical associations.

This screening off is so powerful that even if the relevant conditional probabilities equaled unity, so the EU maximizer could be *certain* of the association between his own behavior and the other player's, he still would not cooperate in a Prisoner's Dilemma and as a potential voter would still abstain (see Gibbard and Harper 1978; Harper 1993, 94–95). He somehow is free to step outside the bundle of behavioral dispositions he is, declaring the statistical associations inoperative. It is this alleged freedom that legitimates his indifference to the information his behavior provides. In this sense, "To regard [a choice] as free is exactly to regard it as *without* the evidential relevance it would have if it were regarded, not as an *act,* but as a bit of behavior" (Kyburg 1988, 80).[5]

Apparently, free will can remain largely implicit in EU theory because its role is essentially negative. In the EU setting free will, whatever it may be, is not a causal force specified within, or corresponding to, the statistical and deterministic relations constituting the subject matter of science, particularly physics. It is a force operating outside those relations, indeed one capable of negating them.[6]

In any case, the distinction between first- and third-person perspectives allows us to see more clearly why the division over causation between EU and CEU theory is only symptomatic. It is much more a disagreement over the rational individual's capacity to override the information her own behavior conveys. Ultimately it is a disagreement over the scientific importance of the distinction between first-person and third-person perspectives. On the one view, the decision maker has a very special status with respect to his own behavior. The agent chooses his own behavioral dispositions. On the other view, the agent acts as if she treats her behavior as an object of analysis like any other.

To the EU maximizer, the free choice producing an act is, in some way, distinct from—an intervention in—the ebb and flow of ordinary behavioral uniformities linking the act with the behavior of others. In choosing this or that behavior, the agent becomes a special causal force amid these uniformities. As Richard Jeffrey (1992, 226) notes with regard to the work of Savage (1972), a leading formulator of the EU scheme, EU-style positions "treat man and nature—acts and events—dualistically." In Savage's formulation, specifically, individual acts are not part of states of affairs but functions from states of affairs to outcomes. Thus as we saw in the voting case, the potential voter is interested precisely in those states of affairs that an individual act can transform into the particular outcome of making or breaking a tie, thereby *causing* a win.

To the CEU maximizer, however, a choice, whether free or not, is still a bit of behavior, to use Kyburg's words, and should be analyzed accordingly. On this view, "The agent is part of nature, and his acts are ingredients in states of nature" (Jeffrey 1992, 228). We also saw this in the voting case. The probability of a given state of affairs—a candidate's winning or losing—conditional on an act is, generally speaking, different from its unconditional probability because the state of affairs encompasses the act. Ellery Eells (1982, 84) makes the point well.

> Savage characterizes outcomes as "anything that may happen to a person." . . . But, since the person is part of the world, anything that may happen to the person is surely a thing that may happen to the world. So it would seem that outcomes ("states of a person") are states ("states of the world") of a kind. So it seems that the distinction between outcomes and states is a distinction between things that may happen to the world *and* the person and things that may happen to the world but *not* the person. Yet it is hard to see why any given place of "drawing the line" would not be arbitrary.

Everything is potentially a relevant part of the state of affairs a decision maker faces, from the remote reaches of the universe to the core of the agent's being. Any element of the state of affairs, including an act, can thereby provide useful information. This is certainly true in the case of voting. Although the potential voter's behavior does not causally affect anyone else's, it is still embedded in social uniformities suggesting the relatively greater chance of turnout from others given that behavior. The agent's special vantage point in the case of her own behavior, the fact that she is a special witness to it, does not change the value of the evidence it provides. The agent's own actions are still part of the state of the world, and ultimately the state of the world, not her act per se, is what interests her. If she is rational, relevant information about any part of the world will interest her.

Since the behavior on which this information is based has not yet occurred, the EU maximizer counters, it cannot provide her irrevocable information. Whatever her final decision *would* say to her or to an observer after the fact, it cannot tell her before the fact. She can freely choose to ignore its message. To the CEU maximizer, of course, the story goes just the other way. For one thing, the information conveyed by future behavior is generally more valuable than past behavior. But the main point of contention, surely, is the EU maximizer's claim that anticipating an event negates its informational significance. The EU maximizer expects to bootstrap himself above the implications associated with any course of action he winds up pursuing. His act may have informational significance, but he, the actor, is somehow not bound by it.

What and where is this actor who is so independent of his acts? The physical boundary of an act, after all, need not be confined to his limbs or to his mouth and vocal cords. It can include every part of his brain involved in the process of acting. The actor needed to embody the freedom of an EU maximizer evidently retreats into a world beyond or prior to the neurophysiology of the act, and his agency becomes "an extensionless point" (Nagel 1979, 35). This ultimately is the separation between actors and states of affairs required by the EU maximization scheme. Indeed Eells (1982, 84) notes that the problem was recognized at the scheme's inception but left unsolved: "Savage remarks that outcomes are 'what the person experiences and what he has preferences for,' but also, in the next sentence, that 'this idea of pure experience, as a good or ill, seems philosophically suspect and is certainly impractical.'" Hard to imagine is more accurate.

V

CEU theory's treatment of causation, I have argued, should not be a focus of controversy. What is controversial, or should be, is EU theory's appeal to an actor standing outside the state of affairs in which he finds himself. His causally efficacious freedom of choice is ultimately what separates him from that state of affairs and reconnects him to it: separates because freedom of choice places the actor outside the statistical web snaring his own body in a state of affairs characterizing the way the world, which includes him, is; connects because freedom of choice initiates a causal chain that transforms that state of affairs into an outcome.

CEU theory's treatment of causation should not be a focus of controversy, but it is. EU theory's reliance on causally efficacious freedom of choice should be highly contentious, particularly among mainstream social scientists, but it is not. This is an awkward combination. Why has scholarly discussion proceeded so incorrectly, from my point of view? Ultimately, I think, the answer lies in the joint goal widely shared by rational choice theorists of all stripes to explain behavior *and* to provide normative recommendations about how others should behave. Rationality is an assumption about behavior as well as a basis for telling people how best to achieve their goals. Free will seems to be an essential presupposition for the latter role, since normative advice is relatively useless for people who are not free to change their behavior. We will explore this issue more thoroughly in chapter 5. For now, there is a more direct way to get a better grasp of why assumptions that should be controversial have not been. We can temporarily abandon our "third-person" vantage point on the debate itself and explore how discussion between EU and CEU theorists has actually proceeded from the inside so to speak.

The inside debate between EU and CEU theorists has tended to revolve around their contrasting analyses of what is called Newcomb's Problem (Nozick 1969). I have skirted this problem until now in favor of its very close and more realistic proxy, the Prisoner's Dilemma (see Lewis 1979). But for analyzing the role of freedom, Newcomb's Problem works somewhat better than does either voting or the Prisoner's Dilemma. Perhaps this is one reason decision theorists have lavished so much more attention on it.

Newcomb's Problem concerns a decision maker's choice between receiving (1) the contents of an opaque box or (2) the contents of that opaque box plus $1,000 in a transparent box. What makes the choice interesting is that an extremely accurate predictor of the decision maker's behavior has put $1,000,000 in the opaque box if it predicted that the decision maker would choose (1), while it put nothing in the opaque box if it predicted the decision maker would choose (2). Extremely accurate prediction in this case means that the probability of $1,000,000 conditional on the choice of (1) and the probability of $1,000 conditional on the choice of (2) are both extremely high. The decision maker's choice, then, is between choosing on the basis of CEU maximization, which recommends (1), and choosing on the basis of EU maximization, which recommends (2) since, in the absence of the decision maker's causal influence on the contents of the opaque box, (2) weakly dominates (1) by guaranteeing at least $1,000 when (1) guarantees only $0.[7]

The parallel with the choice between lotteries (I) and (II) discussed previously should be clear. As before, the decision maker's alleged ability to exercise free choice in favor of alternative (1) or (2) does not hinder the CEU maximizer's recognition of the statistical interdependence between her behavior and the predictor's. Decision makers who choose both boxes choose, in all likelihood, an empty opaque box.

According to Causal Decision theorists, however, there is a clear distinction between the two cases (cf. Eells 1985). In the case of the lotteries (I) and (II), the decision maker is construed not to have any causal influence over the way either lottery was resolved but to have a choice over which resolved lottery he will select. The probability that his choice produces $1,000,000 depends on what he chooses. In Newcomb's Problem, the prediction and action of the predictor are similarly prior to the decision maker's choice, but the truth of the prediction is not. Barring backward causation, if the agent makes the prediction true by choosing (1) he cannot make it true by choosing (2). If choosing (1) would make the prediction true, then choosing (2) would make it false and vice versa. So, the argument concludes, the decision maker is no more able to cause himself to find $1,000,000 in the opaque box when choosing (1) than when choosing (2).

A decision maker following the maxims of Causal Decision Theory in this case should not worry about the predictor's predictions, whose monetary consequences have already been determined. On the other hand, the causal impact of choices on probabilities is relevant when the decision maker chooses between lotteries (I) and (II) and thus decides whether he gets a lottery with a high unconditional probability of $1,000,000 or one with a low unconditional probability.

The CEU maximizer, of course, sees no such distinction. In both cases, the $1,000,000 is or is not in (I) or (II) and is or is not in the opaque box. The decision maker, both sides agree, cannot affect this. The decision maker's actions, both sides also agree, determine whether (I) or (II) is chosen and whether (1) or (2) is chosen. In both cases, when the first alternative is chosen the decision maker becomes a millionaire with high probability, and when the second alternative is chosen the decision maker does not. CEU theory follows the same logic in both situations. What is needed from Causal Decision Theory, as Isaac Levi (1983) observes, is similar consistency.[8]

The immediate conflict between the two sides, at any rate, is now plain. Causal Decision theorists believe the role of correct predictions in Newcomb's Problem makes it substantially different from the choice between (I) and (II). CEU maximizers, in contrast, regard the decision problems as structurally parallel. By choosing (I) or by choosing (1) the decision maker's choice causes it to be the case, with high probability, that she winds up a millionaire; in brief, the one event, her choice, causes the other, whether or not this causal connection can be subsumed under a satisfying causal explanation. The CEU maximizer's account thus assumes the truth of the relevant conditional probabilities, however they happen to be true. Of course neither side disputes their truth, only their application.

The Causal Decision theorist, on the other hand, finds the conditions under which the probabilities become true relevant. For CEU theory's recommendations to hold water, the causal explanation for the high probability connection in the case of Newcomb's Problem must account for the prediction's remaining true across both possible choices by the decision maker just as, uncontroversially, a causal explanation in the case of (I) and (II) must account for the fixed probabilities associated with these lotteries. The Causal Decision theorist does not see how the former requirement can be met.

The Causal Decision theorist envisions the decision maker temporarily standing outside the decision context in order to decide which causal path to initiate, with the prediction fixed as the decision maker contemplates his alternatives. From the standpoint of the CEU theorist, however, the question this causal approach implies—"What should I do?" or equivalently, "What causal chain should I initiate?"—is misconceived. The appropriate question is, "Would I rather be in the situation in which I have chosen (1) or in which I have chosen (2)?" or its third-person equivalent, "Which decision maker would I bet on to become a millionaire, the one who chose (1) or the one who chose (2)?" From this perspective, the decision maker cannot hope to fix one part of the world, the truth of the prediction, and manipulate another part, her own behavior and its causal consequences. The world of the decision maker is uniformly fixed.

The more homogeneous character of the CEU approach is one reason why the special case of complete certainty is so illuminating (this case has been highlighted by Levi [1975] and Seidenfeld [1985]). When the decision maker is *certain* that (1) makes her a millionaire and (2) does not, there is no longer wriggle room for expecting any other outcome, say, on the grounds that the predictor's actions are already fixed and determined, while the decision maker's are not. Nor in this case does the possibility that a low probability event will be realized fuel the illusion that the agent has some additional freedom to dodge the statistical facts. Since the predictor is perfect, the CEU of (1) is $U(\$1,000,000)$ and the CEU of (2) is $U(\$1,000)$. Again, the CEU maximizer insists, (1) is the rational choice.

Causal Decision theorists still advocate (2). Allan Gibbard and William Harper (1978), for example, claim that the infallibility of the predictor is merely epistemic, whereas objective causal relations ensure that (2) remains at least as good as (1). But this kind of rational decision making transcends the beliefs, indeed the certainties of the decision maker. Epistemic probabilities, in the end, are all the decision maker has. If coherent, the probabilities representing his beliefs cannot be contradicted by causal hypotheses he also believes since the probabilities incorporate those hypotheses. His subjective probabilities concerning (1) and (2) cannot be *certainties* if the decision maker has some reason to *prefer* (2) over (1).

Recognizing this problem, N. Jacobi (1993), also in the Causal Decision Theory camp, argues that the special case of infallibility renders the idea of rational choice meaningless, again barring backward causation. Infallibility, according to Jacobi, implies either that the predictor's actions causally influence the decision maker's choice or that the predictor's and decision maker's actions are correlated "presumably through them [*sic*] *both* being causally influenced by some other unknown property or aspect of the universe" (6).[9] In either case, Jacobi (12) concludes, "Rational choice is, by any pragmatic definition, completely absent from these situations, although [the decision maker] may *subjectively* experience the act of choosing."

It is striking that Jacobi's self-pronounced "realist" approach to Newcomb's Problem trades so clearly on the rather metaphysical idea that freedom of choice can be found within the uncertainties defined by probabilities short of certainty. This formulation seems to assume that causation is deterministic and that freedom feeds on the relaxation of causation that probability represents. On this view, Causal Decision Theory ultimately demands an oddly restricted definition of causation.

In any case, this restriction does not establish the association between probability and human freedom Jacobi requires. If probabilities adhere in objective chances, then these are irreducibly embodied in the (causal) behavior of objects, as many physicists contend, and therefore do not disappear with an exercise of freedom at the macrophysical level. If probabilities adhere in subjective uncertainty, this undermines Jacobi's contrast between the subjective experience of freedom and actual freedom reflected in those probabilities.

In sum, if there are causal processes governing human behavior, objectively probabilistic or not, then some of these might be characterized as the exercise of free choice, but they remain causal processes. If freedom is a characteristic of these causal processes, then freedom carries no explanatory weight. Finally, if our part of the universe is not organized by causal processes but by free choices, then the exact point behind Causal Decision Theory is obscure.

The history of philosophy is rich with deep and thoughtful examinations of freedom of will and its compatibility with causation and determination. The claims made here are not meant as substitutes for or serious additions to that literature. But for purposes of rational choice theory, the issue, I have suggested, is fairly narrow. Suppose, for the sake of argument, there is such a thing as freedom and it is compatible with causal processes. This is the best of all possible worlds for Causal Decision Theory. Yet Causal Decision theorists invoking freedom as an antidote to probabilistic dependencies need more than this. Freedom must not simply be compatible with causal processes. It must function in the world as a distinct causal entity. Yet one finds in physics, the science devoted to studying the basic entities of the universe, no appeal to such things, nor the acceptance within physics of an explanatory gap that a serious concept of human freedom can fill. Currently, free choice has all the explanatory power of a miracle.[10]

I say currently. Physics presumably is not immutable. However, if it is redesigned to accommodate free will as a distinct physical force then, as advocates of this accommodation concede, the resulting changes will be "radical" (e.g., Penrose 1989, 298). Given the highly programmatic nature of Roger

Penrose's own proposal and others with which I am familiar, choice-free rational choice theory does not seem to be much of a gamble.

The case of certainty that serves to motivate CEU maximization, I conclude, is not substantively different in the end from the less extreme probabilities with which Causal Decision theorists like Jacobi feel more comfortable. To understand and explain a rational agent's free choices, one still must find the causes of the particular beliefs and desires that, in aggregate, cause her behavior. After we provide an account of those causes and their consequences, no further scientific puzzle is resolved by saying the consequences were chosen.[11]

When decision makers judge what they can and cannot do—what possible outcomes lie in their causal powers—they are reflecting not the openness of the world, its otherwise indeterminate state freely resolved through choice, but the agent's practical ignorance of the way things will be. In this sense, the causal powers of the decision maker, the notion that she can do this versus that, are, "contrary to first appearances, fundamentally epistemic" (Dennett 1984, 148). This confounds those Causal Decision theorists like Gibbard and Harper who find the decision maker's freedom in causal powers subsisting beyond the epistemic certainties of infallible predictors or of infallibly predictive behavior. They properly appreciate that the causal realm encompassing decision makers and everything else is, as they rely on it, nonepistemic but fail to appreciate that the substantive freedom of the decision maker to operate in and on this realm, the freedom to do X when Y is predicted with certainty, is precisely epistemic.

Of course, there is no denying that when Causal Decision theorists invoke choice as the crucial causal element in turnout or Newcomb's Problem, they appeal to a capacity of agency that many find introspectively valid, although I am not sure that anyone, on second thought, actually imagines himself an eyewitness to his own creative act of choice, as opposed to being an eyewitness to the resolution of his choice process. "We do not witness [our decision] being *made;* we witness its *arrival*" (Dennett 1984, 78). Or as Nietzsche (1954, 398) puts it in *Beyond Good and Evil,* "a thought comes when 'it' wishes, and not when 'I' wish."

In the end, the "choice" in rational choice theory is a manner of speaking, like *rise* in *sunrise.* Strictly understood, rational choice explanations merely require determinate beliefs and desires expressed in a particular kind of behavior. Once we drop the idea of free choice, we lose the metaphysical scaffolding of the traditional conception of rationality. We also let science and flattering intuitions about human freedom go their separate ways. Once again, I find it no small irony that a seemingly hardheaded approach, whose proponents are quick to charge CEU theorists with wishful thinking and insensitivity to causal structure, weds a metaphysical notion of free choice to its own version of causality.

VI

To this point, I have treated EU theory and CEU theory as monolithic positions. In the former case, this is not a terrible simplification since EU theory is not the position developed and applied in subsequent chapters. In the latter case, the simplification is more awkward. For one thing, it is unfair to attribute the anti-free-will assumption to CEU theorists who do not in fact share it. Some advocates of CEU theory do not accept the justification for it adopted here. For another thing, simplifications of this sort can easily confuse those who try to interpret the present version of CEU theory through the lens of the existing literature. This section, therefore, emphasizes what is distinctive about *this* version of CEU theory. Beyond clarifying these intratheoretical differences, this section also offers one further and important clarification of the CEU theory I propose.

The present version is empirically oriented. CEU theory is invoked as an explanation of political behavior. It is striking that so much of decision theory is normative, including Jeffrey's (1983) version. "The framework is normative in much the same way as deductive logic is: it is not put forth as a descriptive psychological theory of belief or value or behavior, but as a useful representation of some very general norms for the formulation and critique of belief and decision" (210–11). And as a normative framework, Jeffrey's construction is a natural vehicle for representing first-person considerations. Indeed one can imagine the decision theorist sitting down with a subject to advise him of the best course of action from his perspective. "If you were rational then, given your beliefs and preferences and in light of my CEU analysis, here is what you would (and therefore should) do." The resulting advice is generated by reconstructing the reasoning of an ideally rational agent having those particular beliefs and preferences.

An ideally rational decision maker, of course, would not be dependent on outside counsel. In fact, an agent conceived in Jeffrey's fashion can act as his own constant advisor, monitoring his own deliberations to see what additional information they provide to guide him toward a truly rational decision. Indeed, Jeffrey (1983) exploits this possibility in order to reach a very different conclusion about rational behavior in the Prisoner's Dilemma and similar decision problems than the conclusion reached through the CEU analysis developed here.

Crudely, his idea applied to a Prisoner's Dilemma in which players' behavior exhibits high statistical interdependence is that an agent's decision making will initially follow the direction indicated by those statistical dependencies, namely, cooperation (C). But on the verge of making the actual decision to cooperate, the agent will impute a probability of nearly one to this dominated choice since he knows he is about to make it. Due to the statistical interdependence, moreover, he will also expect the other player to play C with high probability. Therefore, in light of this important and additional piece of information about the other player, the player will no longer find his dominated choice to be rational since the other player's decision not to confess is nearly certain. In this sense, the decision to cooperate is not a "stable" choice. Indeed with the other player's actions nearly fixed in the decision maker's mind, the dominant strategy (D) now becomes appealing.

At the last minute, ideally rational agents pull out from what Jeffrey sees as the mistaken decision to cooperate (or vote, or pick one box). Under this reasoning, then, CEU and EU theory's recommendations not only converge but converge based on the same assumption: rational agents, in this analysis, are ultimately free to choose and thereby *avoid* the statistical implications of their behavior in the Prisoner's Dilemma, the voting decision, and Newcomb's Problem.

Jeffrey no longer fully supports his (1983) "solution" to CEU's supposed problem with the Prisoner's Dilemma—its recommendation to cooperate when these deliberation dynamics are ignored—so I will not belabor difficulties with his proposal that others have identified. From our standpoint, the core problem with his approach is that agents should be making conditional probability judgments about the behavior of others based on their own *behavior*. In other words, they should be making these judgments using the best possible evidence. Prior deliberations, decisions not acted upon, ruminations, and so forth, even those very close to the point of decision, are not the best evidence.[12] Accordingly, the CEU theory developed in this book concerns rational behavior, not the dynamics of the decision making leading to behavior. When the focus remains on behavior, there is no dramatic point in the agent's deliberations at which she breaks away from the path a similar or an identical agent is still destined to follow. If their *behavior* is statistically interdependent, it is interdependent through thick and thin.

Jeffrey's (1993) more recent dissatisfaction with CEU theory's atypical judgment about the Prisoner's Dilemma does recognize the central importance of agency or free will. Formally speaking, he argues, the problem posed by the Prisoner's Dilemma and similar cases is that they provide too much information for a well-posed decision problem. By telling agents not only the probabilities of states of nature (e.g., the behavior of the other player) conditional on their acts but, in effect, the probability of their own acts conditional on states of nature, the decision problem fixes in advance the unconditional probability of acting (141). This fact about the agent's behavior suggests that the decision maker is not free to make up her own mind, since what she decides is already dictated by the stated conditions of the problem. Since the unconditional probability of her own acts is already determined, the point of further decision making is lost. She "is not so much trying to make up her mind as trying to discover how it is already made up" (143).

To Jeffrey, then, the symptomatic problem with these kinds of decisions is the agent's loss of freedom to make a decision. Yet, Jeffrey (1993, 143–44) acknowledges, this is not necessarily an unusual state of affairs: "this may be equally true in ordinary deliberation, where the question 'What do I really want to do?' is often understood as a question about the sort of person I am, a question of which option I am already committed to, unknowingly." Of course the idea of choice-free rationality implies that this situation is characteristic of decision making. Sometimes science or everyday insight gives us sufficient information to recognize it; sometimes ignorance spares us.[13]

Thus Jeffrey's more recent analysis of the Prisoner's Dilemma and related problems comes close to transcending the traditional, voluntaristic foundation of decision theory. He is disturbed, however, by the way the agent's loss of freedom in these cases seems to be linked to an incoherent decision problem. The unconditional probability of acting a particular way presumably is given by nature in the broadest sense, which may include the shared ethnicity of voters or the shared criminal experiences of individuals facing the Prisoner's Dilemma. If these unconditional probabilities reflect causes of the agent's acts, what role can there be for the epistemic conditional probabilities available to the agent who is supposedly still making up his mind? "The diagnostic mark of [these] problems is a strange linkage of this question [What do I really want to do?] with the question of which state of nature is actual" (1993, 144).

On the one hand, the agent is caused to act a certain way. On the other hand, the conditional probabilities allowing the agent to learn her fate are also what seem to determine the fate itself, since unconditional probabilities of acting are calculated from these conditional probabilities. The agent decides using a calculus that reveals her inability to decide, or at least it reveals a decision already made. As a result, Jeffrey (1993, 150) argues, these "problems are like Escher's famous staircase on which an unbroken ascent takes you back to where you started. We know there can be no such things, but see no local flaw; each step makes sense, but there is no way to make sense of the whole picture; that's the art of it."

The point in examining Jeffrey's interpretation of CEU maximization is, of course, to clarify my own. This additional clarification is now upon us, and it forces me to be even less discreet about choice-free CEU theory's break from even Jeffrey's version of the theory. The additional information available in Prisoner's Dilemma and related problems, we now see, can determine the unconditional probability of the act under consideration, which represents a loss of freedom in Jeffrey's view, a coming to grips with reality in my own view. But this determination, Jeffrey suggests, contrasts with the situation found in ordinary decision problems, which do not dictate fixed unconditional probabilities. In the latter case, the agent's introspection about what he will do is not idle, since there is something left for him to decide, some remaining free will to exert.

I note this distinction, which is important to Jeffrey's approach, because one still may be inclined to think a similar distinction can be found in the CEU approach adopted here. For until we began focusing on the problem posed by unconditional probabilities, I characterized rational agents as *using* the additional information that their own behavior may provide. So one may well ask, does not this formulation assume that the agent can freely choose to use this controversial kind of information? Have I not dismissed EU theory's appeal to free will, all the while using it? And does not the role of unconditional probabilities in Prisoner's Dilemma games undermine this strategy?

To be clear (or clearer), then, the notion that agents choose to use the information provided by their own behavior is simply a manner of speaking. It was and will remain a heuristic device designed to aid the transition from the familiar, namely, EU theory, to the less familiar CEU alternative. Choice-free CEU theory, in my view, is not a synopsis of the psychology of conscious decision making. Rational agents facing a static decision problem with particular beliefs and preferences behave in a particular fashion, one that maximizes their CEU. CEU theory makes no additional claims about how agents in a static decision use information, deliberate, or choose from their perspective. In a sense, the theory is not even "as if." It does not claim that agents behave as if they are really using information, choosing, formulating opinions about their own opinions, and so on. The theory says how they behave. It is third person, not first person.

Specifically, when I wrote in the preceding that agents are entitled to use information about their own behavior, this really amounted to saying that the agent's analytic role dissolves into the observer's. Hence, from the standpoint of this theory agents are not torn by a conflict between their desires and their behavior. These conflicts are not internal to the theory or the people the theory studies. Rather, assuming an accurate imputation of beliefs and preferences, any such conflict is a conflict between the theory and the evidence.

I do not mean to dismiss the phenomenon of internal conflict—smokers who in some sense desire to quit (Jeffrey 1993), politicians who act expediently but suffer pangs of conscience, and, more trivially, individuals who stumble down the stairs without desiring to do so. I recognize there is much more to the problem of internal conflict. The dynamics of decision making deserve careful study.

At some point, nonetheless, one is inclined to say that actions speak louder than words, even words appearing in internal monologues. We are not apt to trust the professions of people whose behavior somehow always deviates from their professions. In an important sense, behavior is constitutive of what we take an agent's beliefs and preferences to be (see, e.g., Davidson 1984; Dennett 1987). Hence the complications of internal conflict, in my view, are not a good place to start a tractable analysis of the basic relation between preferences and behavior, which is the foundation on which complications can be erected. Rational is as rational does, in John Hey's (1993) apt words.

CEU theory, in short, imposes a requirement of consistency between preferences (given the agent's beliefs) and behavior. With this important requirement in mind, let us reexamine the problematic cases that worry Jeffrey. To begin, consider an agent who has some condition C affecting his behavior. Perhaps for reasons deeply rooted in evolution he is naturally disposed to respect taller people and therefore is naturally disposed to prefer taller political candidates. If so, given this information we are in a position to assign an unconditional probability prob(A) > .5 to the act A of voting for a taller over a shorter candidate. When the actual decision arises, needless to say, the agent cannot vote prob(A) for the taller and $1 - \text{prob}(A)$ for the shorter candidate. The mixed act, as Jeffrey (1993) refers to it, must be resolved into a discrete choice for one or the other.[14]

Thus we might say that the agent's preexisting condition influences his preferences, but these preferences in any particular election ultimately lead to a CEU for the taller candidate that is greater, smaller, or equal to the CEU for the shorter candidate. In the first instance, his action helps produce a victory V_T for the taller candidate; in the last instance he abstains. In formal terms, prob($V_T \mid A$ and C) = prob($V_T \mid A$ and $\neg C$): given the agent's action, the dispositional condition C has no additional impact on the outcome. The statistical relation between C and V_T is transmitted solely through the agent's decision. As described earlier, A screens off C from V_T.

In this example, the unconditional probability prob(A) functions as a true prior. It reflects initial and general information about the agent that loses its relevance when he decides in a particular election. The problematic cases arise when, substantively speaking, the unconditional probability continues to be relevant at the point of decision. This occurs when the condition does not operate solely through A but operates in some fashion on both A and V_T. In ordinary statistical parlance, analysis solely in terms of A and V_T suffers from an omitted variables problem.

Thus one can imagine ethnicity influencing the agent's vote and, through the votes of others, prob(V_T). Formally, prob($V_T \mid A$) − prob($V_T \mid \neg A$) is not constant as prob(A) varies, where constancy is Jeffrey's (1993) statistical interpretation of causation. Instead, as prob(C) varies, prob(A) varies and alters the ostensibly causal relation. This is because prob(A) is no longer derived from general and prior information but is determined from the conditional probabilities prob($A \mid C$) and prob($A \mid \neg C$) along with the unconditional probability prob(C) and operates throughout the decision process. As Jeffrey sees it, the common effect of C on A and V_T yields the special information available in Newcomb's Problem and the Prisoner's Dilemma. The two possibilities are diagrammed in figures 4a and 4b.

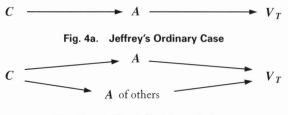

Fig. 4a.   Jeffrey's Ordinary Case

Fig. 4b.   Jeffrey's Problematic Case

In the problematic case, the conflict between the uncertainty of the mixed act, measured by the unconditional probability prob(A), and the certainty of the discrete choice A (or $\neg A$) is no longer merely apparent. It cannot be resolved by the agent's eventual decision in concrete circumstances. Generally, even though $0 < \text{prob}(A) < 1$, prob(A) is controlling throughout the decision process despite the fact that the actual and discrete CEU maximizing decision to perform A or $\neg A$ seems to imply $\text{prob}(A) \approx 1$ or $\text{prob}(A) \approx 0$ ("$\approx$" rather than "=" to allow for the occasional stumble, mistake, or "tremble" in game theoretic parlance).[15] In violation of the consistency requirement emphasized earlier, the maximization of CEU induces the preferred act A with $\text{prob}(A) \approx 1$, yet actual behavior is governed by $\text{prob}(A) < 1$. This discrepancy is acceptable for normative theory, since agents need not, or perhaps cannot, always do what is rational (see Jeffrey 1988, 250). It is unacceptable for an empirical theory of rational behavior.

If prob(C) along with the relevant conditional probabilities is taken to be true and fixed, then only one reconciliation between the two readings of prob(A) seems possible. Since the relevance of C cannot be screened off through the agent's acts but will continue to inform prob(A), it must be the case that the agent's preferences introduced into the calculation of CEU vary randomly. At any given time, in other words, the agent does and must make some decision. But this decision will change over replays of the same decision problem because the agent's preferences change. Without this supposition about preferences, the agent will as a matter of fact tend to perform A a certain proportion of the time, specifically prob(A), but the proportion predicted by CEU theory will approach 100 percent. Under these circumstances, the probability calculus rational choice theory employs would wind up predicting systematically irrational behavior.

Jeffrey (1993) illustrates the resulting, "rationally unstable" behavior using the statistician Ronald Fisher's (1959) speculation that smoking does not really cause cancer but rather the propensity to smoke (A) and the propensity to get lung cancer (V) have a common genetic cause C. According to this speculation, the statistical relation between smoking and cancer is spurious. But the causal connection is not: if Fisher's hypothesis is correct, C dictates a certain prob(A) < 1 of smoking. On the other hand, a straightforward CEU calculation may "recommend" smoking outright, which seems to make prob(A) $\approx$ 1. Indeed the conflict between the recommendation and the behavior is more troubling still. If Fisher's hypothesis is correct then, the CEU recommendation notwithstanding, the pure act A of continuing to smoke and the pure act $\neg A$ of quitting are not options, since C dictates mixed acts.

Here the smoker's behavior belies the supposed power of his decision calculus: "those of us who have repeatedly 'quit' easily appreciate the smoker's dilemma as humdrum entrapment in some mixed act, willy nilly. That the details of the entrapment are describable as cycles of temptation, resolution, and betrayal makes the history no less believable—only more petty" (Jeffrey 1993, 149).

To reestablish the consistency between this probabilistic behavior and the rational behavior predicted, we must put the smoker's dilemma less sympathetically. He does not really have a persistent and true desire to quit dictated by constant preferences that somehow fail to govern his behavior; rather he prefers to quit sometimes and prefers to continue other times. In order to rationalize this smoker's behavior, then, we imagine his smoking gene (or genes) switching and reswitching his preferences, radically enough under some circumstances to establish a perverse preference for illness. Although genetic in origin, such behavior now becomes rational and therefore can still be given meaning. Perhaps smoking, for such individuals, reflects an intermittent "death wish" or a pleasure derived from tempting death (see Klein 1993). The underlying reality, in any case, is that the gene controls behavior. When this agent defies EU theory's recommendation to continue smoking for good, he is being no more irrational than were he to defy a recommendation to solve his decision problem by discovering a cure for cancer or choosing to live forever.[16]

Fortunately for our peace of mind, in most situations causal influences on our behavior are funneled through our discrete and constant choices. Prob(A) is truly a prior and is resolved into 1 or 0 as the decision unfolds. This is not to grant the agent a spurious freedom to will her independence from statistical regularities. Rather, we are now in the more normal realm of decision making in which the relevant statistical regularities are propagated through decisions. The operative probabilities are those constituting her beliefs, not the priors imputed to her in abstraction from her particular case. Put another way, the agent's conditional probabilities are operative here, not the general priors we determine.[17]

In this sense, the situation facing an ill individual deciding whether to see a doctor is much more typical. Illness, or its symptoms, has its impact by prompting the agent to see a physician; it is not independently associated with the visit. Although we may regard prob(A) as being relatively high when illness reveals itself through symptoms, we recognize that the discrete decision to seek treatment or not screens off the statistical bearing of illness on the visit. As in the case of the newlyweds, inferences about the individual case do not always follow from the unconditional probabilities (see Price 1986).

If Jeffrey's (1993) conception of CEU theory is correct, then, it faces two paradigmatic situations with different results. One is the normal case just considered, which resembles the case of voting for the taller candidate. In this situation, there is an underlying condition such as an illness or a genetic predisposition that has a statistical bearing on the outcomes associated with the agent's acts, be it a doctor's treatment or a candidate's victory. This impact is channeled entirely through the agent's decisions. As a result, the agent's decision to see the doctor, for example, screens off the misleading statistical association between doctors and illness. Incidentally, it was noted in the preceding that earlier attempts to grapple with this problem (e.g., Eells 1982; Jeffrey 1983) focused on the ability of agents to monitor their own beliefs and preferences, which naturally provoked the empirical objection that agents sometimes lack this capacity. Jeffrey (1993) takes the important step of allowing CEU maximizers to possess the causal information permitted EU maximizers in critical comparisons of the two theories. Of course, Jeffrey has appropriately translated these causal conditions into a probability constraint or "rigidity condition."[18]

The other paradigmatic situation is the abnormal case such as smoking under the Fisher hypothesis. Here acts do not screen off the relation between the underlying condition and outcome. In Jeffrey's view, Fisher-style cases render the decision calculus itself irrelevant. In the view presented here, however, they force rational choice theory to realign imputed preferences with the stochastic behavior predicted by the underlying condition.

If, as Jeffrey suggests, this typology is exhaustive, Newcomb's Problem, the Prisoner's Dilemma, and the electoral participation decision are all instances of the second, abnormal situation in which decision making is rendered irrelevant. The otherworldly character of Newcomb's Problem, Jeffrey (1993, 149) argues, encourages the idea that we simply can engage in the pure acts of taking one box or two, but there is presumably a hidden causal condition leading to accurate predictions about what the agent ostensibly decides (cf. Jacobi 1993). Similarly, agents facing the Prisoner's Dilemma and voting decision are assumed to be governed by identical or similar causal processes, so their behavior can be represented as independent draws from a common urn whose contents dictate cooperate or defect, vote or abstain (as with standard quantitative studies of voting). When the decision maker is nearly sure what they will both do, he is nearly sure about the kind of urn both players are using; therefore defecting against the other player, or abstaining, becomes desirable. Yet in both these ostensible decision problems the urn continues to dictate actual behavior.

In this two-category typology, Newcomb's Problem is seen as just a science fiction version of the smoker's problem, exploiting the absence of a plausible or even specified condition C in order to achieve a more mysterious or dramatic effect (Jeffrey 1993, 145). Within the context of choice-free CEU theory, by contrast, Newcomb's Problem reflects an important change of focus to the agent's behavior and away from possible causal conditions, which are not even acknowledged in the traditional formulation of Newcomb's Problem.

Indeed for choice-free CEU theory, the key to Newcomb's Problem is that an agent cannot analytically back out from it in order to calculate the consequences when a predictor draws from an urn and thereby fixes the contents of the boxes independently of her own choice. Rather, the agent's act is, once again, an "ingredient" in the very state of nature being predicted. The agent either has or does not have the good fortune of being a potential millionaire, and agents who take one box are more likely to be millionaires. Put another way, the agent's information takes the form of millionaire probabilities conditional on acts. The kind of unconditional probability relevant to the smoking problem is, in this case, not only derived in the literal mathematical sense but in the sense that the derivation imports the very idea of a common cause (the urn) into the problem.

Although the voting decision and the Prisoner's Dilemma are more down to earth, they belong in the same third category as Newcomb's Problem. Whatever roundabout route an agent may have taken to decide whether to vote, she may still be assured that others will have reached the same decision with reasonably high probability. She cannot duck out a mental side door, so to speak, and watch the others pass by on their way to the polls. Likewise, when she is a prisoner her certainty about the other player's cooperation based on her own imminent cooperation cannot survive her own deviation from what had just been certain about her. Reference to an underlying cause in these cases amounts to little more than hand waving, since the possibility of a common cause, in any serious sense of cause, is by no means guaranteed. Certainly the complexity of the social and political environment in which these decisions are made gives us no such assurance.

VII

We now have a case for preferring CEU maximization over EU maximization. CEU maximization, I have suggested, performs better empirically. The case of voting and evolutionary cooperation are important examples, and future chapters will produce others. Yet empirical superiority alone makes CEU theory a better theory. It does not necessarily make it a better rational choice theory. Perhaps it would be preferable to defend CEU theory on empirical grounds alone, rather than diluting the meaning of rationality by adapting it opportunistically to fit the evidence it is supposed to explain.

I am not inclined to concede the concept so easily. Rationality, let us recall, was originally defined in the 1700s as the maximization of expected gain. In calculating expected gain, each monetary outcome, not the utility of that outcome, is multiplied by the probability of its occurring. When Daniel Bernoulli proposed in 1738 that rational agents calculate their expected utility instead, the evidence on which this revision was based was generally considered to be paradoxical (Munier 1988, 14). The EU thesis now the industry standard also once represented a radical, perhaps suspiciously ad hoc revision of the concept of rationality.

As a more recent illustration, Paul Samuelson's (1937) introduction of temporal discounting into EU theory was largely a concession to overwhelming empirical evidence that even guaranteed future benefits are less highly regarded than equal current benefits. This was a reluctant concession since theorists can and have wondered why rational agents would treat the two kinds of benefits unequally. Yet Samuelson's innovation is now so well entrenched that questions about its empirical adequacy are often treated as questions about EU theory itself (e.g., Loewenstein 1992).[19]

It is worth claiming the title of rationality for CEU maximization because this puts in stark relief CEU theory's third-person perspective, which I associate with science generally. The free choice invoked by EU theory as a distinct intervening event, on the other hand, does not correspond to any distinguished cause in the universe at least insofar as physics outlines science's causal inventory. Jon Elster (1989a, 6), I think, reflects the ultimate implications of this freedom by insisting that rationality cannot be "the plaything of psychic processes that, unbeknownst to oneself, shape one's desires and values." This is a difficult standard to meet. Whatever it is called, empirically oriented rational choice theory should not be metaphysical in this sense.

The absence of free choice does not prevent a CEU maximizer from being pleased when she discovers she has behaved rationally, pleased at the good news her behavior brings. She may also be pleased to learn she has a good ear for music or terrific eye-hand coordination. But these are facts about her, not products of decision or choice. Neither her freedom nor her rationality awards her a special power to intervene in her own rational decision processes by making them irrational at will or making them falsify the statistical information they convey. Such special power, guided by first-person intuitions, would place the decision making "she" executes outside the processes that scientific third-person perspectives best describe. In this world, first is last.

Choice-free rationality, then, is more than the name for a brand of decision making in which agents pay attention to what their own behavior reveals. This is the standard approach to CEU maximization, which may or may not be defensible against EU theory, but wrongly does battle on EU theory's own turf. As noted previously, it is even misleading to describe choice-free rationality as claiming that agents act as if they pay attention to the information provided by their own behavior. Rationality is a characterization of an agent's dispositions to behave, nothing more and nothing less. Maximizing CEU, in other words, is a full-time occupation, not a useful description of decision makers who are ultimately free to reveal their power to maximize CEU or not.

CHAPTER 2

Group Identity

For purposes of exposition, chapter 1 largely ignored the existence of other agents in the decision maker's environment, a drastic simplification for any rational choice theory expecting to be applied within political science. This chapter remedies this deficiency by applying CEU theory to multivoter elections in which each of the individuals deciding whether and for whom to vote is aware that other voters are making parallel calculations about their own participation. We will find that CEU theory's conclusions about turnout survive when transplanted into game theoretic models of two-candidate elections involving electorates of any size. These conclusions were previously obtained by Grafstein (1991, 1992) with respect to electorates populated by two political groups each homogeneously supporting one of the candidates. Here CEU theory's conclusions about turnout are extended to electorates populated by multiple groups with divided political loyalties (see Grafstein 1995). Links among the agents studied in this chapter, in sum, are not statistically homogeneous. The strength of the statistical dependence between one agent's acts and another's varies depending on the particular combinations of social and political characteristics each of the agents embodies.

This formal extension to multiple groups has important substantive implications for a theory of political groups and group identity. Politically relevant groups, after all, are not just elements of some abstract partition of the population or mere artifacts of the political divisions of the moment. Religious, ethnic, and other identities play a significant role in the lives of many human beings. They can inspire strong reactions and commitments, notwithstanding the inroads made by modernity, science, urbanization, and any of a host of purported solvents of these "irrational" loyalties. Whatever crude rational choice models may suggest, in other words, human beings do not behave as socially denuded atoms. Their identification with a group, many of whose members they may not even know, can have a far-reaching impact on their own behavior.

Concerns about the atomistic character of traditional rational choice theory are hardly new. Hobbes and Locke faced the same questions. Despite considerable advance warning, however, contemporary rational choice theory has failed to develop a persuasive response to the charge of atomism. Indeed judging from the relative paucity of strict rational choice analyses of group identity, the most common response has been to ignore it. Still, there have been some innovative approaches that the next section will address by way of introducing an analysis rooted in CEU theory.

I

In much of what is commonly regarded as enlightened political discourse, diversity is advocated and even celebrated. In truth, it can pose definite political problems. Religious, class, ethnic, and racial distinctions have a reputation for causing deep social and political divisions. Do these distinctions deserve their reputation? Must these distinctions invariably translate into divisions? Is there some theoretical or practical reason why such hardening of political life must occur? To understand the basis of group conflict or cooperation, we need to understand how and in what sense the conflicting or cooperating groups exist in the first place.

Sometimes, the instrumental value of group distinctions is not hard to see. Ronald Rogowski (1974, 71), for example, argues that a trademark of a salient group is that its members can be distinguished at relatively low cost, owing at one extreme to stigmatic physical characteristics. Serving as easily monitored proxies for economic, status, or other "real" divisions, group distinctions permit the members of a group to exclude nonmembers from otherwise available goods. On this basis, ethnic, racial, and religious classifications can be used to provide material benefits to those who are included and materially injure those who are excluded (Banton 1983; Hardin 1995).[1] Given these potential distinctions, a political entrepreneur may even manufacture group conflict in order to extract rents or tribute from members of her own or other groups. In some models, those interested in maintaining their leadership roles adopt a group-oriented strategy of divide and conquer (e.g., Roemer 1979).

Instrumental explanations of this kind, however, fail paradoxically on instrumental grounds. They are unable to explain the crucial fact of group-based mobilization from instrumentally rational actors in the context of anonymous mass elections, where behavior is difficult to monitor. Although groups are still associated with turnout in this case (e.g., Nelson 1979; Verba and Nie 1972), their participation remains a challenge even to an instrumental rational choice theory sensitized to groups and group identification (cf. Uhlaner 1989a,b).[2]

One alternative, of course, is simply to regard individual preferences for groups as in the nature of the beast. On this analysis, basic preferences deposited by the forces of human evolution ultimately explain group identity and attachments. Howard Margolis (1984), for example, argues that a generalized concern for the group, instilled by evolution, is represented in each individual's calculations as a distinct, group-oriented component self demanding its "fair share" of utility vis-à-vis the traditional self-interested component self. Each bifurcated individual must, loosely speaking, trade off contributions to her self-interest and contributions to her group interest. In the case of electoral participation, for example, tipping the election in favor of a preferred candidate can have a large perceived impact on the individual's group-oriented interest. Even when discounted by the probability of a pivotal vote occurring, this benefit can rationalize participation despite the small perceived impact on self-interest.

In many ways, positing social preferences solves the problem of group-oriented behavior handily. Sometimes, however, a straight line is not the shortest explanatory distance between two points. The reason in this case is that the biological genesis of group attachments is still obscure. As Russell Hardin (1995, 8) notes, "Objective identity tells almost none of the story." Evolutionary explanations in terms of group selection, moreover, are not in great favor (although see Samuelson 1993). By extension, biological explanations of group orientations in politics face an uphill battle.

One reason they face difficulties is the standard set of problems associated with free riding. Since each member can benefit by taking opportunistic advantage of the existence of the group, the group's advantages for its members may be insufficient to insure its survival. In fact, intragroup relations arguably reproduce the conflict-inducing characteristics of intergroup relations.

Second, while numerous folk theorems in game theory offer hope of rationalizing intragroup cooperation when the strategy of each individual can be made contingent on the past behavior of others, the information requirements in these games seem to limit cooperative solutions to small groups or hierarchies of collective discipline built on small groups (e.g., Hechter 1990). Small group dynamics might have provided a useful launching pad for cooperative dispositions, but their immediate application to anonymous political behavior and to diffuse groups in large-scale societies is doubtful (recall Skyrms 1996). True, there is an important strain of analysis showing positive participation when an entrepreneur operating within a group can help rational agents hampered by uncertainty over whether there will be a critical threshold number of contributors without them (e.g., Ainsworth and Sened 1993). Likewise instrumentally rational agents may bear the cost of participation in order to signal leaders about the size of support for a particular policy (e.g., Lohmann 1993). But the finding of positive participation in a large population is not the same as finding substantial participation in such a population. Qualitatively, epsilon ain't zero, but it ain't one hundred million either.

The difficulty of extending biological explanations to larger social and political settings is particularly troubling for Margolis's (1984) analysis. The problem is that individuals who care about the consequences of their actions for, let us say, their ethnic group can find it a difficult interest to implement. "It would be impossible to demonstrate any close connection between the decisions made by members . . . and the economic well-being (much less biological fitness) of those members" (Simon 1993, 159).

Focusing more on instrumental rather than on objective sources of political identity, Hardin (1995) observes that ethnicity and other forms of identification promote the coordination of individual actions that, in turn, encourages the identification. The simplest coordination problems arise when individual benefits depend on all doing the same thing, such as all driving on the right or all driving on the left. Coordination in the driving case poses a problem to participants because neither solution, left or right, is intrinsically better than the other and therefore individuals, despite their best intentions, can get into serious head-on collisions before coordination is achieved. Group identity provides some assurance that these coordination problems will be solved.

In political situations, the advantages to those who solve the coordination problem are equally striking, since a coordinated group has advantages over an uncoordinated group or over a group whose political survival depends on divisions among its opponents. Members of politically atomistic economic classes and religious or ethnic groups can be easily suppressed, whereas those who successfully coordinate may find the resources to resist. As Hardin notes, the sheer weight of numbers in a group, even if it assembled for other purposes, can provide its members with enough individual protection to defy authorities, whose hidden weakness is thereby exposed. The once feared emperor is shown to have no clothes. On a less positive note, the newly coordinated entity is in a better position to impose its will on nonmembers.

Hardin's astute analysis shows that many problems of collective action are not subject to the stringencies of the Prisoner's Dilemma. Hardin recognizes, of course, that collective action dilemmas abound, but he shows that they are not nearly as universal as one might think. Unfortunately for Hardin's analysis, elections are in part Prisoner's Dilemmas, and, to the exent they are not, they are not strict coordination games either.

Consider, again, the two-candidate election in which ties are broken by a coin toss. As Thomas Palfrey and Howard Rosenthal (1983) observe, the two groups of supporters may face a Prisoner's Dilemma insofar as the dominant strategy for each side is to participate even when universal nonparticipation, in expectation, produces the same result without incurring the cost of voting. Elections in this sense are socially inefficient. Within each side, however, each member typically plays a game of Chicken with the other members, not coordination. Abstaining, in particular, is equivalent to not swerving. If most in the group abstain the election probably will be lost, but for each individual it is better to let the others do the work of voting. If just enough are participating to win, no voter can deviate without a net loss.

To Hardin, political participation is a coordination phenomenon. "On the coordination view, it is not the individual voter who is powerful; rather, it is the coordinated mass of voters who vote together that is powerful" (1995, 37). Yet the power emerging from joint participation is not contingent on any individual's participation. What an EU maximizer's participation requires, Hardin recognizes, is some additional "moral commitment" in order to "tip the scales toward action" (1995, 40). Moral commitment, in effect, is Downs's (1957) civic duty motivation for voting. "This norm typically cannot be outcome-oriented in the sense that in a major election I cannot generally affect the outcome with my vote. Indeed, this norm is of value at all because the individual would not vote if the only consideration were her effect on the outcome of the action" (Hardin 1995, 108–9).

While there is no technical obstacle to introducing pure "consumption goods" into the rational choice calculus of voting, critics (e.g., Barry 1970) complain that this formal solution is empty, a variant of saying that the chicken crossed the road to get to the other side. Not that invoking moral commitments or noninstrumental norms makes rational choice theory any *worse* than alternative approaches using the same easy explanatory trick. But rational choice theorists have tried to do better; they have tried to get behind the surface phenomena. In so doing, they purport to offer a very different picture of human behavior, not just the relatively empty claim that all behavior is *formally* rational.

We have not really captured the phenomenon of moral behavior if we cannot explain why some people behave fairly decently when no one is looking. Similarly, I suggest, EU theory has not captured the phenomenon of turnout and, in particular, the role of ethnic and religious identity in turnout if it cannot explain why some people's group identity matters to them in the privacy of the voting booth when even their participation is relatively anonymous. Many forms of group identity no doubt involve coordination, and much of it involves crudely instrumental behavior. But if we limit our understanding of group identity in this way, we may have missed some of its real motivating power.

II

Both the direct evolutionary approach to group identity and the indirect instrumental approach appear to be inadequate. If so, we seem to have steered ourselves into a cul-de-sac. One way out, I suggest, is to recognize that both approaches rely primarily on preference as the vehicle for group-oriented behavior: direct preferences for the group's well-being or indirect preferences for one's own well-being enhanced by the success of one's group. The innovation of CEU theory versus EU theory, of course, lies with beliefs, specifically conditional expectations. Beliefs provide a better way to model group identity.

While in no way denying the existence of preference-based group distinctions, I question whether they capture all that group identities represent in social and political interactions. If group identity in a deeper sense does matter, then simple instrumental explanations of intergroup interactions fail on their own terms, for Elster's (1989b) point with regard to norms applies to group identity as well. One can explain the *exploitation* of group identity (or norms) only if one can explain the identities (or beliefs in norms) themselves (although cf. chap. 4 for some limitations on this argument). It is impossible to exploit something that does not matter in the first place.

We are ultimately interested, then, in types of group membership reflecting who people believe they collectively are (see, e.g., Geertz 1963). Ties of group membership in this sense go to the heart of the identity connecting individuals. Moreover, according to James Q. Wilson (1993, 46–50), this fundamental sense of similarity among members anchors the basic sympathy that leads to sociability, loyalty, and altruism among members of a group.

By the same token, a sense of identification does not necessarily generate altruism (cf. Monroe 1996). The reason is a corollary of Nozick's (1974) observation that we rely on differences to establish individual worth and dignity: we might just as easily see those with whom we most identify as our greatest competitors. Sprinters, for example, are unlikely to be dejected by their inability to outrun cheetahs but will experience the spirit of competition against humans. Altruism is not an automatic consequence of identification.

Fortunately, the difference between identity and altruism does not pose a problem for our analysis since, as we will see, group identity, modeled in terms of CEU maximization, ultimately enhances the utility of the identifier. It is instrumentally valuable. I view this as a positive result insofar as instrumental explanations are deeper, and probably less under the suspicion of being ad hoc, than explanations that take the phenomenon in question to be a brute fact about behavior or preferences (remember the explanation for why chickens cross the road). Finally, intuitions and anthropological assumptions notwithstanding, substantial experimental evidence (e.g., Dawes, van de Kragt, and Orbell 1990; Turner 1982) and nonexperimental evidence (e.g., Banton 1983; Horowitz 1985, 44–49, 66–67; Waters 1990) suggest that for all the personal, social, and political ramifications of group distinctions, individuals are fairly malleable, even opportunistic, when it comes to adopting group identities.

An explanation of why groups can become so socially and politically potent evidently must also explain the relative flexibility of group identification.[3] The CEU model of group-based electoral mobilization developed in this chapter can account for these two aspects of group identification: its role in political mobilization despite its flexible, instrumental use by group members. The key to the model, of course, is how it defines group identities in terms of CEU maximization.

III

In light of the limitations of a preference-based approach to group identity, we are looking for beliefs capable of cognitively connecting members of groups to one another, yet serving some instrumental purpose for those who are connected. Within CEU theory, beliefs in general obviously influence the formation of expectations. Perhaps in the case of groups, or collections of individuals with the potential to become groups, the relevant expectations concern the behavior of other members. Expectations, in this sense, are predictions about their behavior.

I need not belabor the obvious. The ability to predict behavior can be a very useful skill. But in order to predict the behavior of anything, an agent needs some way to categorize it. Children cannot learn from painful experiences with fire if things on fire are indistinguishable from things not on fire. *On fire* is therefore a useful classification. Group stereotypes, bad press aside, work similarly in social and political interactions. They can be useful forecasting tools.

Walter Lippmann (1965, 60) elegantly describes one value of group stereotypes: "there are uniformities sufficiently accurate, and the need of economizing attention is so inevitable, that the abandonment of all stereotypes for a wholly innocent approach to experience would impoverish human life." No rational agent, as Lippmann recognizes, uses stereotypes in disregard of case-specific information. Agents, first of all, will adjust their original expectations in light of this evidence. If they are Bayesians, their new expectation will lie between the prior probability and the probability suggested by the evidence when unfiltered by their initial belief.[4] Second, new evidence may suggest switching to an alternative system of categories—a different way of subdividing populations—if it promises to outperform the current scheme. The choice of category schemes is modeled in the next chapter.

For now the message is that group categorizations are salient sorting devices in part because they provide effective predictions of behavior (see also Lakoff 1987). This is no less true in the political realm. "We tend to assume that people's characteristics are a guide to the actions they will take, and we are concerned with the characteristics of our legislators for just this reason" (Pitkin 1967, 89).

Agents can use a group classification to forecast how others will behave or be treated and, if they are so inclined, may be able to use the same classification to predict what they themselves will do or how they will be treated (see chap. 1). Yet this use of classification seems to be a far cry from group identification in the ordinary sense. An agent's classification scheme presumably summarizes the actual causes of others' behavior—their beliefs and preferences—in order to determine how others will behave or to predict the summaries others will use in dealing with him. Yet these uses, however valuable, do not necessarily tell us why a group classification "matters" to the individuals who are classified. To do so, the fact of a *shared* group classification should directly affect the user's own behavior. The agent who classifies, in other words, may continue to behave as his beliefs and preferences dictate; the fact that a given category applies to him as well as others could be irrelevant to his calculations.

Should an instrumentally rational agent's behavior be sensitive to whether or not his classification scheme subsumes his own behavior along with the behavior of others? Could sharing a category with others matter to a rational agent? The remainder of this section explores this possibility. In some cases, we shall see, a shared classification can directly influence the choices of CEU maximizers by providing them with useful information about the behavior of others. A rational agent who identifies with other members of a group—sees himself as falling under their categorization—can read their behavior from his own.

Suppose Sally, whom we will now designate by S, has some beliefs about a particular ethnic group and these beliefs anchor some fairly accurate predictions. As one example, S predicts that Italians are more likely to be in a Catholic than in a Protestant church on Sunday. In other cases, however, S's predictions are much less clear. Suppose, for example, members of this same group must choose between going to an Italian restaurant or having a dinner at home The subjective probability of the one alternative may be no higher than the probability of the other.

In both examples, S is using conditional probabilities, probabilities of behavior conditional on individuals' being Italian. But this probability can be refined. Following the lead of chapter 1, our analysis of group identification will assume that when an individual like S shares an appropriate classification with those whose behavior she predicts, she can also condition on her own behavior. If, then, S is Italian, her own choice between going to an Italian restaurant and having dinner at home can alter her estimate of the behavior of other Italians from what her general knowledge of their shared ethnic identity suggests. Given their shared ethnic background, S can treat her own choice as conveying additional information about the behavior of others.

As I pointed out in chapter 1's discussion of voting, this much of S's analysis should be uncontroversial. Since we have not yet assessed the impact of S's analysis on her actions, we are dealing only with distinctions among beliefs. To represent these distinctions formally with regard to two agents, S and H: prob[H does A | S and H are Italian and S does A and I_S] > prob[H does A | H is Italian and S does A and I_S] ≥ prob[H does A | S and H are Italian and I_S], where $A \in$ {going to an Italian restaurant; having dinner at home} and I_S is S's other information. Thus S may believe that there is a .7 chance of B's eating at an Italian restaurant when both are Italian and S chooses to go, when if S were not Italian the conditional probability would only be .3.

We now generalize to groups of all kinds. When agent j has a *group identity* with respect to group G then, for any other group member k, j believes there is some action x such that

$$\text{prob}(x_k \mid j,k \in G \text{ and } x_j \text{ and } I_j) > \text{prob}(x_k \mid j \in G \text{ and } k \notin G$$
$$\text{and } x_j \text{ and } I_j), \tag{2.1}$$

where x_m means that agent m does x and $m \in G$ means that m belongs to group G and where again I_m designates m's background information. We will say a *group identity* exists with respect to G when the belief characterized by expression (2.1) is correct for any arbitrary group member.

When expression (2.1) obtains, then the probability S assigns to some action by H increases when S behaves that way compared to situations in which they do not share a group identity. This conclusion can be plugged into the analysis of chapter 1. If now $A \in \{\text{voting, not voting}\}$, then S's belief that H or any other fellow member of G will participate, conditional on S's own participation, increases. By the same logic, the subjective probability of participation by other group members, conditional on S's abstention, declines.[5] This variation will matter to S should it turn out that members of the group with which she identifies also support S's favorite candidate.[6] If group identity is strong enough, it may matter enough to S to prompt her to vote.

Chapter 1, however, is decision theoretic, while S's calculation might be sophisticated enough to recognize that the very individuals with whom she identifies use the same calculus to determine the likelihood of her participation, as well as the participation of others. Their behavior is statistically dependent on hers and vice versa. Also, S must reckon with parallel calculations by members of other groups. The issue is not whether S's perception of the statistical dependence is correct after all. I will assume it is, although variations in turnout could lead S to update her estimates (see Grafstein 1991, 1002–3). Rather, the issue is whether S can exploit that dependence in game theoretic as well as decision theoretic settings. Will group identification produce positive turnout in mass elections when the implications of identification are generalized to the rational decisions of all potential voters?

The next section formally explores this question (although my answer is by now no mystery). It does this by integrating the two characteristics of group identification explored previously. On the one hand, a group classification is not, in this model, a neutral typology whose significance is determined solely by the instrumental use to which it may be put. Group classifications become the basis for group identification when they connect the individuals who fall under them. When there is group identity, in other words, the classification formally reflects the interdependence of behavior that makes the existence of groups relevant to behavior. The schema embodied in expression (2.1) operationalizes the idea that group identity introduces a certain "we-ness" into people's thinking (and, correlatively, distinctions with respect to others). Whether this captures the phenomenology of group identification is less important to me than a behavioral consideration. The fact of shared group classification affects the behavior of those who find themselves meriting the classification.

On the other hand, group identities affect behavior because they are instrumentally valuable. In the following model of voting, for example, an individual voter is prompted to participate because of her group identity, but it is strictly her conditional expected utility she thereby increases. She participates because, in part, she thinks her group membership tells her something about the behavior of others. She does not participate in order to benefit them or their group as a whole.

IV

In order to explore the impact of ethnic identity on voting participation in a game theoretic setting, we will need to complicate the formal apparatus substantially. We consider a population of $N + 1$ potential voters divided into n mutually exclusive and exhaustive groups $G_1, G_2, \ldots, G_k, \ldots, G_n$. There is a two-candidate majority-rule contest between Θ and Ψ, which might be candidates, parties, or coalitions. Members of each group G_k are not politically homogeneous; $G_{k\Theta}$ supports Θ and $G_{k\psi}$ supports Ψ. To avoid forcing the assumption that everyone is in a group, $G_{n\Theta}$ and $G_{n\psi}$ can, if one prefers, represent residual collections of nongroup members who support Θ and Ψ respectively.

Departing from the analysis of chapter 1, if the election is a tie, Ψ wins (the impact of a coin toss tiebreaker is considered subsequently). The two-candidate (two-party, two-coalition) contest is clearly the simplest to analyze and continues to be the workhorse of turnout models, most notably for the present discussion, those of John Ledyard (1984), Palfrey and Rosenthal (1985), and Grafstein (1991, 1995). These provide the framework for the approach used in the chapter.

Potential voters maximize their CEU when deciding whether to participate. The utility for $i \in G_k$ of Θ's winning, $U_i(x,\Theta)$, is a function of Θ's policy position, represented by Θ, as well as i's individual characteristics x, including group membership; the utility from Ψ's winning is $U_i(x,\Psi)$. Although group membership does not completely determine i's utility, membership is related to utility in this sense: $U_i(x,\Theta) > U_i(x,\Psi)$ if and only if $i \in G_{k\Theta}$ and analogously for $i \in G_{k\psi}$. As in chapter 1, we make the standard simplifying assumption that costs enter the agent's utility function linearly. This allows us to normalize the net utility of i's candidate (party, coalition) winning as 1, the net utility of that candidate losing as 0, and the cost of voting as c_i.[7] In what follows, it is assumed that i prefers Θ.

Repeating the CEU decision rule from chapter 1, $i \in G_{k\theta}$ votes if and only if

$$\text{prob}_i(W_\theta \mid V_i)(1 - c_i) + [1 - \text{prob}_i(W_\theta \mid V_i)](-c_i) = \text{prob}_i(W_\theta \mid V_i) - c_i$$
$$> \text{prob}_i(W_\theta \mid A_i),$$

where $\text{prob}_i(W_\theta \mid V_i)$ is shorthand for i's belief that Θ wins (W) given that i votes (V) and $\text{prob}_i(W_\theta \mid A_i)$ is i's belief that Θ wins given that i abstains (A). Thus i votes for Θ whenever

$$P_{i\theta} = \text{prob}_i(W_\theta \mid V_i) - \text{prob}_i(W_\theta \mid A_i) > c_i, \qquad (2.2)$$

that is, whenever the increase in the conditional probability of Θ's winning when i votes exceeds the cost of voting. Analogous expressions hold for supporters of Ψ.

For a voter who identifies with a group, her private information about her own participation decision provides additional insight into the participation decisions of others in the group. To represent the difference this private information makes, let $Q_{\theta k}$ be the common probability estimate that an individual chosen randomly from the eligible population is from $G_{k\theta}$ and votes for Θ. This estimate is based on universally available statistical information about the population's voting costs, the distribution of preferences within the group, and the group's relative size. But the participation of $i \in G_{k\theta}$ influences i's own estimate. Let $f_{Vk\theta}(Q_{\theta k})$ denote i's revised estimate given i's participation and $f_{Ak\theta}(Q_{\theta k})$ i's revised estimate given i's abstention, where $f_{Vk\theta}$ is a monotone increasing function, and $f_{Ak\theta}$ is a monotone decreasing function, of $Q_{\theta k}$, with $0 \le f_{Ak\theta}(Q_{\theta k}) \le Q_{\theta k} \le f_{Vk\theta}(Q_{\theta k}) \le 1$. Thus when i participates, the participation she predicts from supporters of Θ in her group is at least as great as the predicted participation without her private information, while when she abstains the participation she predicts is no higher than when she knows only what everyone else knows.

Parallel restrictions hold for $i \in G_{k\theta}$ concerning fellow group members $j \in G_{k\psi}$, except insofar as shared political preferences suggest additional similarities in political behavior, $f_{Ak\theta}(Q_{\theta k}) \le f_{Ak\theta}(Q_{\psi k}) \le Q_{\psi k} \le f_{Vk\theta}(Q_{\psi k}) \le f_{Vk\theta}(Q_{\theta k})$. Note that $f_{Ak\theta}(Q_{\psi k})$ and $f_{Vk\theta}(Q_{\psi k})$ reflect the "cross-dependence" of subgroup members $j \in G_{k\psi}$ on $i \in G_{k\theta}$. For the sake of generality, these expressions include as a special case, $f_{Vk\theta} = f_{Ak\theta} = Q_{\theta k}$ and $f_{Vk\psi} = f_{Ak\psi} = Q_{\psi k}$.

Here i's participation offers i no additional information about the likelihood that other members of G_k will participate.

As I mentioned previously, i understands that G_k does not have exclusive rights to group identification. If so, the universal impact of group identity might negate each group's impact on participation, although we will see it does not. In any case, i models members of other groups as CEU maximizers, subject to the same restrictions imposed on $f_{Vk\psi}$ and $f_{Ak\psi}$. Although the decision to participate is private, the parameters of group identification, like the estimates $Q_{\theta k}$ and $Q_{\psi k}$, are known to all potential voters.

We now have expressions for the probabilities in expression (2.2). For $i \in G_{k\theta}$ this means the probability of Θ's winning with i's participation, $\text{prob}_i(W_\theta \mid V_i)$, minus the probability of Θ's winning without i's participation, $\text{prob}_i(W_\psi \mid A_i)$. It is convenient to calculate the probability of Θ's winning by $t + 1$ votes with i's participation as the probability of Θ's being t votes ahead without i's vote:

$$\sum_{s=0}^{\|N/2\|} \sum_{t=0}^{N-2s} \frac{N!}{(s+t)!s!(N-2s-t)!} [[f_{Vk\theta}(Q_{\theta k}) + Q_{\theta\backslash k}]^{s+t}[Q_{\psi\backslash k} + f_{Vk\theta}Q_{\psi k})]^s$$

$$\times [1 - [f_{Vk\theta}(Q_{\theta k}) + Q_{\theta\backslash k} + Q_{\psi\backslash k} + f_{Vk\theta}(Q_{\psi k})]]^{N-2s-t}$$

$$- \sum_{s=0}^{\|N/2\|} \sum_{t=1}^{N-2s} \frac{N!}{(s+t)!s!(N-2s-t)!} [f_{Ak\theta}(Q_{\theta k}) + Q_{\theta\backslash k}]^{s+t}[Q_{\psi\backslash k}$$

$$+ f_{Ak\theta}(Q_{\psi k})]^s[1 - [f_{Ak\theta}(Q_{\theta k}) + Q_{\theta\backslash k} + Q_{\psi\backslash k} + f_{Ak\theta}(Q_{\psi k})]]^{N-2s-t},$$

where $\|N/2\|$ denotes the greatest integer $s \leq N/2$; t denotes the vote difference between Θ and Ψ; $Q_{\theta\backslash q}$ denotes the joint probability that an individual randomly chosen from the population is a voting member of a group, other than G_q, supporting Θ; and similarly $Q_{\psi\backslash q}$ is the joint probability that a randomly chosen individual is a voting member of a group, other than G_q, supporting Ψ. We calculate $Q_{\theta\backslash q}$ and $Q_{\psi\backslash q}$ respectively as

$$Q_{\theta\backslash q} = \sum_{r \neq q} Q_{\theta r}, \qquad Q_{\psi\backslash q} = \sum_{r \neq q} Q_{\psi r}, \tag{2.3}$$

where $r \in \{1, 2, \ldots, n\}$. Thus:

$$Q_\theta = Q_{\theta q} + Q_{\theta\backslash q}, \qquad Q_\psi = Q_{\psi q} + Q_{\psi\backslash q}. \tag{2.4}$$

The function $\xi_\theta(Q_{\theta k}, Q_{\theta\backslash k}, Q_\psi, Q_{\psi\backslash k}, f_{Vk\theta}, f_{Ak\theta})$ is the expected difference occasioned by i's participation:

$$P_{i\theta} = \xi_\theta(Q_{\theta k}, Q_{\theta\backslash k}, Q_\psi, Q_{\psi\backslash k}, f_{Vk\theta}, f_{Ak\theta}). \tag{2.5}$$

Individuals $j \in G_{m\psi}$, who support Θ, participate if and only if

$$P_{j\psi} = \text{prob}_j(W_\psi \mid V_j) - \text{prob}_j(W_\psi \mid A_j) > c_j. \tag{2.6}$$

While this formula is analogous to expression (2.2), the calculation of the component probabilities must reflect the fact that Ψ wins in the event of a tie:

$$\sum_{s=1}^{\|N/2\|} \frac{N!}{s!(s-1)!(N-2s)} [Q_{\Theta\backslash m} + f_{Vm\psi}(Q_{\Theta m})]^s [f_{Vm\psi}(Q_{\psi m}) + Q_{\psi\backslash m}]^{s-1}$$

$$\times [1 - [Q_{\Theta\backslash m} + Q_{\psi\backslash m} + f_{Vm\psi}(Q_{\psi m}) + f_{Vm\psi}(Q_{\Theta m})]]^{N-2s-1}$$

$$+ \sum_{s=0}^{\|N/2\|} \sum_{t=0}^{N-2s} \frac{N!}{s!(s+t)!(N-2s-t)!} [Q_{\Theta\backslash m} + f_{Vm\psi}(Q_{\Theta m})]^s$$

$$\times [f_{Vm\psi}(Q_{\psi m}) + Q_{\psi\backslash m}]^{s+t} [1 - [Q_{\Theta\backslash m} + Q_{\psi\backslash m} + f_{Vm\psi}(Q_{\psi m})$$

$$+ f_{Vm\psi}(Q_{\Theta m})]]^{N-2s-t}$$

$$- \sum_{s=0}^{\|N/2\|} \sum_{t=0}^{N-2s} \frac{N!}{s!(s+t)!(N-2s-t)!} [Q_{\Theta\backslash m} + f_\psi(Q_{\Theta m})]^s$$

$$\times [f_{Am\psi}(Q_{\psi m}) + Q_{\psi\backslash m}]^{s+1}$$

$$\times [1 - [Q_{\Theta\backslash m} + Q_{\psi\backslash m} + f_{Am\psi}(Q_{\Theta m}) + f_{Am\psi}(Q_{\psi m})]]^{N-2s-t}.$$

The result, $\xi_\psi(Q_{\psi m}, Q_{\psi\backslash m}, Q_{\Theta m}, Q_{\Theta\backslash m}, f_{Vm\psi}, f_{Am\psi})$, gives the expected difference occasioned by a member of $G_{m\psi}$'s participation:

$$P_{j\psi} = \xi_\psi(Q_{\psi m}, Q_{\psi\backslash m}, Q_{\Theta m}, Q_{\Theta\backslash m}, f_{Vm\psi}, f_{Am\psi}). \tag{2.7}$$

To this point, we have simply presented a more elaborate version of the decision theoretic model of voting from chapter 1. In the game theoretic setting, however, each individual's identification with a group does not blind him to the group identification and other factors influencing the decisions of others. The subjective probability that a randomly chosen individual participates is itself a function of the expected costs and benefits he ascribes to members of the other groups, weighted by the estimated size of those groups. The additional insight provided by the individual's own decision on voting does not come at the expense of his understanding that other individuals are guided by personal analogues of expressions (2.2) and (2.6). Thus an individual's group identification is only one part of a comprehensive estimate of Θ and Ψ's chances of winning, although group identification still plays a crucial role. Finally, if there is no group identity, meaning complete statistical independence for all groups, the model presented here reduces to the models of Ledyard (1984) and Palfrey and Rosenthal (1985).

Initial beliefs about the voting costs of individuals belonging to $G_{q\theta}$ and $G_{q\psi}$ are represented by the continuous probability density functions $h_{q\theta}(c)$ and $h_{q\psi}(c)$ $(0 \leq c < \infty)$. The restricted lower bound on c is designed to limit the analysis to the nontrivial case of voters with nonnegative voting costs. For when $c_i < 0$, i participates regardless of her candidate's chances. We retain the possibility of voting costs that are so high that even the certainty of the candidate's victory with participation does not lead to voting. This arises when $c_i \geq 1$.

We assume the cost functions $G_{q\theta}$ and $G_{q\psi}$ are independently and identically distributed (i.i.d.) with respect to the relevant potential voters. We make analogous assumptions about the shared uncertainty concerning the size of groups in the form of density functions $g_{q\theta}(y)$ and $g_{q\psi}(y)$, where $y \in [0,1]$ is the decimal fraction of individuals belonging to the relevant subgroup of G_q. These functions are also i.i.d. with respect to the relevant individuals. The assumption of common uncertainty about cost and size, I concede, is probably unrealistic, since individuals are likely to be more knowledgeable about their own group than about others. The assumption is maintained for analytical convenience. The same can be said for the next simplification. Following Palfrey and Rosenthal (1985), we assume that relative to the normalization we have adopted, $c_i = c_j$ for $i, j \in G_{q\theta}$ and $i, j \in G_{q\psi}$, which allows us to use the identical c to represent any subgroup member's requirement for participation. Thus we need distinguish only among the $P_{k\theta}$, $P_{m\theta}$, $P_{k\psi}$, and $P_{m\psi}$, where $k\theta$ stands for any $i \in G_{k\theta}$ and $m\psi$ stands for any $j \in G_{m\psi}$.

With knowledge of $h_{q\theta}(c)$ and $g_{q\theta}(y)$, $1 \leq q \leq n$, members of a particular subgroup supporting Θ can calculate the probability of a randomly selected individual voting for Θ by summing the component probabilities for each of Θ's subgroups. The calculation for the particular subgroup $G_{q\theta}$ is

$$Q_{\theta q} = \int_0^1 \int_0^{P_{q\theta}} h_{q\theta}(c) g_{q\theta}(y) dc \, dy \equiv t_{q\theta}(P_{q\theta}, g_{q\theta}, h_{q\theta}), \qquad (2.8)$$

subject of course to

$$\int_0^1 g_{q\theta}(y) dy = \int_0^1 g_{q\psi}(y) dy = 1.$$

The inside integral involving $h_{q\theta}(c)$ will also be denoted $H_{q\theta}(c)$. Parallel formulas apply to each $G_{q\psi}$. By analogy to equation (2.8) there exists a function t whose arguments are the union of the arguments of either the $t_{q\theta}$ or the $t_{q\psi}$.

V

We have now characterized a number of conditions. First, there is each individual's calculation that his participation is worthwhile, which is determined by comparing the probability of Θ's winning (or Ψ's, depending on the individual), with and without his participation. In shorthand, each individual calculates the CEU of voting. Second, the probability of making a worthwhile contribution to Θ's victory depends on expected turnout. This expected turnout is a function of the very decision to participate just described. In terms of our formulas, the $P_{i\theta}$ and $P_{j\psi}$ are functions of Q_{θ} and Q_{ψ}, which in turn are functions of the $P_{q\theta}$ and $P_{m\psi}$ by way of equations (2.4) and (2.8).

The result is a circle but not a vicious one so long as some values of the variables satisfy the first and second sets of conditions simultaneously. Such an equilibrium exists if there are Q_{θ}^*, Q_{ψ}^*, $P_{k\theta}^*$, and $P_{m\psi}^*$ that solve equations (2.4), (2.5), and (2.7), where again k's stand for representative members of the subgroups supporting Θ and m's stand for representative members of the subgroups supporting Ψ (Ledyard 1984). The following propositions are proved in appendix A.

PROPOSITION 1: *There is an equilibrium.*

More important for our purposes, there is turnout from voters who have a positive cost to participating.

PROPOSITION 2: *If for some $1 \leq q \leq n$, $H_{q\theta}(c) > 0$ for $c > 0$, then there is positive turnout at equilibrium.*

Technically, this turnout could be exclusively for Θ or Ψ. The following corollary provides a more complicated condition for the more realistic case of turnout for both.

COROLLARY: *If there are k and m ($1 \leq k, m \leq n$), and $o = \theta, \psi$; $p = \psi, \theta$, such that $f_{Vko}(Q_{ok}) > f_{Vko}(Q_{pk})$; $f_{Vmp}(Q_{pm}) > f_{Vmp}(Q_{om})$; $H_{ko}(c), H_{kp}(c), H_{mp}(c)$, $H_{mo}(c) > 0$ for all $c_{ko}, c_{kp}, c_{mo}, c_{mp} > 0$; and $[Q_{o\backslash k} + Q_{o\backslash m} + f_{Vko}(Q_{ok}) + f_{Vko}(Q_{pk})]$, $[Q_{p\backslash m} + Q_{p\backslash k} + f_{Vmp}(Q_{pm}) + f_{Vmp}(Q_{om})] < 1$, then $Q_o, Q_p > 0$.*

For this corollary to work, some abstention must be expected; the corollary also implies turnout when ties are broken by a coin toss.

These qualitative findings offer a useful corrective to the Downsian literature's general skepticism about turnout from instrumentally rational voters. As evidence in favor of CEU theory, however, these findings must counter potential challenges from two directions. On the one hand, the present model replicates the positive results on participation developed by Ledyard (1984), who does not rely on group identification or, for that matter, CEU maximization. On the other hand, Palfrey and Rosenthal (1985) show that in Ledyard's model turnout from individuals with positive voting costs limits to 0 as the size of the electorate goes to infinity. Positive turnout, in other words, is not enough. To be empirically plausible, it must be robust to increases in the size of the electorate. The next proposition shows that, unlike in Ledyard's model, turnout in the group identification model does not hinge on relatively small electorates.

PROPOSITION 3: *If for some* k $[f_{Vko}(Q_{ok}) + Q_{o\backslash k}] > [Q_{p\backslash k} + f_{Vko}(Q_{pk})]$ *and* $[f_{Ako}(Q_{ok}) + Q_{o\backslash k}] \leq [Q_{p\backslash k} + f_{Ako}(Q_{pk})];$ *or* $[f_{Vko}(Q_{ok}) + Q_{o\backslash k}] = [Q_{p\backslash k} + f_{Vko}(Q_{pk})]$ *and* $[f_{Ako}(Q_{ok}) + Q_{o\backslash k}] < [Q_{p\backslash k} + f_{Ako}(Q_{pk})],$ $1 \leq k \leq n$ *and* $o = \Theta, \Psi;$ $p = \Psi, \Theta,$ *then the equilibrium turnout does not limit to* 0 *as* $N \to \infty.$

Group identification, then, is a crucial ingredient in producing turnout.[8] An individual's willingness to participate, which depends on her increased expectation of supporting a winner given her participation, is itself contingent on her degree of group identification as well as on the distribution of intragroup interests. Although proposition 3 encompasses the case in which the prospective voter breaks a tie, we know from the literature motivating Downsian-style analysis that this prospect is highly improbable in a large electorate (e.g., Chamberlain and Rothschild 1981). So for all practical purposes, we can interpret proposition 3 in terms of strict inequalities. Turnout occurs when participants believe that the group with which they identify is, given their participation, likely to secure a win. These group identifiers are not limited to a decision theoretic calculus. There is turnout even in the more comprehensive game theoretic environment in which decision makers factor in the parallel decisions of others. Palfrey and Rosenthal's (1985) analysis, which seemed fatal to realistic game theoretic models of instrumental voting in mass elections, no longer applies.[9]

Of course, this analysis only covers group identification as defined in the text. What might be called alienated groups, like those corresponding to Marx's *lumpenproletariat,* will look more Downsian in their behavior. To use more modern political science terminology, these are potential groups without any sense of their own identity as groups. The greater the level of this alienation, the less participation in general.[10]

VI

If the preceding model is correct, the link between interest and group identification provides a powerful impetus to mobilization. Yet the definition of group identity embodied in expression (2.1) allows interest (preference) and identity (belief) to vary independently. This suggests that the impact of group membership should be quite ephemeral. It is striking, then, that certain group identities, such as those based on a combination of religion and ethnicity, are so often both salient and tenacious. Why do their members resist crosscutting pressures?[11]

This question also arises on purely analytic grounds. For any population of size N there are $2^N - N - 1$ potential groups, assuming any two or more individuals can constitute a group (this very large number of potential groups ought to be kept in mind when one characterizes a given society's politics as riven by group distinctions). The manifest groups, as David Truman (1951) notes, are bound to be a small fraction of the latent groups, and what we standardly view as the latent groups are bound to be a small fraction of the potential groups. This puts our original question in sharper relief. Why given this multitude of potential groups are some groups constantly in the political arena while others never mobilize or do so only sporadically?

Finally, to sharpen the question one more time recall that the criterion for group identity embodied in expression (2.1) makes the probability of common action conditional not only on the decision maker's action but also on her total information. In some cases, this additional information will help explain, let us say, ethnic income differences (see Sowell 1983). Therefore it may weaken group identity by the pure definitional criterion of expression (2.1). If, for example, I have a large family and also belong to a group associated with large families, this additional piece of information about family size can, apparently, attenuate the distinct impact of group identity. As we know with regard to research design, the addition of controls in an experimental design may well decrease estimates of statistical dependence.

To address the successively sharpened question of why some groups and not others persist, we can begin with the last sharpening. Ultimately, satisfying the criterion of group identity built into expression (2.1) is not the issue, behavior is. For reasons to do with large families or other factors, the decision maker may still be confident in the predictive powers of his behavior with respect to members of the group and, for all the world, may act as if he is motivated by group identity defined by expression (2.1). His bottom line is the predictive power of his own behavior; he does not share the social scientist's fussiness over multicollinearity. Over time, in fact, the resulting uniformities in the group's behavior can encourage or allow reasonable statistical inferences based on group membership alone: to the extent the factors embodied in the decision maker's information overlap with group membership, his "signal extraction" problem becomes more difficult and, fortunately for him, less pressing. The evidence from his own behavior, initially motivated for whatever reason, helps forge and reinforce a basis for deepening group identity.

I am suggesting, then, that the very sharp question posed in the preceding is wrongly stated. To use expression (2.1) as a club against the possibility of durable groups is to assume some prior or natural ethnic sense that agents bring to their group membership or experience. Group-oriented behavior, according to the CEU approach, is not an expression of a prior group orientation, whose distinguished role in the agent's life needs explaining. Rather, group-oriented behavior represents those survivors among the $2^N - N - 1$ possibilities for which joint action based on each individual's conditional probabilities confirms those probabilities. For successful groups, the formation of group identity is a virtuous circle.

These successful ethnic and religious groups, for example, are more likely to involve members in mutual interactions and shared customs, involvement encouraging the inference that members will engage in similar (political) behavior. A relationship of comembership based on mutual interaction, common customs, and shared experience is in many cases less artificial than a relationship based, say, on common identification with a political party, although the importance of such identification for turnout (e.g., Dalton 1988) is consistent with the present model, as was the encompassing role of the great historical fascist, socialist, and communist parties in the lives of their members (for example, the "minisociety" of French communists discussed in Kriegel 1972). Communism was a religion in more ways than one.

Further, as modernization dissolves familiar and traditional economic, residential, and other social patterns, individuals seeking some predictive markers in unchartered or at least more fluid circumstances may well turn to or resurrect ethnic or religious identities as useful supplements. These identities need not fully counteract either the causes or effects of modernization. But given a mobile and nontraditional world in other respects, ethnicity and religion can have an enhanced comparative advantage in the competition among cognitive frameworks for getting a handle on things. The absolute size of the conditional probabilities associated with these groups can still be modest so long as they are larger than alternatives. Individuals may be forced to depend on predictive devices they know are not very powerful.

Given patterns of interaction, inculcated preferences, and the motives for instrumentally enforced distinctions noted by Rogowski (1974) and Hardin (1995), it is not surprising to find even in pluralistic societies that membership in certain distinguished groups is often statistically related to political and economic interest. Northern Ireland is only one extreme and well-known example of a common phenomenon. The historically active groups thus are more likely to have a degree of political homogeneity sufficient for mobilization.

We see, then, that certain group memberships are more likely to justify the inference, necessary for mobilization based on group identity, that the *conditional* probability of identical actions is reasonably high. This conditional probability, linking one member's behavior to expectations about the behavior of others, is distinct from the weaker and insufficient belief that members of the group happen to behave the same way (see Jeffrey 1981, 485).

In sum, conditional probability formalizes behavioral aspects of those "primordial" ethnic and religious ties associated with turnout. Conditional probabilities do not tell us, of course, how it feels to identify with a group, just as the study of human physiology cannot tell us how it feels to drown. But this failing, if it is a failing, does not detract from the important behavioral implications of rational identification or from the behavioral importance of drowning.

Moreover, I have suggested, the historical fact that ethnicity has been among the most salient and persistent bases for identification does not reflect its ontological distinctiveness compared to other kinds of groups, manifest or latent. The physical, genetic, and social proximity of potential members, their evolving pattern of interactions, and the selective incentives for victimizing or being victimized help create the conditions for these groups and their political mobilization. In terms used by Arthur Miller et al. (1981), interest plus belief induces group consciousness, which occurs when members in a social stratum have a sense of belonging and a political awareness targeted at collective action. But in the end, I suspect, we are apt to label as ethnic the social identities that seem to persist and matter most. CEU theory thus can capture the instrumental character of group identity without contradicting what we know about the tenacious grip some of these identities can have.

VII

Ethnic politics offers a particularly useful application of the CEU model since the relative contribution of interest and ethnicity to political mobilization has received extensive theoretical and empirical discussion. Is ethnicity a factor facilitating interest-based mobilization rooted in class or occupation? Or is it a competing interest in its own right? And if it is a distinct interest, what role in mobilization does it play?

These stubborn questions have been answered in at least five different ways, and it will be useful to explore how the CEU approach fits within this literature. According to what has been called the developmental model, modernization substitutes class interest for ethnicity as the primary vehicle of political mobilization (e.g., Butler and Stokes 1974). While the developmental model recognizes that class and ethnicity can covary, it questions whether ethnicity adds substantially to class-based mobilization. Indeed in some historical settings they are rivals.

As an alternative possibility, ethnicity becomes important precisely because of the stresses modernization imposes on traditional society. According to Michael Hechter (1975), ethnic mobilization is a reaction to modernization and class organization, constituting an alternative, status interest. Yet Hechter

(1978) quickly introduced a corrective to his own hypothesis. As he saw it, neither the developmental nor his simple reactive model explains how either ethnic or class interests solve the problem of group formation understood in standard rational choice terms. Free riding should dissolve any group effort.

Accordingly, Hechter (1978) hypothesizes a special role for ethnicity. Suppose that for some reason a society's ethnic membership and its system of stratification or occupational structure are highly correlated. Hechter calls this a "cultural division of labor." Under these circumstances, he suggests, class defines the interests of the participants whereas ethnicity facilitates mobilization by building communities capable of overcoming their free-rider problems. Ethnicity allows mobilization; class gives mobilization its point.

A fourth and widely discussed approach is the ethnic competition model (e.g., Banton 1983; Bates 1974; Melson and Wolpe 1970, 1114–18). In this model, ethnicity also facilitates mobilization, but mobilization results not from class divisions but rather from universal and therefore cross-ethnic interests in scarce resources.

Finally, Eric Leifer (1981) agrees that ethnicity is best understood as a facilitating condition for mobilization and not as a mobilizable interest in its own right. Yet class and ethnicity, he argues, do not tell the whole story. The available institutional channels also help determine whether group mobilization is incorporated into the national political system. There must be facilitating institutional conditions for the mobilization to have an object and a means to reach it.

The CEU model of group identification, I suggest, synthesizes the core insights of all these approaches, with the possible exception of the developmental model.[12] To take up Leifer's approach first, the CEU model clearly recognizes the role of institutional channels. In a sense, Θ and Ψ are institutionally defined objects. Moreover, due to institutionalized electoral arrangements, voting occurs through legally well-defined as well as physically discrete acts. The structure provided by these institutional arrangements, therefore, is apt to increase the conditional probabilities on which mobilization relies (see Grafstein 1992).

The CEU model also easily accommodates Hechter's notion of a cultural division of labor. Like Hechter's, the CEU model does not treat ethnicity as an interest in its own right. Ethnicity mobilizes interests, here operationalized using the more abstract concept of preference. Ethnics do not derive direct utility from their identity since their identity is not an interest per se. Yet in both models the coincidence of interest and identity leads to mobilization. Specifically, a cultural division of labor implies an uneven distribution of group members' interests, and in the CEU model turnout is partly a function of the relative sizes of the two subgroups into which each group is divided. Indeed for this reason equal distribution can completely negate the effect of group identity.[13] A cultural division of labor, then, is a natural way to generate the statistical preconditions for mobilization.

"[W]hile for earlier and most traditional nationalisms the reactive or developmental models may hold good . . . , for almost all the new nationalisms that have been investigated the competitive model fits the data far better" (Rogowski 1985, 337). The CEU model of course easily accommodates this last approach. Insofar as ethnic groups compete over scarce goods, the resulting allocation determines competing preferences. Against a backdrop of ethnic identification, competing preferences, in turn, lead to mobilization.

For those with a more sociological view of political life, the cohesiveness of ethnic groups does not revolve solely around interest but is cemented, to borrow Elster's (1989b) term, by norms. According to James Coleman (1990, 825–28), for example, the existence of a norm of voting explains participation and, in turn, is explained by its usefulness as a sanctioning instrument allowing an actor to gain some control over the externalities represented by the participation decisions of others—a positive externality if they support the actor's candidate and a negative externality if they oppose the actor's candidate. The result is a "demand for a norm to vote" (291) whenever the norm's positive impact on fellow supporters of a candidate exceeds the value of the demander's own net contribution to the candidate's election.[14]

Still, Coleman notes, this creates a second-order free-rider problem since a sanctioning system is also a public good. Satisfying the demand for a voting norm, therefore, "depends on the existence of social relationships among potential beneficiaries of the norm. . . . Unless the social networks that link persons together are somewhat distinct, so there is a correlation between the political preferences of friends, these normative systems cannot function" (1990, 291–92).[15] The difficulty with this explanation is that networks capable of anchoring norms by somehow removing the anonymity of the participation choice are too small to matter in the overall election. Alternatively, one can simply postulate an internally sanctioned norm of voting, which essentially is the civic duty norm already discussed.

Once again, the CEU maximization principle tracks the same phenomenon without the attendant problems. Ethnic groups polarized by political preference are not only fertile targets for sociological expeditions in search of norms but are also, we have seen, vehicles for the rational pursuit of CEU through voting. Differential association, as Coleman puts it, creates the combination of interest and behavioral interdependence necessary for large-scale participation without assuming a premodern way of living ethnically.

VIII

Although contemporary communitarians and champions of ethnic diversity tend to be optimistic about the resulting divisions, Hardin's (1995) worry about diversity's potential to promote violence and fanaticism represents a much more standard reaction among pluralist democrats. Historically, clear ethnic or religious divisions have troubled many moderate political observers. Accordingly, the attenuation of these divisions has been seen as a formula for political peace: "Multiple and politically inconsistent affiliations, loyalties, and stimuli reduce the emotion and aggressiveness involved in political choice" (Lipset 1960, 77).

It is interesting in this regard that the CEU theory of turnout challenges the common wisdom that the conditions for (ethnic) group formation not only help mobilize a population but mobilize it in the direction of extremism. Granted, electoral mobilization is a special case that already assumes a certain taming of political impulses. But ethnic electoral mobilization is important enough to constitute an interesting if weak test of the extremism hypothesis.

Is electoral politics more likely to be polarized when ethnic identification contributes to political mobilization? The CEU model presented earlier answers in the negative. The question is subtle, however, since a negative answer is not the same as denying the existence of extremist ethnic politics. I am not asking whether strong ethnic identity is often found among extremists. Rather, I am asking whether ethnic identification independently exacerbates polarization or whether polarization occurs because those who are mobilized through their ethnic identification happen to have polarizing preferences.

In contrast to much of the empirical and normative literature, existing formal analysis tends to absolve ethnicity but not decisively. To Rogowski (1974), for example, ethnic categorization is clearly a powerful mobilizing instrument in the hands of competing groups. Yet these categorizations do not cause the competition. Alvin Rabushka and Kenneth Shepsle (1972) do argue that any consensus in an ethnically divided society is fragile because it can be undermined by politicians or parties adopting unambiguously extremist positions. Still, they trace both the possibility of a temporary consensus and the likelihood of its unraveling to the intense and competing preferences of different politicized ethnic groups, interpreting intensity in terms of risk acceptance (technically, strictly convex utility functions). The culprit in their analysis of polarization, then, is the kind of preference ethnics in these settings have rather than the fact that they identify with one another. Still, Rabushka and Shepsle do not explicitly model ethnic identity, and therefore its full role in generating polarization is left vague.

The importance of preference as an influence on polarization is partly confirmed by Rebecca Morton's (1991) group-oriented model of turnout. One implication of her model is that candidates maximizing expected plurality from risk averse voters converge to a unique equilibrium, although she does argue (1987) that risk aversion across all alternatives is unlikely. In any case, the kinds of pressures driving standard median voter results for unidimensional

Downsian models imply a "moderation" in candidate behavior notwithstanding greatly divergent preferences among voters linked to ethnic or other group loyalties.

Finally, Ledyard's (1984, theorem 1) Bayesian framework, which is adopted in this chapter, shows that when candidates frictionlessly attempt to maximize the probability of winning the election, then any candidate or party equilibrium is unique and symmetric, again so long as voters are risk averse. Preference is again the decisive factor determining the political impact of mobilization.

Ledyard's model, of course, does not incorporate group identification. When identification is introduced, one might think, his convergence result will disappear because a reduction in the distance between candidates or parties—convergence—can weaken the political significance of group membership. As a result, the effective, as opposed to the underlying, distribution of voter ideal points is altered, and candidates or parties may feel compelled to maintain the mobilization of their supporters by maintaining distinct positions.

It can be verified formally, nonetheless, that Ledyard's crucial theorem 1 holds for the CEU model incorporating group identification, so long as identification "parameters" that vary with changes in candidate or party platforms vary continuously. In hitching the CEU model to Ledyard's result, I am not suggesting that mass elections actually do produce convergence, either with or without group identification.[16] My more analytical point concerns the supposed connection between ethnicity and political extremism. While ethnicity aids political mobilization, identity is not itself the source of polarization since it is consistent with convergence. Group identity enhances turnout when there is a sufficient statistical relation between group identity and interest. If polarization results, the culprit is not identification as such but the original intensity of the preferences group identities mobilize.

IX

In our review of the main approaches to ethnic political mobilization, it became clear that for many observers ethnicity interacted with, or even substituted for, class. So far, however, we have not examined class explicitly. The idea that conditional beliefs form a basis for political action was fleshed out using ethnicity, but the other side of the rational choice coin, preference, was left abstract. A brief discussion of class in relation to our CEU theory of mobilization is one illustrative remedy for this gap.

There is another reason why the political role of class looms large in any examination of the CEU theory of mobilization. While, historically speaking, religion and ethnicity seem to be the most persistent bases for group mobilization, class must be given pride of place as an object of theoreticians' interest.

Moreover, there is certainly continued support for class-based empirical political analysis within modern political science (e.g., Manley 1983; but cf. Offe 1985). Walter Dean Burnham (1980) and G. Bingham Powell, Jr. (1980), for example, argue for the continuing electoral influence of class position.

Marxism has been the wellspring for theories that take classes to be distinct political forces. Ironically, the political failure of the Marxist program has not stanched the flow of theoretical reconsiderations and reformulations of its class analysis. If anything, it seems, political roadblocks have provoked a more rigorous and even formal examination of Marxist theory's underlying structure (e.g., Elster 1985a; Roemer 1982).

Marxism is primarily a theory of revolution, and its theory of class is designed to explain and predict revolutions, not voting patterns. Yet it is important to note that Marxists have increasingly come to appreciate that a systematic analysis of the worker's ongoing political participation in a liberal democratic society and a systematic analysis of his decision whether to use his class to overthrow it are simply two sides of the same coin. A distinct Dr. Jekyll and Mr. Hyde do not cohabit in each laboring body. Rather, there is one unified actor who as worker-citizen calculates the relative merits of the two options, revolution and consent to a capitalist order (Przeworski and Wallerstein 1982; Przeworski 1985a). This more modern Marxism explains the absence of revolution by arguing that the material benefits workers receive under a capitalism reformed through political pressure may outweigh those contemplated under socialism, particularly when they recognize the risks and sacrifices associated with revolution and its immediate aftermath. The study of revolution thus entails the study of elections and vice versa (see also Lancaster 1973, 1094; Mehrling 1986, 1282, 1297–98). For this reason, the once dominant Marxist approach to class analysis is not merely a historically significant model for theorists concerned with class and revolution; its increasing recognition of the importance of class mobilization for a theory of electoral politics means that it remains an interesting laboratory for applying the CEU theory of elections presented here.

It is an interesting laboratory because the Marxist analysis of class formation and class politics faces the familiar collective goods problem, namely, explaining how individual workers can act as a class to produce results benefiting their class. Thus in his seminal analysis, Mancur Olson (1971, 102–10) criticizes Marxist theory for its failure to explain the predicted socialist revolution as the calculated product of rational self-interested workers. Since the benefits of revolution are public goods—they are enjoyed by nonparticipants—and the sacrifices revolutionaries must make are individual and substantial, Olson notes, a universal preference for revolution among workers is insufficient to produce it. This criticism of Marxist theory has now received extensive theoretical attention (e.g., Buchanan 1982, 86–102; Elster 1985a, 349–71; Hardin 1995, 39–42).

It is crucial to emphasize, however, the two-sided nature of the calculation Marxist theory imputes to workers. Their capacity for revolution is not all that is at stake. In the absence of revolution, their class's influence on the political class compromise institutionalized in liberal democracies also depends on their capacity to solve a collective action problem. Only then can Marxists explain the mobilizing of electoral and other kinds of political support within the boundaries of democratic politics. "There are good reasons to believe that workers as well as capitalists are placed by a compromise into a prisoner's dilemma, in which each participant may find it preferable not to pay the costs of the compromise even if such a compromise is collectively optimal for the class" (Przeworski and Wallerstein 1982, 221). So having shown that workers can be induced not to revolt by the material benefits of welfare state capitalism, Marxist theory is still obligated to show that the liberal democratic alternative can survive virtually the same dilemma plaguing the revolutionary course of action.

For the working class to resolve this dilemma, it must solve its collective action problem. To solve its collective action problem it must be organized as a class. According to the CEU model of electoral participation, of course, the working class can do so if circumstances in their lives increase the appropriate conditional probabilities for common behavior.[17] It is not enough, recall, for individuals to find themselves in common circumstances such as identical positions in a Prisoner's Dilemma. Common circumstances only raise the unconditional probability of identical action. For there to be either collective revolutionary action or collective action in the voting booth, CEU theory says that the probability of one worker's action, conditional on another's, must be higher than the unconditional probability of the action.[18] Here is Marx's (Marx and Engels 1968, 171–72) famous exposition of this crucial distinction.

The small-holding peasants form a vast mass, the members of which live in similar conditions but without entering into manifold relations with one another. Their mode of production isolates them from one another instead of bringing them into mutual intercourse. . . . In this way, the great mass of the French nation is formed by simple addition of homologous magnitudes, much as potatoes in a sack form a sack of potatoes. Insofar as millions of families live under economic conditions of existence that separate their mode of life, their interests and their culture from those of the other classes, and put them in hostile opposition to the latter, they form a class. Insofar as there is merely a local interconnection among these small land-holding peasants, and the identity of their interests begets no community, no national bond and no political organization among them, they do not form a class.

Class consciousness is the common term for the additional ingredient constituting a class. In the preceding analysis of ethnic and religious groups, it was called group identity. And in the formal terms of expression (2.1), it is the situation in which the probability of one class member's behavior conditional on another's is higher than its unconditional probability.[19]

As in the case of ethnic group identity, there is a sense in which the existence of a class within CEU theory reflects the collective actions and interdependencies of its individual members, relations beyond "the simple addition of homologous magnitudes." In this sense, a CEU theory of class avoids a rather common objection to standard rational choice analyses of social phenomena: "What is thus wrong with methodological individualism, I believe, is not the idea that collective actions must be explained by referring to individual rationality but the idea that society is a collection of undifferentiated and unrelated individuals" (Przeworski 1985b, 393). In the CEU model, individuals are not only differentiated but their differentiation affects their rational behavior.

For their own part, Marxist theoreticians have offered a number of explanations for how the revolutionary's dilemma could be surmounted, some of which are simple applications of existing Prisoner's Dilemma proposals and others of which have been improvised for the specific purposes at hand.[20] One possibility is to recognize that the dilemma is actually a supergame, an iterated series of Prisoner's Dilemma games allowing participants to retaliate against previous defections from the cooperative solution (Edel 1979; Taylor 1987). Retaliation, however, presupposes observability, which, we noted earlier, is difficult to assure in large n-person games.

Workers are not limited to learning about the behavior of others. According to Offe and Wiesenthal (1980) workers may also engage in a dialogue modifying their own preferences into a less individualistic form. This is nice work, if workers can get it. Yet the dialogue contains no guarantee that the new preferences will be more sociable. Indeed workers may learn more about their fellow class members than they wanted to know (cf. Elster 1985a, 363). Nor are we given a precise description of the process of change. It is not even clear why individual preferences should *anticipate* the new, noncompetitive society for which these preferences are best adapted. Finally, the special case of liberal democratic elections continues to represent a problem. Their anonymity and size are not necessarily conducive to dialogue.

Perhaps workers simply abandon the individualist model motivating the Prisoner's Dilemma and adopt, under the pressure of their situation under capitalism, a scheme of "collective rationality" (Roemer 1978). Other problems aside, this hardly seems consistent with the relative promise of capitalism under the Przeworski and Wallerstein (1982) model invoked here. At any rate, for purposes of analyzing individually rational behavior, it seems to declare the problem solved rather than to solve it.

A functionally related idea is to assume that workers have ethical inhibitions about free riding. Yet there certainly are strong doubts about the role of moral appeals in a strictly Marxist solution (e.g., Buchanan 1982). Moreover, it is unclear that ethical inhibitions will have the desired results when the collective production of the public good is precisely what is in doubt (Elster 1985b; Godwin and Mitchell 1982; Hardin 1982, 118–22).[21]

The final possibility we will consider is a communitarian solution. According to Michael Taylor (1988), peasant revolts have been able to overcome the free-rider problem because people living in fairly tight-knit communities can successfully monitor the contributions of each member. In some respects, organizations and factories may perform an analogous function for the working class. On the other hand, this communitarian solution, Taylor (85) concedes, cannot account for large-scale demonstrations and secret voting in mass elections.

In sum, these proposals for solving the revolutionary's dilemma tend either to assume that workers change radically or that they change the collective nature of the problem they face. In the first case, the workers themselves are transformed into more social or ethical creatures. In the second case, as with the communitarian solution, individuals are not socialized but rather the collective problem is individualized for each participant, who becomes subject to discrete sanctions from other individuals. Yet in the original dilemma, those rational self-interested workers who overcome their collective action problem must somehow recognize the genuinely social nature of the problem they face, without losing their analytically isolated status as individuals.

In the case of mass elections, in particular, rational individuals cannot be herded into socially optimal behavior but rather must develop their own, more abstract sense of their collective problem, in a word, class consciousness. Indeed, Elster (1985a, 347) goes so far as to define class consciousness "as the ability to overcome the free-rider problem in realizing class interests" (emphasis deleted). CEU theory models that ability. The empirical question it leaves is whether workers in fact learn about statistical dependencies related to class.

Elster's test for class consciousness can be formulated more generally. Group consciousness is the ability of group members to overcome their free-rider problem. Accordingly, each of the proposed solutions to the Marxist problem of class mobilization will have its counterpart whenever theorists confront the generic problem of explaining voting and mobilization. For example, civic duty, as an answer to this problem, hypothesizes that individuals identify with a "group" coextensive with the polity as a whole. The ongoing problem faced by Marxists attempting to explain variations in class mobilization, in short, is worth considering if only as representative of the general problem of mass political participation.

X

Whether they are rooted in classes, religions, or ethnicity, group identities are associated with behavioral interdependencies. Rational agents will not disregard them and cannot, at any given moment, transcend them. Group identities, as a result, are politically exploitable, whether it be for mobilization in mass elections or for staging revolutions. In the latter case, however, higher costs and a weaker institutional structure are imposed on the relevant acts. Accordingly, electoral participation will be more common.

Group identities, we have found, are worth exploiting when interest and identity coincide sufficiently. In these cases, group identities can become powerful and persistent. This has suggested to some that they are also politically unsettling. In and of themselves, however, group identities do not polarize. Under appropriate circumstances, the interests they mobilize do.

Despite its political salience, group identity is surprisingly malleable and opportunistic. This is a paradox for views that trace important social phenomena to important and deep psychological orientations. In the CEU model, however, there is no paradox. Identities are corrigible inductions from behavioral evidence, not ingrained preferences. Typically, there is more than one way for behavioral interdependence to develop. If so, rational agents can certainly learn or conjecture about these alternatives. The means by which these agents acquire one identity is the means by which they acquire another.

Identities, on the CEU model, can become deeply important to the individual when they become socially or politically important. Under these circumstances, their role and meaning are hardly illusory. Yet as crucial navigating instruments within so many societies, they remain hostage to the circumstances to which they respond. Ethnic and racial identities ultimately reflect the context in which identifiers must behave. The resulting divisions are not given by nature even though in some societies it pays to act as though they are.

CHAPTER 3

Ideology

The decisions made by CEU maximizers are greatly influenced by the way they categorize themselves and other people. If they see the world through ethnic lenses, their decisions will not likely be the ones they would reach if they looked through religious lenses. Marxists certainly recognize that workers who unite on the basis of class must in some sense ignore or transcend both of these sources of intraclass division. Unfortunately, despite the importance of conceptual schemes for CEU theory generally, chapter 2 is quite casual about them. It tells us they are chosen based on their usefulness in making predictions. It does not tell us how these schemes are compared or revised.

When the agents modeled in chapter 2 condition their choices on a category such as ethnicity, all their other beliefs are subsumed under the nondescript title of additional information. This suggests, quite unreasonably, that categories such as ethnicity exist in isolation as arbitrary elements of an agent's entire set of beliefs. A rational agent's beliefs presumably are coherent and systematic. Indeed in politics coherent sets of beliefs are so important that they have been given a special name. A system of beliefs constituting a coherent and systematic guide to action is typically termed an *ideology*.

Yet calling the beliefs systems invoked in chapter 2 ideologies only alerts us to additional gaps in that chapter's discussion. For while a coherent belief system—an ideology—seems to be just the sort of thing a rational agent would have, ideologues hardly fit anyone's common-sense view of rational agents. Moreover, a substantial literature to be discussed subsequently argues that only a fraction of modern mass publics has a working ideology. The majority is ideologically challenged. But if rationality and ideology are intimately related and most people do not have an ideology, what happens to the assumption of universal rationality?

This chapter addresses these issues. We will see that while particular categories may be the innovations of specific rational agents, the existence of a system of categories is an inherent part of rational choice, not just a product of it. By the same token, there is no reason to suppose that rationality implies a shared system of categories and beliefs. Rationality plus exposure to new information does not necessarily lead to a convergence in belief systems, an end to ideology, or even an end to ideological disagreement. Ideology and ideological difference are in the nature of rational behavior.

I

Two conceptions of ideology—the "empiricist" and the "rationalist" (Stimson 1975)—predominate in contemporary political science. To Philip Converse (1964, 1975, 84–85), the leading advocate of the empiricist approach, an ideology is a logically and psychologically constrained belief system used to organize the substantial body of political information ideologues happen to have. Since individuals who think ideologically fit newer experiences into their ideological preconceptions (Converse 1966a), their political beliefs generally will not converge, even when these individuals are exposed to large amounts of the same political information. Thus Converse is comfortable with the idea of agents who reason in a distinctly ideological way. He is also comfortable with the idea that the mass public is unwilling or unable to reason in this fashion and therefore displays a set of incoherent and unstable nonattitudes concerning a variety of political issues.

Whereas Converse treats ideology as a belief system whose distinct constraints influence the use of information, the "rationalist" program initiated by Downs (1957) suggests the opposite. As clarified and revised by James Enelow and Melvin Hinich (1984) and Hinich and Michael Munger (1992, 1994), the Downsian approach conceives of ideology not as a psychological constraint on induction but as a means of avoiding the costs associated with induction. Because particular political parties and candidates are identified with particular systems of ideas, economizing voters can use ideological labels to determine their preferences instead of acquiring information specific to the electoral contest. If voters' political beliefs do not converge, this is not because they think in distinctly ideological ways but because they have not been subjected to the same political information. In short, voters who use ideologies do not process information differently than their more informed counterparts; they simply have less information to process.

This chapter draws from both conceptions of ideology. On the one hand, it reverts to the empiricist approach by defining ideology as a psychological feature of the way political actors see the world and process information about it. On the other hand, it maintains the rational actor assumption. An ideology will be understood as a coherent view of the world—a consistent set of beliefs updated in a rational manner—coupled with preferences for the way the world should be. Specifically, I define ideology in terms of four elements characterizing an agent's conceptual scheme and preferences:

1. a set of categories partitioning (some portion of) an individual's experience

2. a set of propositions constructed with those categories
3. a coherent probability distribution defined over these propositions, and
4. a coherent preference function also defined over them.[1]

The categories *liberal* and *conservative* are classic examples of categories, while "Franklin Roosevelt was a liberal leader" and "Ronald Reagan was a conservative leader" are propositions constructed from them. The propositions "Franklin Roosevelt was a conservative leader" and "Ronald Reagan was a liberal leader" illustrate why element (3) is necessary. Since agents will believe in some propositions more strongly than others, we reflect their varying degrees of belief by means of a probability function. Probability 1 is assigned to propositions about which the agent is certain, probability 0 to propositions the agent believes are impossible. Most propositions fall between these two values. Strong belief, however, should not be confused with support, just as strong disbelief should not be confused with aversion. Element (4) therefore recognizes the separate dimension of preference concerning the propositions about which the agent has beliefs. Preferences may concern the historical claims I have used as examples, future economic outcomes, or more abstract objects like justice (e.g., Kalt and Zupan 1984; Dougan and Munger 1989), and they may be rooted in the agent's social role (Elster 1985c).

In effect, the list (1)–(4) defines someone with an ideology as rational but does so by distinguishing elements (1) and (4), which are often merged. When combined with the rationality assumption, this implies that everyone has an ideology of some sort, if not one of the "isms" often taken to characterize, if not caricature, ideology. As a result, instead of dichotomizing the population into ideology holders and nonholders, we essentially start from Robert Higgs's (1987, 38) premise: "Every sane adult, unless he is completely apathetic politically, has an ideology. The notion that ideology is only the distorted, fanatical thought of one's intellectual or political opponents cannot be sustained."

Obviously, this stands in marked contrast to the empiricist tradition, which is very much captivated by the task of defining what an ideology "really" is, how political or abstract it must be, and how politically active its adherents should be. I do not deny that these variables may indeed be linked to interesting variations in political behavior. I do deny the value of using these variations to dichotomize the population into ideology holders and, let us say, pragmatists, just as I deny the utility of characterizing only those who have very abstract theories of the world as being truly rational. Small wonder that after all the discussion about measuring ideology, basic conceptual issues remain, such as whether the detailed and rich political ideology is the most "sophisticated" or whether sophistication is marked by simplicity and organizing power. Distinctions between those who do and those who do not have ideologies tend to disguise the more important elements they share, including their basic rational ways of behaving.

Consistent with the preceding two chapters, my analysis of ideology and ideological behavior emphasizes the belief rather than the preference component of the rational choice apparatus. In traditional language, I shall emphasize ideology's status as a "conceptual scheme" influencing the processing of information. This is why elements (1) and (2) of the definition will be particularly important. Yet what motivates this analysis is not merely the definition of a term or the desire to reconcile two opposing traditions. As defined here, ideology's role in human decision making has important implications for our understanding of the way individuals interact with their political environment, whatever the terminology.

One, we will see that the rationality assumption is consistent with the extensively confirmed finding that a subject's framework for organizing beliefs and information "distorts" his decision making (e.g., Peffley, Feldman, and Sigelman 1987; Tversky and Kahneman 1987; Iyengar 1991). Cognitive and political psychologists, by contrast, argue that individuals who process information through schemas or other systems of categorization are being "miserly" in their use of political information rather than inductively rational.[2] By integrating conceptual schemes into a notion of rational ideology, we challenge this conclusion and, by extension, Giovanni Sartori's (1969) influential distinction between the nonrational, "deductive" style of ideologues and the "inductive," pragmatic style of nonideologues.

Two, we therefore will see that the Downsian program's neat distinction between ideologies defined as public, "disembodied ideas" (Hinich and Munger 1992, 29) on the one hand, and operative systems of belief and preference on the other, may mask a specific feature of decision making historically associated with ideology, namely, the influence of conceptual structure on decisions or, in other terms, the nonneutrality of conceptual frames.

Three, it is often assumed that because ideology influences the assimilation of information, ideological belief should be much more stable than nonideological belief. We will see, however, that the pattern of volatility in public opinion documented in Converse 1964 can be modeled as the rational response of individuals to a dynamic political environment. Using his dichotomous "black and white model," by contrast, Converse attributes this pattern to nonideologues with unconstrained, nonrational psychologies.

Finally, having rationalized both "closed-minded" and volatile opinions, we rationalize this apparent divergence by modeling factors governing the choice of ideology itself: individuals rationally decide among ideologies that can have a varying impact on the stability of their opinions. Political parties recognize this possibility of ideological change when they attempt to influence how their policies and policy commitments are interpreted (Riker 1986, 1990). As we shall see, neither citizen opinion nor ideology is exogenous to the political system, even in a democracy (see, e.g., Margolis and Mauser 1989).

The next section develops the theoretical basis for reconciling CEU maximization and a more psychological view of ideology and thereby begins to confront the challenge ideology poses to rational choice theory. The challenges are that, contrary to the implications of the rational actor assumption, (i) ideology influences how information is processed into changes in belief, (ii) the typical citizen does not use a stable ideology to resolve the problem of information costs, evidenced by the instability of the typical citizen's political opinions, and (iii) choices can be politically manipulated by alternative ways of framing a given decision. Challenge (i) will be addressed by showing that this ideological effect is consistent with rational decision making. Challenges (ii) and (iii) will be addressed by showing that both phenomena are consistent with a model embedding ideologically minded rational citizens in dynamic models of electoral competition.

II

Seeing is believing: a rational agent's opinions should be affected by the evidence and not vice versa. To those in the grip of an old-fashioned ideology, however, beliefs influence the interpretation of evidence. To them, believing is seeing. For this reason, ideology is often associated with fanaticism since ideologues apparently can maintain a belief that would have been undermined had they any sensitivity to evidence. In more coolly cognitive terms, ideologues seem particularly adept at reducing the "cognitive dissonance" (Festinger 1957) between their current beliefs and new conflicting information. In this section, we show why this ideologically induced stubbornness, which cannot be attributed solely to the relative costs of information, is consistent with inductive rationality, which in turn is consistent with ideology as defined in the preceding. In brief, the term *rational ideologue* is no oxymoron.

As John Broome (1990, 1991a,b) and George Tsebelis (1990, 45–46) argue, rationality is such a core principle that attempts to fix a faulty rational choice explanation should first try to preserve the rationality assumption itself. In that spirit, our diagnosis of ideological stubbornness will look for causes consistent with the overall rationality hypothesis embodied in the definition of ideology given previously. Since belief is not a function of preference, element (4) of that definition, preference, cannot explain ideological characteristics of belief (although Elster [1985c] attributes alleged ideological peccadilloes like wishful thinking to the contamination of belief by preference). Nor do elements (2) and (3), beliefs, explain stubbornness, since they reflect symptoms of the problem, not the cause. The culprit is element (1), the system of categories in which evidence is introduced. The process of belief formation may seem radically different across individuals—rational in some, irrational in others— because of variations in the category schemes those individuals use. And as

Pamela Conover and Stanley Feldman (1989, 914) note, "Cognitive and social psychologists have shown that one of the basic cognitive activities is categorization."

It is well known that the ascription of rationality is not independent of how subjects perceive their alternatives, how those alternatives are "framed." To take a crude example, presidents may be more likely to implement a certain policy when it is described to them in terms of employment rates than when it is described in terms of unemployment rates. Analogously, it has been found that doctors will be more positive about a medical procedure characterized in terms of survival rates than the same procedure characterized in terms of the complementary mortality rates (e.g., Tversky and Kahneman 1987).

We can attribute these choices to an irrational preference reversal induced by framing effects. But it is better, following Broome (1990, 138–41), to explain these apparent failures of rationality by appealing to differences in categorization. Thus we can rationalize these choices by presidents and doctors by assuming that different ways of framing the alternatives actually define different causal outcomes in the minds of respondents. In the case of doctors, for example, characterizing a procedure in terms of survival rates may represent it as a form of rescue from a prior probability of a bad outcome; mortality rates suggest the unintended consequence of death from the treatment. Similarly, for presidents employment statistics may suggest the causal utility of a particular policy, whereas unemployment may imply a different causal structure involving welfare dependence. Again, Broome would prefer to maintain the rationality assumption so long as the rationalization is plausible. But the larger point is that seeing someone as rational or irrational seems relatively arbitrary. At least there is no simple fact of the matter as to a subject's "true" rationality. We now apply this general insight to the dynamics of belief to show how the role of categorization can rationalize observed cases of ideological stubbornness.

Consider classic Marxist ideologues—true believers—who continually receive data on the absence of class warfare in capitalist societies but do not change their initial prediction of revolution. Is it possible that these ideologues are rationally updating their opinions although they somehow continue to infer that revolution is on the horizon, say, by the year 2010?

I suggest that different rational agents can reach different conclusions about the likelihood of revolution. I do not mean simply that at any given time rational individuals can have different opinions. That goes without saying. Rather, the idea that more and more evidence necessarily brings agents ever closer to the same posterior beliefs or some best system of political categories represents wishful thinking. *Formally speaking, rational inductions oriented toward the proposition that capitalism is peaceful or toward the proposition that capitalism is unstable converge in the same way, although toward different beliefs.* Ideologies can survive what appear to be repeated instances of disconfirmation.

Like the ordinary analyst, I will argue, the Marxist may have a coherent set of beliefs rationally supported by the evidence as the Marxist interprets it.[3] Both the Marxist ideologue and the ordinary analyst predicting capitalist peace can be rational even though identical evidence equally strengthens their divergent convictions. There need be no formal distinction between the rational thought processes of those who make these very different predictions about capitalism. Both sides may be sustaining their hypotheses by filtering information through very different sets of rationally supportable categories.

As noted, we operate on the assumption that the Marxist conceptual framework—corresponding to (1) in the preceding—rationalizes the Marxist's conclusions. Fortunately, Nelson Goodman's (1983) widely discussed analysis of induction, although devised with a different purpose in mind and using a different example, suggests what such a framework would look like. Suppose Marxist ideology is constructed around the category I will designate by *labor peace**, which is defined *in our terms* as labor peace for the period through 2009 and revolution for years thereafter. Note that I have distinguished the expressions *labor peace** and *labor peace* only for conceptual accounting purposes. To Marxists, the concept of *labor peace** is not only natural, but nothing about the classification of current or past evidence, except their distinct view of the future, would suggest to them that their vocabulary is different at all. In fact, given the identical spellings and pronunciations, users of these terms will not be aware of the need for translation at all. Still, I am assuming by hypothesis that there is indeed a proper translation.

To Marxists, then, the continuation of the current strike pattern—or strike* pattern—is precisely what rationally grounds the prediction of revolution in the year 2010 since each year's labor peace* reinforces the Marxist hypothesis. By *rational* here, I mean inductively rational. It is easy to show that the application of Bayes's Rule leads to a posterior belief in revolution converging to unity.

$$\text{Lim}_{n \to \infty} \text{prob}_M(P_t^* \mid P_{t-1}^*, P_{t-2}^*, \ldots, P_{t-n}^*) = 1, \tag{3.1a}$$

where prob_M is the Marxist's rational degree of belief and P_t^* is labor peace* at time t, meaning revolution for $t = 2010$. Given the Marxist conceptual scheme, the expectation of revolution is rational. Repeated instances of labor peace* add up to a revolutionary future. However, to those unaware of the translation, indeed unaware that there is anything to translate, the Marxist's confidence in revolution seems irrational, even bizarre.

This rationalization of the Marxist inference may seem artificial. Does it not rest on the temporally defined, ad hoc category *labor peace**? Is not the concept just a gimmick? The problem with this natural judgment is twofold. Most important, the oddness of the category is purely in the eyes of the beholder. We already saw how doctors and presidents may have their own ways of categorizing that are unappreciated by experimental psychologists. To see this in the case of Marxists, imagine that in their effort to understand the opposing viewpoint and its odd refusal to acknowledge the coming revolution—in their effort to decode capitalist ideology—Marxists also develop the concept of *labor peace***, defined *in our terms* as revolution for the period through 2009 and labor peace thereafter.[4] To Marxists armed with this vocabulary, the non-Marxist analysis predicting labor peace introduces an unmotivated transition from *labor peace** to *labor peace*** on January 1, 2010, instead of using the concept of *labor peace** throughout. Perhaps class interest dictates this transition. In any case, from the Marxist standpoint, it is the concept of *labor peace** that is homogeneous and "objectively" more natural than *labor peace.*

In judging capitalist ideology this way, Marxists would be assuming the validity of their own. Similarly, when judging the Marxist category to be unnatural, we presuppose the appropriateness of our own. Each of us operates with a homogeneous concept from her own perspective, and each of us operates with a heterogeneous concept from the perspective of the other, assuming, again, we know the translation. If not, we assume a common language and attribute our disagreement to a breakdown of shared rationality.

There is a second reason to think the preceding rationalization is not as artificial as it may first appear. While it is true that an isolated concept like *labor peace** cannot fully represent a full-blown ideology, it does distill the way in which ideological schemes can rationally support their characteristic inferences while looking irrationally stubborn from the outside. In key respects, moreover, *labor peace** is representative of Marxist ideology since, on the classic Marxist view, processes within capitalism lead to transformations of capitalism. Note Marx's (1967, 309) appeal, exploited by dialectical materialists, to "the law . . . that merely quantitative differences beyond a certain point pass into qualitative changes."[5]

While this bivariate Marxist theory is not very exciting social science, the larger and more accurate theory, with its more complex "laws of motion," may, for all logical purposes, simply represent a system of belief in which the category *labor peace** is "distributed" over a larger conceptual structure. Remember, we are not trying to understand Marxism as a detached scientific theory attended to by specialists, mostly in Western universities. We are trying to capture its role as an ideology motivating and filtering the political judgments and decisions of actual political agents who are assumed to be rational. In short, we are after the "lived relation" (Althusser 1971) between people and their society.

So while Marxism is not just an ideology but a theory, and one concept does not a theory or an ideology make, our focus on a few concepts can tell us how the net conceptual differences between theories or ideologies can produce dramatically and seemingly pathologically different conclusions in their adherents. In fact, one conclusion to draw is that theories can easily be mistaken for ideologies.

Given the concept of *labor peace**, the Marxist is being as inductively rational as the non-Marxist who uses *labor peace*. And since evidence available to this point, in whatever quantities, formally confirms both their conclusions, there is no formal basis for arguing that the one category scheme is rationally preferable to the other. Those still inclined to reject this rationalization of the Marxist's inferences as obviously too bizarre should recognize the truth that both the previously noted Marxist inference and the non-Marxist inference are valid:

$$\text{Lim}_{n \to \infty} \text{prob}_M(P_t^* \mid P_{t-1}^*, P_{t-2}^*, \ldots, P_{t-n}^*) = 1, \qquad (3.1a)$$

$$\text{Lim}_{n \to \infty} \text{prob}_{NM}(P_t \mid P_{t-1}, P_{t-2}, \ldots, P_{t-n}) = 1, \qquad (3.1b)$$

where prob_M is, again, the Marxist's rational degree of belief, prob_{NM} is the non-Marxist's rational degree of belief, P_t is labor peace at time t, and P_t^* is, again, labor peace* at time t, meaning revolution for $t \geq 2010$. When equally rational decision makers draw incompatible conclusions like equations (3.1a) and (3.1b), the political scientist wrongly attributes "deductive" ideological thinking to an actor who is simply ideologically divergent. Nonetheless, the absence of ideological convergence explains why some ideologies are popularly associated with fanaticism.

When supplemented by the concept of rational ideology, then, standard Bayesian analysis does not preclude sustained ideological divergence, notwithstanding technical findings on the convergence of belief from different priors, that is, initial probability estimates (e.g., Kadane 1984).[6] Since agents with ideologies do not partition the universe of possible events the same way, arguments that common priors lead to convergent belief are irrelevant. Standard Bayesian inference, however valid in other respects, thus fails to treat the underlying conceptual scheme as a variable. Rational ideologues, in any case, can react differently to shared evidence, can stick to their divergent opinions, and can even bet with one another and trade (cf. Aumann 1976; Milgrom and Stokey 1982).[7] Also, ideologies can survive despite the general tendency of (political) markets to eliminate or at least compensate for agents who are subject to preconceptions (Wittman 1991, 408–11).

Although ideologies can be stubborn, this stubbornness differs from ideological conviction as defined by Roger Congleton (1991, 67): "An individual's ideological conviction is simply the extent to which his priors for specific theories approach unity." Congleton's formulation does not explain how distinct ideologies can each become so secure, particularly in light of the Bayesian argument noted earlier that rational agents will generally converge to the same beliefs when subjected to enough of the same information. In the view presented here, convergence between ideologically different agents need not occur even in the face of common and abundant information, freely available and freely believed (cf. Hinich and Munger 1994).

Furthermore, since ideologies are active, rational constraints on individual reasoning, we have not purchased ideological coherence at the cost of interpreting them as timeless and disembodied normative systems such as the world's great "isms" (Hinich and Munger 1992, 1994).[8] I think this interpretation is troubling. For one thing, specifying these systems presents enormous problems: exactly how many disembodied Marxisms and Islams are there, and how are they demarcated?

Second, the notion of ideologies as discrete systems of disembodied ideas, corporately providing policy cues to voters, seems ill suited to the continuity of a public, predictive ideological dimension like liberal-conservative (see Sartori 1976, 334). If these are latent dimensions constructed out of political debate and confrontation—which I agree with Hinich and Munger they are—then the points along the dimension linking these bulky ideologies are still not easy to understand. If ideologies are discrete and coherent systems, what, say, is a "moderate" ideological point between them?

Third, the Hinich and Munger approach treats ideology as a legitimating motivation for individual behavior in a deeper sense than the motivation provided by the ordinary beliefs and desires of any rational agent. This notion of legitimacy reintroduces those problems with the traditional sociological framework that rational choice theory has understandably tried to avoid (e.g., Hechter 1987, 19–30; Grafstein 1992), problems partially raised in our discussion of civic duty as an explanation for turnout. In brief, either a legitimating ideology's grip on the individual's behavior is turned into a brute fact about human life, or the individual's relation to the legitimating norms and values raises all the original questions about motivation. What exacerbates this problem of motivation, moreover, is that fully worked up ideologies like liberalism and Marxism, which serve as paradigms of disembodied belief systems, are typically too vague, abstract, and even self-contradictory to function directly in anybody's active belief system.

The elaborate, even ornate ideologies that function as "isms" may be useful for academics, theologians, and party theoreticians, but for ordinary political actors they are not the stuff that dreams are made on. In this regard, the Marxist theoretician Antonio Gramsci (1971, 339) once speculated that believers on the street, who lack the intellectual resources to win debates with ideological opponents, are reassured by the existence of the full construction. Somewhere, they are convinced, there are supporters who could carry on the argument. More likely, however, the paradigmatic "isms" are more academic museum pieces, only parts of which are used by those directly involved in political struggles.

Fourth, disconnecting ideologies from the individual decision maker merely postpones rational choice theory's reckoning with the well-documented influence of conceptual schemes on information processing. Whether one calls them ideologies or schemas, their behavioral consequences must be rationalized if rational choice theory is to remain a theory of individual behavior. Defining ideologies as abstract entities, moreover, compounds this problem of linking rational choice and ideology; the puzzle of how physical creatures like human beings interact with such entities is now into its third millennium. Even a solution to this puzzle may be a Pyrrhic victory so long as parsimony remains one criterion for good scientific theorizing. After one posits distinctly ideological beliefs, preferences, moral and normative commitments, and perhaps group solidarity (Higgs 1987), how much of individual behavior is left to explain?

The approach to ideology developed in this chapter, in sum, does not only answer to the special needs of CEU theory. In comparison to other strategies, it has advantages for rational choice theory generally, most important, for the prospect of rationalizing the role of conceptual schemes in orienting rational behavior.

Returning to rational ideologies, we are now in a position to confront the first challenge noted earlier: ideologies do color the way *rational* actors interpret evidence and process information. As conceptual frameworks, they are not neutral with respect to decisions. We have shown this in detail for a particular model of Marxist ideology, but the moral is quite general. Indeed closer to home, Conover and Feldman (1981, 624) find that "liberals and conservatives view the political world not from different sides of the same coin, but . . . from the perspective of entirely different currencies."

"Indifference" to evidence may characterize any ideological position when viewed from the outside, that is, from the standpoint of another rational ideology. To the observer, truly rational agents may behave like "cognitive misers" who are hesitant to change their beliefs in the face of apparently contradicting evidence (see, e.g., Peffley, Feldman, and Sigelman 1987, 102–5). They will act like misers even if it costs them nothing to obtain or process the new information. Still, ideologies are not substitutes for, but integral components of, formally rational decision making.[9]

Cognitive schemas for organizing information are entirely consistent with rational choice. More accurately, cognitive schemas are necessary for rational choice. Individuals cannot learn without a system for categorizing information. Their choice of system is, in one sense, arbitrary, since many alternatives are equally rational (assuming some sufficiently neutral vantage point from which to survey them). Yet despite this arbitrariness, the choice of conceptual system is extremely important since different schemas rationalize different behavior.

Cognitive political psychologists have documented the influence of schemas but have denied its rationality. Rational choice theorists implicitly accept the existence of a category scheme, but tend to deny its influence. Like money in classical macroeconomics, they treat categories as an accounting scheme or unit of measure, necessary but purely conventional.

In the case of ideologies, however, categories affect behavior since they affect the expectations and therefore the political evaluations of rational agents. Some arbitrariness may be unavoidable since rational selection among alternative ideologies based solely on predictive power can leave a degree of indeterminacy. But since the resulting predictions generally will be different, this arbitrary choice can have far-reaching consequences.

It is worth noting that Morris Fiorina (1981, 200) rationalizes the parallel impact of "selective perception" and party identification on voters' divergent evaluations of the same events by arguing that the voters' previous experiences are simply showing their accumulating effect. On this view, socialization is an independent influence on evaluation manifested as a constant bias linearly added to that experiential effect (75–76).

This section offers a more integrated picture. Socialization is not a separate bias added to experience (cf. Achen 1992 for the limits of linear models when Bayesian learning takes place). It provides future political actors with the ideology within which politically relevant information is first accumulated. As a necessary feature of rational information processing, this ideology's "biasing" of cognition has a continuing impact on the mature actor's choices and apparent cognitive miserliness.

I will conclude this section with a defensive comment. From my experience, two objections are often raised against this approach to ideology. To those who make them, the objections often seem obvious and devastating, although recognition that they point in opposite directions may cause some critics to pause. The first objection is that the approach taken here is easily refuted since actual Marxists clearly have converted en masse. Evidently, even ideologues eventually feel the pressure of reality. The second objection is that the approach is empirically empty. Ideologies imputed this way cannot be falsified since they can be rigged to fit any ostensibly bizarre pattern of behavior. The idea of rational ideology is no more a solution to the problem of cognitive miserliness than the assumption of altruism is a resolution of the Prisoner's Dilemma.

The first objection is wrong because a rational ideology is perfectly consistent with failure and rationally compelled changes in belief. The fact that "ideologized" Bayesian learning is relative to a way of seeing the world does not make belief completely relative to ideology. There may still be a fact of the matter to choosing between inferences rooted in alternative ideologies. These variable ideologies can be falsified. To take our earlier illustration, one of the two ideologies, Marxist or capitalist, will fail after 2010. For many of Marxism's actual adherents, it failed sometime in the post–World War II period.

Ideological variability, then, does not immunize ideologies from reality. Indeed ideological change will be considered more systematically in section V of this chapter. Yet to understand it, one must recognize that the ideology or conceptual scheme in which learning takes place is a variable, not a constant. Standard Bayesian induction, however valid, presupposes a fixed underlying conceptual scheme. The idea of rational ideology proposed here does not.

The second objection raises a more pragmatic worry. Even if ideologies are not insulated from reality, this conception of ideology is. Any behavior can be rationalized by positing a sufficiently bizarre conceptual scheme. The idea of rational ideologies, according to this criticism, tests only the imagination of the observer.

This serious objection goes to the heart of a behaviorally oriented conception of rationality. If a theory of ideology must recover the actual ideology of specific actors, our power to rationalize their Marxism, Islamic fundamentalism, fascism, or liberalism by making untestable adjustments in the belief system we impute to them will be singularly unimpressive. All reasonable philosophies of science justly condemn the intellectual sin of adhockery.

Still, one saving grace remains. Any particular ideological hypothesis can be falsified. Since rational agents can learn about their ideological mistakes, specific ascriptions of ideologies to them, however bizarre, will be falsified when these agents continue to use them after such learning should have taken place. It clearly is difficult to nail down a decisive empirical test for the imputation of one particular ideology. Still, in principle there are points beyond which a specific ideology should not persist.

I also have a more radical answer to this objection. If virtually any behavior can be rationalized by appending an appropriate conceptual scheme, this does not reflect a looseness in our understanding of conceptual schemes. Rather it confirms a looseness in their status. Conceptual schemes are not independent psychological anchors for testing the rationality hypothesis but flexible and nevertheless unavoidable ways to fill out the rational choice hypothesis. Their very malleability helps call into question precisely the assumption that an individual's ideology is a particular and determinate psychological state or mechanism (see Kripke 1982).

The arbitrariness of the version of Marxist ideology we have used in this section would be troubling if, in the process, we did not also show that, from a rational standpoint, the ideological scheme from which we judge arbitrariness is equally arbitrary. What ours has going for it, Goodman (1983) essentially shows, is the sheer fact that we have used it successfully. In Goodman's words, it is entrenched. Had we used the Marxist scheme elaborated in the preceding, it too would be entrenched. We did not and therefore it is not.

So the idea of rational ideology is not a plea for an indulgent tolerance of behavioral quirks; the issue is how to make sense of anomalous behavior when we recognize that its anomalousness may simply consist of failing to conform to what would be rational relative to our conceptual scheme. This point becomes crucial when, moving beyond philosophical possibility, we find evidence in the real world that millions of people do not seem to think the way we do. What are we to make of that? I suggest we make as much of it as we did those millions of anomalous souls who have turned out in election after election.

With this multitude in mind, one may object to rational ideology from another direction. Rationality is a property of individuals, one might say, yet ideology, like ethnicity and religion, is social in nature. The very notion of an individually rooted ideology is misconceived: "To embrace an ideology is to join a community of like-minded people" (Higgs 1987, 42). I see no contradiction. Ideology, like ethnicity, religion, or party identification, provides a useful cue for political actors calculating the CEU of their acts. It is most likely to be useful when it is widely shared. More accurately, an ideology will be judged to be widely shared—by observers and adherents alike—when it proves useful.[10]

To sum up, we have rationalized ideology. This historically important political phenomenon is perfectly consistent with rigorous rationality. While significant for rational choice theory generally, this finding is particularly crucial for CEU theory. CEU theory relies extensively on the existence of categorizations or conceptual schemes to orient agents deciding whether to vote or provide public goods generally. If the existence of these politically potent schemes represented a challenge to the rationality assumption, CEU theory would be in serious difficulty. If variations in these schemes represented a challenge to the rationality assumption, CEU theory would be nearly equally stymied. For it is very unappealing to posit individuals who rationally condition on conceptual schemes that are themselves held irrationally.

III

In arguing for the typical citizen's ideological innocence, Converse (1964) anticipates the preceding section's conclusion that ostensibly idiosyncratic behavior or reasoning is consistent with having an ideology.[11] Whatever subtle and diverse forms individual ideologies might take, Converse responds, they should nonetheless provide a stable source of political opinions (see also Converse 1975, 88–89). Instead, he finds that the key political opinions of a large segment of the population are unstable, reflecting citizen nonattitudes. In particular, he finds the greatest instability for "a domestic issue concerning the relative role of government and private enterprise" (1964, 241).

This section will show that when citizens' opinions develop in an environment containing rational political parties, the existence of rational ideologues is consistent with the pattern of opinion instability Converse observed.[12] I develop a model in which citizens form opinions about an economic variable, inflation, over which a governing party is assumed to have substantial influence. Of course, opinions about inflation do not exhaust the scope or substance of the attitude items worrying Converse. Yet they allow us to assess whether his finding is a generically appropriate inference about ideology, whose existence the CEU approach assumes. Moreover, Stimson (1991) and Christopher Wlezien (1995), among others, find that the public's policy preferences move in sync over a wide range of issues, while there is also substantial evidence that political opinions are low dimensional (Enelow and Hinich 1984; Hinich and Munger 1994).

Following Alberto Alesina and Howard Rosenthal (1995), consider an election involving two presidential candidates with distinct policy preferences. There is no possibility of reelecting the winner. In this game, accordingly, the lame-duck president has no incentive to accommodate the preferences of the voters. Because the voters can anticipate their abandonment, they in turn have no reason to put any stock in promises or policies that suggest anything else. In brief, a candidate cannot make a credible commitment to pursue lame-duck policies that would please the voters. Thus Alesina and Rosenthal adopt the partisan view of party electoral competition, but they do not recognize the voters' preferences as either direct or indirect arguments in the president's utility function.

Although Alesina and Rosenthal do not allow an incumbent president to cater to voters, their model does generate a policy dynamic over his two-period term. Suppose, in particular, one of the presidential parties prefers relatively less inflation than the other and that the inflation preferences of most voters lie strictly between those of the parties. In this situation, "moderate" voters know that when one party dominates government, its inflation policies will be relatively extreme from their standpoint. Going into a presidential election, therefore, moderate voters who are uncertain about the outcome may still split their legislative votes between the parties in order to use the legislature as a hedge against the policy of the new executive. Once their uncertainty about the election is resolved, however, voters no longer have an incentive to hedge. They will tilt the legislature against the incumbent even more. In this way, Alesina and Rosenthal explain the phenomenon of midterm losses by the party holding the U.S. presidency. Since in their model actual policy outcomes reflect not only the preferences of the executive but the balance of power between the two parties in the legislature, policy will in general change when a left-wing executive's policy is shifted right as a result of the midterm election or a right-wing executive's policy is shifted left.[13]

In this model, the executive branch behaves as though it did not care about its popularity. This does not mean the incumbent suffers no disutility from a hostile electorate. At the very least, the executive dislikes the midterm backlash against its initial policy. In addition, it may derive utility from holding office or even from the sheer fact of victory. Nonetheless, so long as the incumbent's relative popularity does not enter into the utility function characterizing its policy, it does not matter since there is nothing the executive can do about it. The executive, in particular, cannot moderate its policies in hopes of maintaining the voters' loyalty since the voters know this loyalty will go unrewarded after the midterm election: if they moderate their backlash, they will merely facilitate a more extreme policy.

For our purposes, the important result is that the midterm election causes the executive's party to lose strength in the legislature, which is characteristic of U.S. elections, and therefore the incumbent executive's policies are moderated. This policy movement will be crucial to our rationalization of the opinion volatility Converse documents. There is, however, one problem with the model that should be addressed.

While the electorate in this model actively calculates the policy consequences of its votes, the executive has a fixed policy ideal it rigidly pursues. This seems an odd asymmetry. Presumably, a clever executive would follow the voters in distinguishing between the policy it adopts and the actual outcome emerging from its relation with the legislature. A rational executive may take stands in anticipation of the interbranch compromise producing the actual outcome. By staking out a more extreme position, the executive may influence the bargaining to follow. Tracking this more complex set of considerations requires us to substitute a somewhat different formal model for the verbal description on which we have so far relied.

Consider, then, the decision problem of a president from party $i \in \{\Theta, \Psi\}$ who knows that voters will attempt to anticipate any policy he adopts by installing a legislature to offset it. On taking office at time t, president i maximizes his utility U_{it}, which is sensitive to the gap between his own policy ideal and the actual policy outcome:

$$U_{it} = E_t \sum_{s=t}^{t+1} - \beta^{s-t} \{\lambda P_s + (1 - \lambda)P_{is}^L - P_i^*\}^2, \qquad (3.2)$$

where P_t is the change in policy, relative to time $t - 1$, initiated by i, with periods occurring in two-year intervals; E_t is mathematical expectation conditioned on information available at time t; β is the executive's discount rate reflecting a preference for the present over the future; P_i^* is i's ideal change in policy, with possible policy bounded by a closed interval $a \leq P_t \leq b, b > a$; and finally $\lambda \in (0,1)$ reflects the determination of the actual political outcome, which is a compromise between the legislature's "preference" P_{it}^L, reflecting the voter-induced composition of the legislature at time t, and the executive's chosen policy.

If legislators behave with fixed preferences in the manner hypothesized by Alesina and Rosenthal, voters effect policy shifts by changing the composition of the legislature. Given the bound on policy, there is an upper limit on the countervailing pressure voters can exert at any given time.[14] The electorate's implicit policy ideal is $\lambda P_i^* + (1 - \lambda)P_{it}^L \equiv P_{it}^v$; without loss of generality, we assume that the executive is to the left of this ideal, that is, $a < P_i^* < P_{it}^v < P_{it}^L < b$.

It is also realistic to assume that voters experience negative utility when legislators take positions deviating from the voters' true ideals. This negative utility can arise, for example, when legislators' policy positions are linked to legislative actions unrelated to the executive-legislative contest, so these positions matter in their own right. Thus we assume, parallel to equation (3.2), that each voter's loss function is not only quadratic in deviations of policy from the voter's ideal but also in deviations of legislators' policy ideals from that of the voter. The former specification follows Alesina and Rosenthal (1995, 108). As a technical point, observe that since the sum of concave functions is concave, voter utility functions remain concave on the policy interval.[15]

President i makes policy given current and past values of all variables. The voters, by contrast, are uncertain about the distribution of their ideal points, which primarily lie between the two relatively extreme positions of the two parties. This uncertainty reflects shocks to turnout (Alesina and Rosenthal 1995, 86–87) or perhaps the survey polling noise emphasized by Christopher Achen (1975). In any event, at the time of the election voters are uncertain about who the next president will be.[16]

By assuming that all voters are fully rational, using their information to make predictions in light of a correct model of the policy process, we have precluded the voter myopia driving the standard theory of political business cycles (e.g., Nordhaus 1975; Tufte 1978). More important, this rational expectations assumption serves to test the claimed inconsistency between the existence of rational belief systems and the pattern of opinion volatility discovered by Converse. If as it turns out this pattern of opinion is consistent with rationality in its strongest form, Converse's inference about the nonideological character of the electorate is most clearly challenged.

We solve equation (3.2) using the technique of dynamic programming (see, e.g., Chow 1975). The first-order condition for the last period is

$$\frac{\partial U_{it+1}}{\partial P_{t+1}} = -\lambda^2 P_{t+1} - \lambda(1 - \lambda)P_{it+1}^L + \lambda P_i^* = 0.$$

Solving for P_{t+1}, substituting the result in equation (3.2), taking the first-order condition with respect to P_t, and solving for P_t yields

$$P_t = \frac{1}{\lambda}\left[P_i^* - (1 - \lambda)P_{it}^L\right].\tag{3.3}$$

This is the policy set by president i at time t and, with a change of time subscripts, for $t + 1$. From equation (3.2), the actual policy outcome is $\lambda P_t + (1 - \lambda) P_{it}^L = \lambda\{\lambda^{-1}[P_i^* - (1 - \lambda) P_{it}^L]\} + (1 - \lambda)P_{it}^L = P_i^*$. This is president i's original policy ideal, so in this analysis he prevails and the electorate is thwarted. Contrary to the implications of Alesina and Rosenthal (1995), the executive may be able to counter the electorate's midterm attempt to influence policy through the composition of the legislature.

Yet this proposed solution for P_t suffers from two possible defects. First, it is infeasible if $P_t < a$. Second, even if feasible it is not necessarily an equilibrium since a rational electorate anticipating equation (3.3) can perhaps change its voting strategy in an attempt to induce its original policy goal P_{it}^v. In effect, the electorate would like to revise the legislature's preference to $2P_{it}^L - P_i^*$, so that actual policy outcomes at time t are now determined by $\lambda P_t + (1 - \lambda)[2P_{it}^L - P_i^*]$, where P_t is given by equation (3.2). Of course, $P_{it}^L - P_i^*$ is not feasible if $2P_{it}^L - P_i^* > P_j^*$, $i \ne j$.

Assuming feasibility for the moment, observe that should the voters revise their original strategy the executive will not continue to operate according to equation (3.3), which is predicated on the electorate's original vote. It will again induce the original policy outcome P^* by selecting strategy (3.3'): $P_t = \lambda^{-1}[(2 - \lambda)P_i^* - 2(1 - \lambda)P_{it}^L]$. This then dictates a voter-induced legislative preference of $3P_{it}^L - 2P_i^*$, which is countered by a new executive policy (3.3''): $P_t = \lambda^{-1}[(3 - 2\lambda)P_i^* - 3(1 - \lambda)P_{it}^L]$. Policy (3''), in turn, induces a legislative preference of $4P_{it}^L - 3P_i^*$. By iterations on equation (3.3), it is clear that, subject to feasibility, the executive changes policy to compensate for each change in the legislature's preference by the amount $(\lambda^{-1} - 1)[P_i^* - P_{it}^L]$, while the legislature's preference changes by the amount $-(P_i^* - P_{it}^L)$. The change in executive policy is a negative function of the change in the legislature's voter-induced preference.

As noted, these changes are subject to the feasibility constraint, which implies three possible cases (setting $i \ne j$): (1) the executive is more extreme than the voters, that is, $P_i^* - a < P_j^* - P_{it}^v$, (2) the executive is less extreme than the voters, that is, $P_i^* - a > P_j^* - P_{it}^v$, and (3) neither is more extreme than the other, that is, $P_i^* - a = P_j^* - P_{it}^v$. Each of these cases generates three possible subcases: (a) $\lambda < 1/2$, (b) $\lambda > 1/2$, and (c) $\lambda = 1/2$. In subcase (a), the executive is less influential over policy than is the legislature, and therefore each voter-induced shift of the legislature from P_{it}^L covers less policy distance than does the executive response; in subcase (b), the relative influence is reversed, and the executive covers less policy distance; and in subcase (c), with equal influence, the distances are equal. I will refer to the issue of relative ideological extremism as the issue of *bargaining position,* while the issue of relative political influence will be termed the issue of *bargaining power.*

According to a standard result of game theory (e.g., Debreu 1952), there is a pure-strategy equilibrium to this game between the president and the voters.[17] In six of the subcases—(1a), (1c), (2b), (2c), (3a), and (3b)—the nature of the equilibrium is particularly clear. The effort of either the executive or the voters to compensate for the movement of the other runs out of policy room. This occurs when a relative lack of bargaining power compounds the problem of weak bargaining position, when equal bargaining power is upset by an inequality of bargaining position, or when equality of bargaining position is upset by unequal bargaining power. For subcases (1a), (1c), and (3a), the voters preserve the policy result of the original model and there is a midterm policy shift; for subcases (2b), (2c), and (3b), the executive achieves its ideal by completely negating the voters' shifts and policy is constant. When policy is constant, moreover, voters stay with P_{it}^L due to the otherwise negligible cost of installing a legislature straying from their policy ideals (see n. 15). Voters are unwilling to elect a more extreme legislature than necessary for modifying executive policy. For subcase (3c), the executive is only required to match the ideological movement of the legislature, and the executive prevails as well.

Subcases (1b) and (2a) are a little more subtle because relative bargaining position and bargaining power have a conflicting impact (e.g., in the period covered by Converse's 1964 panel data, a relatively centrist president faced a strongly organized legislature controlled by the opposing party). The analysis, however, continues to depend on which side, the executive or voters, has sufficient ideological room to adopt the more extreme bargaining position. The executive will prevail if there exists an $x > 0$ such that $P_i^* - a \geq (\lambda^{-1} - 1)(P_i^* - P_{it}^L)x$ and $(P_i^* - P_{it}^L)x \geq P_j^* - P_{it}^v$, in words, if the interaction of bargaining position and power allows the executive to counter any feasible legislative shifts. After algebraic manipulation this condition becomes $(\lambda^{-1} - 1)^{-1}(P_i^* - a) \geq P_j^* - P_{it}^v$. Here too it is disadvantageous to be extreme, but the executive's bargaining power can compensate for its extremism. When this condition is not satisfied, the voters can and will produce a more extreme legislature than they otherwise would want, but their compensation is a moderating swing in policy after the midterm elections.

The preceding finding that in some situations the executive gets its way follows from relaxing the assumption of mechanical executive behavior. Yet it fails to recognize the actual frictions that inhibit changes in executive policy. Presumably a new administration finds it costly to move policy from the status quo it inherits.[18] Furthermore, actual policy outcomes emerge from a political process in which deals are struck, favors granted, and threats carried out. Given this process, the political cost facing an executive wishing to achieve its ideal outcome will likely increase with the policy distance between itself and the legislature. Given both these costs, an executive producing its "ideal" policy would not be optimizing.

An executive concerned with these costs will be indirectly concerned with the popularity of its party's position as reflected in the composition of the legislature. This concern, of course, does not imply the possibility of manipulating public opinion. Nonetheless, public opinion will play an implicit role in the executive's utility function insofar as the greater the distance between the legislature chosen by the public and the executive's ideal, the greater will be the shortfall between the ideal and the actual policy. The claim that incumbents behave as though they do not care about their popularity is clearly counterintuitive. Cost considerations suggest a way to modify this result.

Subject to an initial policy, president i on taking office now maximizes

$$U_{it} = E_t \sum_{s=t}^{t+1} -\beta^{s-t}\{[\lambda P_s + (1 - \lambda)P_{is}^L - P_i^*]^2 + \alpha_i P_s^2\}, \tag{3.4}$$

where the P_s^2 term reflects the cost of changing policy and $\alpha_i > 0$ is the relative weight i gives to the cost of changing policy and also incorporates any objective constraints on the executive's ability to maneuver. Again using dynamic programming, the policy for each period s is

$$P_s = \frac{\lambda}{\lambda^2 + \alpha_i}[P_i^* - (1 - \lambda)P_{is}^L]. \tag{3.5}$$

There are several immediate things to observe about equation (3.5). Most important, the actual policy outcome is

$$\frac{1}{\lambda^2 + \alpha_i}[\lambda^2 P_i^* + \alpha_i(1 - \lambda)P_{is}^L].$$

The policy swing is no longer negated, regardless of the executive's relative bargaining position or power, although the more weight it attaches to satisfying its ideal (or the less friction it encounters in changing policy) the less it tolerates attempted shifts away from its ideal. As $\alpha_i \to 0$, the executive's response to the midterm swing becomes negligible.

Two, although α_i influences the character of the equilibrium to this game, it is straightforward to confirm that the basic dynamics of the previous model hold here as well. Even when the executive's ideal prevails, however, it now incorporates the legislature's preference.

Three, as noted previously, the original model implies that the on-year preference of the legislature is closer to the executive's policy preference than is the off-year legislative preference. It is clear from the equilibrium just established that the resulting policy swing will be proportionately affected. Likewise, the greater the executive's bargaining power, the less important is the legislature's preference.

IV

The preceding section investigated the optimal decision rules for executives and voters. One upshot is an underlying tendency of the actual policy outcome to spike as the executive responds to voter-induced changes in P_t^L between on-year and off-year elections. The policy pendulum associated with the role of P_t^L influences public opinion in turn. Specifically, a voter whose ideal point is within the range of the pendulum will alternately prefer positive and negative changes in the policy outcome, in other words, more and then less of what the government is doing.

Consider, for example, agents responding to the question posed in 1956, 1958, and 1960: "The government in Washington ought to see to it that everybody who wants to work can find a job. Do you have an opinion on this or not?" (e.g., Nie and Andersen 1974). The problem of nonattitudes aside, what does a genuine opinion holder's response indicate in this example?

One possibility, of course, is that respondents have a complete view of jobs policy and its implementation. This would entail a precise definition of unemployment, a conception of the role frictional unemployment should play, a position on the appropriate queuing times for the unemployed, an opinion as to whether the unemployed should have jobs in their field at prevailing wages, at wages prevailing when they lost their job, or at the prevailing wages for just any job, an idea of how to factor in seasonal unemployment, and so on. Even "defenders" of public opinion concede the inaccuracy of this portrait of respondents (e.g., Page and Shapiro 1992; Stimson 1991; Zaller 1992).

A more realistic possibility is that respondents sense the direction policy is moving, either from direct information about the policy or by drawing inferences from the general character or policies of the administration and the reactions of interested reference groups. From this less refined perspective, the typical voter will still find both parties too extreme. In caricature form, this voter sees the Democrats as willing to reward people for holding out for better jobs, for gambling badly on job prospects, or for preparing themselves inadequately. Likewise, to this voter Republicans write off the unemployed as just lazy or fussy. Without knowing the ramifications of the perfect policy for today—their ideal policy level—respondents know what changes they do and do not like. Implicitly, they operate in terms of a general continuum of employment policy about which they have, or act as if they have, rational expectations. Their ideal is implicit in their shifting enthusiasms relative to perceived party extremes they do not support.[19]

The preference volatility generated by the policy pendulum is crucial for evaluating Converse's (1964) famous anti-ideology argument. His argument develops in two stages. First, Converse presents evidence that individuals do not reason in terms of coherent belief systems. Their opinions, for example, do not generally reveal much internal "constraint." But having developed these findings, Converse anticipates the objection that ostensibly unconstrained responses may simply reflect a belief system, like the Marxist, that is alien to the observers who are unsuccessfully attempting to interpret it. If this is the case, his negative results are due to problems with the translation rather than problems with the respondent. This leads to the second and more innovative stage of his argument. However idiosyncratic an individual's belief system might be, Converse suggests, it should be a stable source of political opinions (see also Converse 1975, 88–89). Instead, he discovers that key political opinions of a large segment of the population are unstable, reflecting citizen nonattitudes.

Converse's finding of extreme opinion volatility has, of course, been strongly criticized (e.g., Achen 1975; Nie, Verba, and Petrocik 1976; Sniderman, Brody, and Tetlock 1991). What is striking, however, is that both sides of the ideology-nonattitude debate tend to regard the instability of opinion as inherently problematic for the proconstraint side. Accordingly, most of the debate over Converse's finding has revolved around the actual degree of volatility exhibited by public opinion.[20]

The model developed in this chapter suggests that this debate has been misdirected. It shows that when a citizen's opinions develop in the context of an electoral policy cycle, the existence of a rationally held belief system is consistent with the specific pattern of opinion instability Converse observed. A part of the public may have volatile opinions because it is reacting to changes in the direction of policy. Since Alesina and Rosenthal (1995) suggest a cycle with respect to monetary growth, economic policy is a natural example of systematic, politically induced volatility in individual opinion. This does not mean that all such volatility has systematic contextual causes, political or otherwise. Rather, volatility cannot be addressed, as it so often has been, independently of the context in which the questions eliciting opinion are asked.

This is particularly true of ideology. If one identifies a preference for more of the policy or government activity (e.g., higher inflation) as a "left" orientation and a preference for less of the policy (e.g., lower inflation) as a "right" orientation, the spiking pattern of public opinion might well suggest acute ideological incoherence.[21] Yet the individual voters modeled in the preceding section are not incoherent. Indeed their individual changes of opinion are consistent with rationality. Nor is this instability empirically surprising. According to James Stimson, Michael MacKuen, and Robert Erikson (1995, 543), "political decisions have a directional force to them, and their incremental character is inherently dynamic. Further, most public opinion judgments concern change as well."[22] There is, moreover, substantial evidence that political opinions are endogenous (e.g., Gerber and Jackson 1993) and, specifically, that citizens form "countervailing" opinions about government policies (e.g., Chappell and Keech 1985; Durr 1993; Kiewiet 1983, 8).

As Converse (1964) recognizes, the spiking pattern rationalized here can explain the particular pattern of individual-level volatility he documents. "It would have to be assumed that a person who chose a leftish alternative on a certain issue [e.g., more inflation] . . . would be motivated to remember to seek out the rightish alternative [e.g., less inflation] two years later, the leftish again two years after that, and so on." But he recognizes this possibility only to dismiss it. "Naturally, an assumption that this behavior characterizes one member of the population is sufficiently nonsensical for us to reject it out of hand" (242). This however is precisely the biennial pattern of behavior resulting from our model of the citizen's interaction with a dynamic, optimizing government.[23]

These considerations, of course, do not mean that our model explains instability in general. Rather, lability of opinion does not in itself indicate the absence of rationally held beliefs. In this sense, Converse's inference from instability to ideological innocence, however influential and widely protested on empirical grounds, is a non sequitur.

In fairness, Converse probably interprets preference volatility as movement independent of circumstances. This is because he thinks of ideologues as reasoning deductively. Rather than inductively altering their beliefs, they impose their preconceptions on new experiences (Converse 1966a). Their opinions, he concludes, will be relatively stable since they are relatively impervious to the political context in which they are formed. Even the way he words his dismissal of the spiking mechanism reflects his view of ideologies as closed-minded belief systems. The ideologues responsible for the "nonsensical" behavior he describes do not adapt to changes in their political environment. They are autonomously "motivated to remember to seek out" competing positions over time. From Converse's perspective, therefore, the linear incoherence of mass public opinion undermines any ideological pretensions for it.

In one sense, Converse is right. Preferences that spike independent of context would indeed be difficult to motivate (although there may be individuals who are the ideological equivalent of smokers who intermittently attempt to quit; cf. Converse and Markus 1979, 37). Change seems most appropriate when context-dependent opinions face a changing context. Yet a changing context is precisely what our model of policy formation suggests.

Of course, it may be objected that the preferences invoked here do not truly depend on context. While the *revealed* policy preferences of the government and voters do change, they change relative to a fixed ideal point, explicitly modeled as P_i^* for the parties and implicitly modeled for the centrist voter as an element P_v^* lying in the interval between the parties' ideals. Once we distinguish between true preferences and the choices they produce under varying circumstances, we will see that the individuals involved are more stable than my interpretation suggests.

By way of response, imagine alternative models of context dependence that advocates of this notion, such as William Keech (1995), might have in mind. An *implicit* fixed ideal is likely to be an artifact of any such formal representation of the individual voter. Thus in the simplest case of systematic preference volatility, $P_{vt}^* = dP_{t-1}$, $-1 < d < 0$, not only is the "long-run" ideal 0 but if for some reason $P_{t-1} = 0$, the long-run ideal is reached immediately.[24] As a result, this case of pure context dependence can be interpreted as a process in which revealed preference shifts around a "true" preference for 0. Under either interpretation, an implicit ideal point anchors shifting preferences.

The notion of an implicit ideal is given a more substantive interpretation by Benjamin Page and Robert Shapiro (1992, 16): "over a period of time, each individual has a central tendency of opinion, which might be called a 'true' or *long-term preference,* and which can be ascertained by averaging the opinions expressed by the *same individual* at several different times." This definition of long-term preference grounds their argument for the reality of a generally stable aggregate public opinion. At the lower level of temporal aggregation explored by the present analysis, however, we detect more *systematic* individual variation around what they construe as a long-term preference. Our analysis, in other words, would emphasize the scare quotes Page and Shapiro place around *true.* In this one respect, then, our analysis is closer to Zaller's (1992, 118) conclusion that "'attitudes' in the conventional sense of the term do not exist." Instead individuals exhibit stable "long-term response probabilities" to the extent the information they receive over time is politically stable or balanced.

According to Zaller, however, considerations current in a respondent's mind determine her immediate survey responses, so there is substantial stochastic variation around a statistically induced long-run equilibrium. While his account of opinion formation is clearly different than rational choice theory's (whether EU or CEU), its more important corollary, for our purposes, is that politically loaded information can generate departures from this equilibrium (1992, 64–65, 69–70). Our analysis would similarly emphasize the role of each agent's decision environment in producing (or attenuating) systematic changes in the individual's preferences and corresponding changes in aggregate opinion.

Page and Shapiro (1992, 17) also appreciate the "many ways in which individual (and collective) opinion could respond to new, policy-relevant information." They observe that since unmotivated individual volatility should cancel in the aggregate, change in aggregate opinion is evidence for the public's sensitivity to context. Converse (1964) likewise interprets his finding of aggregate opinion stability as evidence for unmotivated individual volatility. Observe, however, that in the present model policy change that is disapproved by some individuals will be approved by others, so canceling in the aggregate can take place.

The crucial point, as Page and Shapiro (1992, 56) emphasize, is that opinion change does not imply irrationality and that context, such as policy direction, influences the referents of survey questions and, therefore, the responses to them (58–59). In contrast to Page and Shapiro's work, however, the present model is not designed to capture glacial movements of opinion occurring at lower than electoral-cycle frequencies.

The same is true for opinion change at higher than electoral-cycle frequencies (e.g., a few weeks, as indicated by Page and Shapiro 1992, 6; see also Zaller 1992, 30–33). Strict application of the rational choice assumption would attribute this fluctuation of opinion to changes in each agent's specific circumstances, like job loss, or to new information about policies and policy outcomes. Thus Robert Erikson, Norman Luttbeg, and Kent Tedin (1988, 47) highlight the volatility of responses to 1956–58–60 questions about the government's role in desegregating schools. Compared to the issue of government's economic role, these civil rights questions produce somewhat higher uniformity of individual opinion across panel waves but also a higher percentage of "inconsistent" opinions (see Page and Shapiro 1992, 6–8). In assessing this inconsistency, I would suggest, it is difficult not to note the possible impact of the civil rights confrontation in Little Rock, Arkansas, and the dramatic policy change this represented.[25] In addition, some fluctuation is doubtless the result of noise from the survey instrument (e.g., Achen 1975) and the changing salience of the issue.

Not all endogenous preferences, of course, necessarily shift. Agents whose implicit ideal points lie outside or sufficiently near the party extremes will in general see policy as either consistently too much or too little. If so, the population will be divided into two parts, parallel to Converse's (1964) "black and white model" of pure ideologues and a larger group of random, nonideological respondents.[26] The group unaffected by the policy pendulum will appear ideological in Converse's sense since their opinions will view policy as uniformly too "left" or too "right." Those who are affected by the pendulum will appear nonideological. From their standpoint, however, policy itself is inconsistently swinging too far right and then too far left. An observer of public opinion might say that public sentiment and government policy are out of phase (Stimson 1991). By the same token, policy and lagged opinion will appear in phase (Stimson, MacKuen, and Erikson 1995).

V

The common test for coherent ideologies in the mass public is inadequate. Coherence must be evaluated in the context of an explicit model of how voters cognitively interact with their political environment. In the preceding model, for example, this interaction produces unstable opinions about inflation rather than the fixed responses a common-sense view of ideology might suggest. An individual with a developed and systematic set of beliefs and preferences need not have petrified opinions on the issues of the day. Individuals with ideologies, in short, may not be as rare as some have suggested.

Yet we have also seen that, in the eyes of an observer, the ideology held by a group of decision makers can stabilize their opinions in apparent defiance of the evidence generated by their political environment. Because of their particular conceptual scheme they can act as though they were blind to the evidence a rational agent would want to consider. There is instability in the one case, due to the context dependence of preferences, and stability in the other, due to the impact of the conceptual schemes anchoring CEU maximization.

For a stable belief to be seen as a symptom of ideological stubbornness requires at least two conceptual schemes, one as a framework for processing new information into (ideological) beliefs and the other as a standpoint from which to condemn the rigidity of the first. Since the stability of the first is relative to its particular scheme, and may seem suboptimal from the standpoint of the second, it is natural to ask how agents find themselves with one scheme rather than another. It would be helpful to have a way to assess which ideology will be used in a given political environment and to what effect. This section begins to take up this challenge. Granted, as we have seen, it is hopeless to expect evidence to determine a unique optimal framework or ideology. It is worth reemphasizing, however, that the CEU maximizer's use of a particular framework is not completely arbitrary either. Some ideologies will be incompatible with the evidence and therefore will be abandoned by rational adherents.

The attraction of one concrete ideology over another will not be determined, of course, solely by their relative predictive power. Other criteria surely include the ease with which an ideology can be acquired and the rapidity with which the human brain can process information within it—all summarized perhaps by the elusive notion of relative simplicity. Although ideologies occur at varying levels of generality, the question of how ideologies are selected is of a piece with the vexing issue of how scientific theories are selected.

Instead of tackling this complex problem head on, I propose to focus on one of its specifically political aspects, namely, the attempt by political candidates to influence the voter's choice of ideology, when ideologies are chosen on the basis of their predictive power. As William Riker (1990) emphasizes, effective politicians are adept at heresthetics, which includes the art of defining the categories or dimensions organizing the voter's perceptions. Citing numerous examples, he observes (1986, 150–51) that the "manipulation of dimensions is just about the most frequently attempted heresthetical device," with "[m]ost of the great shifts in political life" arising this way. Thus in the United States the nationalization of the slavery issue was part of "the main political maneuver of the nineteenth century." More recently, different candidates have asked voters to interpret their policies in terms of family values, good jobs, and fairness. Parties and candidates, in short, behave as if ideological interpretations can be influenced, which is not surprising. If politics is influenced by the way CEU maximizers categorize their political environment, as I have suggested, their political environment need not be passive in the face of these important decisions about the appropriate categorization.

Riker uses spatial voting theory to explain the consequences of heresthetic maneuvers. In the spatial theory of two-candidate elections, a majority-rule winner, if such exists, is determined by each voter's comparison of the proximity of each candidate's position on the issues to the voter's own ideal (see, e.g., Enelow and Hinich 1984). The voter prefers the closer candidate. The relative measure of distance, however, is defined over a particular space of issue dimensions in such a way that closeness is weighted by the relative importance to the voter of the particular issues at stake. Riker notes that by altering the existing issue dimensions, say, by introducing a new issue into a campaign, the successful heresthetician can create a new majority.

Yet if the motivation for heresthetic maneuvers is clear, why, in rational choice terms, the maneuvers work is not. After all, to tell voters in the mid-1800s that slavery is a dimension of the issue space is not in any obvious way to tell them something new. From this standpoint, "the main political maneuver of the nineteenth century" looks like a pointless redundancy.

Why is publicizing an issue effective with rational voters? One possibility, emphasized by Hinich and Munger (1992, 1994), is that ideological messages do not inform voters about the candidates' positions so much as reinforce the candidates' commitment to those positions. Politicians are happy to underscore their devotion to a particular ideology, in the traditional sense of the term, since nonideological politicians cannot motivate voters to take their platforms seriously. In voters' minds, then, ideological pronouncements reduce the likelihood that candidates will be opportunistic once in office. Heresthetics succeeds when the terms of debate crystallize around competing ideological poles— conservatism versus liberalism, Islam versus Western modernism—with which the heresthetician is positively and negatively identified. It is unclear, however, why professions of ideological fealty are more credible than the platforms themselves. In either case, politicians send a message voters do not have to take at face value.

In the model developed in the preceding, based on Alesina and Rosenthal (1995), the only credible campaign announcements were those that accurately reflected the policies parties would in fact adopt and the outcomes these policies would produce. In actuality, voters may have a more difficult time translating announcements into policy predictions even when they know which party will be in office. Another possible rationalization of heresthetic devices, therefore, goes back to the predictive function of ideologies. Heresthetic announcements send voters an ideologically loaded message encouraging them to estimate future policy within a particular framework, thereby encouraging them to revise their expectations.

Roughly speaking, heresthetics on this view assumes that voters use one of the alternative political interpretations already available to them. To adopt the simplest version, these alternative ideologies will be assumed to coexist in latent form with the agent's operative ideology. On this assumption, each party's policy or message is ideologically ambiguous. In devising its position, each party must anticipate the results of possible heresthetic maneuvers by its opponent as well as the rule by which voters condition on ideological announcements and make electoral decisions. In turn, each voter operates with one of her available ideologies, either by retaining the one she is currently using or by switching to some other in her inventory. Politicians, in brief, are trying to tell the voter not only where they stand but how their positions should be interpreted.

Even under these simplified assumptions and the additional simplifications to follow, it is difficult to characterize party and voter behavior without a formal construction of the players' decision rules. The following formalization is designed to capture what Riker shows is often a dramatic process, in some sense the very essence of politics. The formalization tries to determine conditions under which these announcements can actually change the voter's decision. In contrast to the preceding section, we assume the two parties are entirely office motivated and maximize their expected vote. By focusing on the party's relation with the voter and the opportunism of their strategies, we highlight induced changes in voter ideology and preference when voters are legitimately skeptical of the party's orientation.

Parties Θ and Ψ seek (re)election knowing that the $2N + 1$ voters, all of whom vote, operate with a common inventory of potential one-dimensional ideological frameworks $\mathbf{I}_1, \ldots, \mathbf{I}_n$ with n finite. The parties Θ and Ψ take public positions π_i, $i \in \{\Theta, \Psi\}$, on Π, a closed interval in R^1 representing alternative public positions like liberal and conservative (this terminology and structure are consistent with Enelow and Hinich 1984). At time $t - 1$, Θ, the incumbent, makes an announcement $(\pi_{\Theta(t-1)}, m_{\Theta(t-1)})$ providing both its location on Π and a proposed ideological interpretation $m = 0, 1, 2, \ldots, n$ of that location ($m = 0$ when the announcement is purely positional). At time $t - 1/2$, Ψ, the challenger, also makes an announcement. Thus before t, the voter's calculus has successively incorporated the new data about the parties' positions.[27]

When a party's announced position is translated within a particular ideology, this will be termed an *interpretation*. For example, the selfsame position—say, a call for a balanced budget—may receive an economic interpretation in one ideology, a religious interpretation in another. The voter's utility from each $\mathbf{I}_k$ is determined by considering the net benefit of voting for her preferred party based on the ideological interpretation of each party's position in $\mathbf{I}_k$. Each voter chooses among the $\mathbf{I}_k$ by selecting the ideology whose use is associated with the highest CEU (if two or more frameworks have equal CEU, they are used with equal probability). Ideology, in other words, is not an idle form of contemplation but is action oriented. Guided by different utility calculations, different voters will generally choose different frameworks (see, e.g., Conover and Feldman 1981; Lane 1962).[28]

At time t, the net benefit for party positions $y_{ti} \in \mathbf{I}_k$ is therefore

$$\text{prob}(\mathbf{I}_k)|U_k^j(y_{t\Theta}) - U_k^j(y_{t\Psi})|,$$

where $U_k^j(y_t) = -(y_t - y_{jk}^*)^2$, y_{jk}^* is j's ideal point in $\mathbf{I}_k$, and $\text{prob}_t(\mathbf{I}_k)$ is j's prior degree of belief in the ideology, with $\sum_{k=1}^{n} \text{prob}_t(\mathbf{I}_k) = 1$ and $\text{prob}_t(\mathbf{I}_k) > 0$ for all k. This prior belief summarizes j's initial socialization into an ideology as well as subsequent experience using it. Factors such as the probability of j's vote being pivotal are assumed to be constant across ideologies.

Since actual policies are subject to the vagaries of policy implementation, can evolve, and may intentionally deviate from campaign promises, j must adopt some inferential strategy for translating announced positions into interpretations concerning subsequent policy. We assume j uses ordinary least squares estimates for party i, $i \in \{\Theta, \Psi\}$:

$$y_{ki(t+1)} = a_{ki}\pi_{i(t)} + b_{ki} + u_{ki(t+1)}, \tag{3.6}$$

where the $u_{ki(t+1)}$ are independent and normally distributed scalar random variables with variance $\sigma_{i(t+1)}^2$ and zero mean.[29]

In a sense, the prediction formula (3.6) represents reputation: if $|a_{kij}| = 1$, position announcements are taken at face value. To the extent $|a_{kij}| < 1$, the party's strong ideological reputation means that changes in position encounter skepticism. In this case, a party must execute a relatively large public deviation from a given position in order for the voter's interpretation to "credit" the movement. To the extent $|a_{kij}| > 1$, the party's reputation carries the opposite implication. Since the party's historical rigidity is so well established, even relatively small changes in public announcements have large ideological repercussions (as perhaps in the West's strong interpretive reaction to Mikhail Gorbachev's early public announcements). Finally, if $a_{kij} = 0$ stated positions are simply not credible. The b_{ki} remain the party's reputation no matter what it declares, although $u_{ki(t+1)}$ recognizes some residual uncertainty about the exact implications of this fixed position.[30]

In the present model, reputation is not interpreted as a restriction on the ability of parties to maneuver along Π since, if they so choose, parties can ignore the gradient their reputations create. Our approach to ideology is not inherently frictionless, as the preceding model incorporating party preference shows, but here it is designed to highlight the role of opportunistic heresthetic strategies.

Given equation (3.6), j's expected utility, in $\mathbf{I}_k$, from party i is

$$EU_k^j(y_{ki(t+1)}) = -prob(\mathbf{I}_{kj})[(\bar{y}_{ki(t+1)} - y_{jk}^*)^2 + \sigma_{i(t+1)}^2], \tag{3.7}$$

where $\bar{y}_{ki(t+1)}$ is the mean of $y_{ki(t+1)}$. Thus, suppressing temporal indices, j's net expected utility is given by

$$|EU_k^j(y_{k\theta}) - EU_k^j(y_{k\psi})|. \tag{3.8}$$

This formulation implies that each voter equally values ideal points in the ideologies.

Voters incorporate the parties' position announcements directly by substituting them into the n versions of equations (3.6) and (3.7). Since voters have no new information on actual policy outcomes, the coefficients of equation (3.6) do not change in response to position announcements (in this respect they parallel the linear predictions of Enelow and Hinich 1984). The ideology announcement, in contrast, must be weighed against the previous estimate of the parties' ideologies. If a party recommends a particular ideological interpretation, this information is subject to Bayesian updating of the voters' initial beliefs since voters must weigh the credibility of the announcement.[31] In particular, within $\mathbf{I}_k$ j's updated utility concerning y_t is

$$U_k^j(y_t) = -prob_t(\mathbf{I}_k)(y_t - y_{jk}^*)^2, \tag{3.9}$$

where $prob_t(\mathbf{I}_k) = prob_{t-1}(\mathbf{I}_k) \, prob(\mathbf{I}_m \mid \mathbf{I}_k) \, \{\sum_k [prob_{t-1}(\mathbf{I}_k)prob(\mathbf{I}_m \mid \mathbf{I}_k)]\}^{-1}$ when $1 \leq m \leq n$ ranges over j's inventory of ideologies. For present purposes $prob(\mathbf{I}_m \mid \mathbf{I}_k) = R_{km}/\sum_m R_{km}$, where $R_{km} = 1/2[1 + (R_{mt}^2 - R_{kt}^2)]$ for $k \neq m$, $R_{km} =$

R_{kt}^2 for $k = m$, and R_{mt}^2 and R_{kt}^2 are averages of the parties' individual R^2's (the denominator $\sum_m R_{km}$ ensures $0 \le \text{prob}(\mathbf{I}_m \mid \mathbf{I}_k) \le 1$). When $m = 0$, $\text{prob}_{t-1}(\mathbf{I}_k)$ is unchanged. The motivation for this definition of R_{km} is that when a party announces ideology m, but j's current ideology $\mathbf{I}_k$ performs as well as $\mathbf{I}_m$, j concludes that $\mathbf{I}_m$ is no more plausible than $\mathbf{I}_k$.[32]

We initially consider voters who have, in each of two ideologies k and m, common priors $\text{prob}_{(t-1)}(\mathbf{I}_k)$, $\text{prob}_{(t-1)}(\mathbf{I}_m) > 0$, and common levels of uncertainty concerning Θ and Ψ, $\sigma_{k\theta}^2 = \sigma_{m\theta}^2$ and $\sigma_{k\psi}^2 = \sigma_{m\psi}^2$. All voters use the predictive functions $y_{k\theta} = a_{k\theta}\pi + u_\theta$, $y_{k\psi} = a_{k\psi}\pi + u_\psi$, $y_{m\theta} = a_{m\theta}\pi + u_\theta$, and $y_{m\psi} = a_{m\psi}\pi + u_\psi$. We have simplified the ensuing calculations by assuming zero intercepts, and, for the same reason, we assume a simple linear transformation between m and k such that $a_{mi} = v a_{ki}$, v finite (consistent with our discussion of Marxism, points in different ideologies are intertranslatable). As noted earlier, the u_i are all zero mean and normally distributed, but their second moments may vary between parties. Finally, to maintain our focus on the impact of individual ideologies, we assume a complete information model, aside from the ambiguities already mentioned. As we will see subsequently, analogous results can be derived when parties are uncertain about the distribution of voter ideal points.

We start with minimum ambiguity, which technically is a limiting case, and consider the situation facing the parties conditional on their ideological announcements (the proofs of the following propositions are collected in appendix B).

PROPOSITION 1: *If $\sigma_{k\theta}^2 = \sigma_{m\theta}^2 = \sigma_{k\psi}^2 = \sigma_{m\psi}^2 = 0$, $\text{prob}_t(\mathbf{I}_k)/\text{prob}_t(\mathbf{I}_m) > v^2$, and $y_{rk}^* \ne y_{sk}^*$ for some voters r,s, then the unique Stackelberg equilibrium party announcements are $\pi_{ik}^* = (\text{argmax}_{yki} \text{EU}_k^{M_k})/a_{ki}$, where M_k is the set of voters with the median ideal point in k. If $\text{prob}_t(\mathbf{I}_k)/\text{prob}_t(\mathbf{I}_m) < v^2$, the unique equilibrium announcements for the parties are $\pi_{im}^* = (\text{argmax}_{ymi} \text{EU}_k^{M_m})/a_{mi}$, where M_m is the set of voters with the median ideal point in m.*

In this case, the voters factor the translation between ideologies (v) into their calculations and the introduction of ideologies does not overturn the standard result of spatial theory. Party positions reflect the ideal of the median voter within the dominant ideology, that is, the ideology with higher prior. But there is also an implication for the voter's willingness to change ideologies. The stronger the voter's ideological convictions relative to some alternative, the greater must be the difference between the voter's optimal point and the positions of the parties in order to induce the voter to switch. This is because ceteris paribus these differences increase the usefulness of the associated $\text{prob}(\mathbf{I}_k)$. *In more familiar language, alienation creates opportunities to change the interpretation of party positions.*

Although the parties converge in the relevant ideological space, in general $\pi_\theta^* \neq \pi_\psi^*$: parties do not converge in their public announcements notwithstanding their indifference to policy, the usual path to divergence (e.g., Enelow 1992; Wittman 1990). The historical relation between each party's public announcements and its policies generates a distinct reputation that, in turn, dictates a distinct optimal position.

We now consider the consequences of voter indifference between ideologies.

COROLLARY 1A: *If the assumptions of proposition* 1 *obtain except that* $\mathrm{prob}_t(\mathbf{I}_k)/\mathrm{prob}_t(\mathbf{I}_m) = v^2$, *then there are equilibrium position announcements* $\pi_i^* = (\mathrm{argmax}_{y'_i}\, EU_k^{M_y})/a_{ki}$.

The following corollary is stated without proof.

COROLLARY 1B: *If* $y_{rk}^* = y_{sk}^*$ *for all voters r and s—the exception from proposition* 1*—the results of corollary* 1A *also apply.*

We now drop the assumption of uniformity in voters' comparisons between ideologies.

COROLLARY 1C: *For any mix of voters satisfying the assumptions of proposition* 1, *corollary* 1A, *and corollary* 1B, *there are equilibrium position announcements* $\pi_i^* = (\mathrm{argmax}_{y'ki}\, EU_k^{M_y})/a_{ki}$.

Thus notwithstanding the unidimensionality of y' and Π, *the equilibrium in candidate strategies may be sustained by wholly different ideologies rather than points on a single continuum.* This is consistent with Conover and Feldman's (1981, 624) finding cited previously that liberals and conservatives view the political world from entirely different perspectives. Yet our analysis splits the difference between Conover and Feldman (1981) and Sniderman, Brody, and Tetlock (1991), who argue in favor of a liberal-conservative continuum. We posit a multiplicity of ideologies underlying one public continuum. The present analysis is also consistent with Sniderman, Brody, and Tetlock's finding that voters embrace particular ideologies with different degrees of intensity.

These results can be applied to $n > 2$ ideologies.

PROPOSITION 2: *The optimal candidate strategies are determined for any finite number of ideologies.*

It is now possible to introduce explicit ideological announcements into the framework for position announcements.

PROPOSITION 3: *If $\sigma_{k\theta}^2 = \sigma_{m\theta}^2 = \sigma_{k\psi}^2 = \sigma_{m\psi}^2 = 0$, $y_{rk}^* \neq y_{sk}^*$ for some voters r,s, and* $\text{prob}_{(t-1)}(\mathbf{I}_k)/\text{prob}_{(t-1)}(\mathbf{I}_m) > v^2$, *then Stackelberg equilibrium candidate announcements are* (π_{ik}^*, k), *where* $\pi_{ik}^* = (\text{argmax}_{yki} \; EU_k^{M_k)/a_{ki}}$.

The equilibrium announcement described in proposition 3 is not necessarily unique since $(\pi_{\theta k}^*, m)$ will not be harmed by $(\pi_{\psi m}^*, m)$ when the inequality in the proposition's antecedent is large enough. Yet the incumbent is susceptible to heresthetic maneuvers when voters are indifferent between alternative ideologies but at least one of the median voter positions does not survive as a median in the "merged" dimension y'. *In short, heresthetic possibilities arise when ideological transitions are comparatively easy for voters but their policy preferences across ideologies are polarized.*

COROLLARY 3A: *If the assumptions of proposition 3 obtain except that* $\text{prob}_{(t-1)}(\mathbf{I}_k)/\text{prob}_{(t-1)}(\mathbf{I}_m) = v^2$ *and* (1) *there does not exist a* $\pi_{\theta k}^* = (\text{argmax}_{yk\theta}$ $EU_k^{M_k})/a_{k\theta}$ *such that* $\pi_{\theta k}^* \in (\text{argmax}_{y'} \; EU_k^{M_{y'}})/a_{k\theta}$ *or* (2) *there does not exist a* $\pi_{\theta m}^* = (\text{argmax}_{ym\theta} \; EU_m^{M_m})/a_{m\theta}$ *such that* $\pi_{\theta m}^* \in (\text{argmax}_{y'}$ $EU_m^{M_{my'}})/a_{m\theta}$, *then the incumbent* Θ *loses.*

The "overlap" among median points prohibited by corollary 3A is, in general, less likely to occur to the extent $|v| \neq 1$. In words, *the greater the cognitive difference between ideologies to which the voters are indifferent, the more vulnerable the incumbent is.* We add without proof consideration of the case of overlap.

COROLLARY 3B: *If the assumptions of proposition 3 obtain except that* $\text{prob}_{(t-1)}(\mathbf{I}_k)/\text{prob}_{(t-1)}(\mathbf{I}_m) = v^2$ *and there does exist a* $\pi_{\theta k}^* = (\text{argmax}_{yk\theta}$ $EU_k^{M_k})/a_{k\theta}$ *such that* $\pi_{\theta k}^* \in (\text{argmax}_{y'} \; EU_k^{M_{y'}})/a_{k\theta}$, *then there are equilibrium strategies* π_{ik}^* *for the candidates that evenly split the expected vote.*

Together, proposition 3 and corollaries 3A and 3B are significant not only because they provide conditions for heresthetic success but because they show the relatively limited nature of the opportunity. A model in which successful heresthetics is very common would explain too much.

Our analysis of incumbent vulnerability is predicated on the incumbent's obligation to announce first, albeit in anticipation of how the challenger will react. If the parties move simultaneously, there is no Nash equilibrium in pure strategies under the conditions of proposition 3, that is, no situation from which neither party has an incentive to deviate unilaterally. Thus one potential resource for a party in this situation, or Θ in the case of corollary 3A, is to have mixed strategies over ideological announcements. In effect, this would allow the party to make an ambiguous ideological announcement by presenting voters with a probability distribution over the n ideologies.

There is a substantial literature on the electoral impact of party and candidate ambiguity (e.g., Enelow and Hinich 1984; Glazer 1990). In some ideological contexts, ambiguity hurts for the standard reason that voters are risk averse.

PROPOSITION 4: *If the assumptions of proposition 3 hold except $\sigma^2_{k\psi} = \sigma^2_{m\psi} >$ 0, then Θ wins with announcement* (π_{Mk}, k).

In some heresthetic situations, however, the negative impact of a candidate's ambiguity is outweighed by the weakness of the opponent's existing ideological position.

COROLLARY 4A: *If the assumptions of corollary 3A hold except $\sigma^2_{k\psi} = \sigma^2_{m\psi} > 0$ and neither $(\bar{y}'_{\Theta k} - y^{*}) > 2\sigma^2$ nor $(\bar{y}'_{\Theta m} - y^{*}) > 2\sigma^2$, with $\bar{y}'_{\Theta k}$ and $\bar{y}'_{\Theta m}$ the counterparts in y' of Θ's announcements of $\pi^{*}_{\Theta k}$ and $\pi^{*}_{\Theta m}$ respectively and $y^{*\prime}$ the closest of $M_{y'}$'s ideal points, Ψ wins.*

The main tools of the campaigning party, then, remain position announcements, ideological announcements designed to reinforce its current reputation, and heresthetics. Hinich and Munger (1992, 1994) argue, by contrast, that the party's campaign becomes credible only because its self-identified ideology subjectively restricts its own movement. Yet while a party certainly can have an ideology of its own (see n. 13), presumably its announced ideology becomes credible to the extent the party has acquired an ideological reputation through previous behavior. In the present model, accordingly, the relation between announced positions and actual interpretations by voters is a function of past party policies and the accuracy of past position and ideology announcements. Parties with a long-term horizon would want to develop a reputation for accuracy. A model of heresthetics with weaker information assumptions about the parties is developed in appendix B.

The present approach uses reputation to connect public announcements to the voters' interpretations; Hinich and Munger (1992) appeal to public ideological commitments. Both approaches dissent from Sartori's (1976) claim that since voters have very limited information, a party's ideological identity must become an informationally empty, emotion-filled label. The present dissent is motivated by three considerations. First, even limited information can be processed rationally. This will produce greater volatility of opinion because agents are less sure of their inferences, not because emotion has filled in the gaps in their information. Second, the preceding sections suggest that Sartori's negative inferences about the voter's processing ability are more delicate than is often imagined. Third, there is evidence that voters make cognitive use of public party positions (e.g., Enelow and Hinich 1984).

VI

When voters use ideology to interpret an ideological announcement recommending some alternative, they recognize the position component of the announcement to be ambiguous as among the alternative ideological frameworks. Yet they regard the ideological announcement itself as unambiguous. This simplification has its obvious modeling advantages and is largely justified when candidates or parties are explicit about the terms of debate they believe are appropriate to the campaign. Candidates and parties, however, are not always so cooperative, and their campaign messages often must be deciphered. For one thing, the campaign may be ideologically inarticulate. For another, controversial messages may be deliberately "coded" or perceived to be coded. While not wishing to retrofit the entire model to reflect this additional ambiguity, I do want to indicate several interesting features of a class of models incorporating ambiguous evidence. The first issue is how learning from ambiguous messages might be formally represented.

In everyday life, ambiguity is commonplace. What spice am I tasting? What color bird did I see? Did she look my way? If categorization is the key to ideology, and comparing alternative systems of categorization is the key to ideological choice, then there is potential ambiguity in the ideological categorization of political information. As an examination of Bayes's Rule will show, standard Bayesian conditioning assumes that any evidence E (say, the party's announced ideological recommendation m) is perceived with certainty even while the inference drawn from the evidence is probabilistic. Therefore, on receipt of evidence at time t, the new probability of a given hypothesis H, $\text{prob}_{t+1}(H)$, is directly conditioned on E. The well-known result is $\text{prob}_{t+1}(H)$ $= \text{prob}_t(H \mid E)$, where $\text{prob}_t(H \mid E)$ is the original conditional probability.[33] Thus ambiguity about the evidence is not directly modeled.

It has been argued that decision makers who receive ambiguous information should use Jeffrey conditionalization, a generalization of Bayesian induction (see, e.g., Jeffrey 1983; Diaconis and Zabell 1982). Jeffrey's version of Bayes's Rule is $\text{prob}_{t+1}(H) = \sum_i \text{prob}_t(H \mid E_i)\text{prob}(E_i)$. In the present case, the E_i are distributed across the potential ideological frameworks, $i \in \{I_1, \ldots, I_n\}$. Accordingly, the contribution of ambiguous information to an ideological hypothesis entertained by the decision maker is weighted by the decision maker's subjective probability about how the ambiguity is resolved into alternative ideological frameworks. The application of Jeffrey's Rule, I should add, assumes that $\text{prob}_{t+1}(H \mid E_i) = \text{prob}_t(H \mid E_i)$ for all H and i or more technically that $\{E_i\}$ constitutes a sufficient partition for the two probability functions. Although the partition is discrete in the present example, it need not be.

The elegance of this resolution of the problem of ambiguous evidence is, for our purposes, less interesting than its ability to make sense of the ideological path dependence of learning (for comments on this dependence see North 1990, 76). Individuals may not only stubbornly cling to ideologies that seem obsolete to the observer. Their ideological frameworks may seem to have an additional, historical character, for experimental evidence as well as more casual observation suggests that how individuals come to hold their opinions—the order in which they receive information—influences their current opinions. The same aggregate information, in other words, will lead to different conclusions when received in different sequences. Thus an individual's ideological framework helps determine the significance of information and the way it will affect his beliefs. Such path dependence does not hold under standard Bayesian conditioning, and therefore the substantial evidence for it has been taken as one indication that political actors are not inductively rational (e.g., Popkin 1991).

In contrast to Bayesian conditioning, however, Jeffrey conditionalization is not commutative. The order in which information is received does matter to individuals updating their beliefs according to Jeffrey's Rule. More formally, conclusions drawn from successive updating based on evidence $\{E_i\}_{i=1}^{n}$ and then $\{F_j\}_{j=1}^{m}$ will differ from inferences based on the same evidence received in reverse order. In general, the newer information will dominate in the receiver's calculations, which is the standard finding. The decision makers studied by cognitive psychologists seem most impressed by recent events.

Compare this general result to the specific path dependence characteristic of ideological thinking. For example, agents who switch ideologies—say, former U.S. communists who became conservatives—do not seem to see their earlier selves as suffering merely from a shortage of information; they believe they misinterpreted the information they had. They were blind but now they see. On the other hand, one has the sense that they would not necessarily have become staunch conservatives had they not started out as staunch communists. Their present position is in part a reaction to their previous decisions.

The violation of path independence not only runs counter to the standard Bayesian result of commutativity, it may seem counterintuitive to those who have informally absorbed Bayesianism's lessons. After all, it might be objected, one's total information ought to matter, not the order in which it was acquired. Yet path dependence, I suggest, is consistent with rationality in the generic or intuitive sense. An individual who first experiences $\{E_i\}$ is cognitively different than one who first experiences $\{F_i\}$. There is no reason to expect convergence in their final judgments. Once again, the framework in which information is interpreted matters not only in its own right but even when it is transcended (for somewhat more technical considerations on path dependence, see Diaconis and Zabell 1982, 827).

The failure of commutativity implies that agents will not necessarily draw the same conclusions from logically equivalent but temporally distinct statements (e.g., P_t and Q_{t+1} versus Q_t and P_{t+1}). Samuel Popkin (1991, 72–73) interprets this persistent experimental finding as challenging rational choice theory. The failure of commutativity, according to Popkin, occurs because subjects are attempting to fit new evidence into individual narratives about their experiences. As a result, previous ways of making sense of information influence the use of later information. This formulation should be familiar. It is essentially Converse's (1966a) diagnosis of ideological thinking. However, we now see there is an alternative interpretation consistent with the rationality assumption. These subjects may be behaving as if they learn by Jeffrey conditionalization, a formalized path dependent process. They are ideological, but in a rational way.

VII

At first sight, ideology represents a difficult dilemma for rational choice theory. Those individuals whom we identify as ideologues tend to act as extreme "cognitive misers" ignoring evidence contradicting their beliefs. Yet those in the mass public whose political thinking we do not associate with ideology often do not seem to think much about politics at all; and if they do, their use of schemas and information seems to violate ordinary conceptions of rationality.

Our analysis of ideological framing, learning, and heresthetics leads, however, to a new respect for rational choice theory's resources as an empirical theory. Under some circumstances, we have seen, ideologies can induce in their adherents behavior widely considered to be the hallmark of nonrational or even irrational ideologues. Under other circumstances, those with ideologies can revise their beliefs in such an inductively ideal way that ideological influence seems out of the question. Indeed even highly volatile opinions are consistent with rational ideology.

Thus we find that ostensibly irrational ways of thinking may have less to do with the peculiar ways individuals use information than with the ideological distance between those who observe and judge and those who are observed and judged. When the ideological distance is great, the resulting "irrational" behavior is often explained in unflattering psychological or social terms. As Clifford Geertz (1964, 47) summarizes this attitude, "I have a social philosophy; . . . he has an ideology." Contrary to this widespread opinion, however, rationality goes hand in hand with ideological thinking.

We are most directly interested in ideological frameworks because they provide the categories CEU maximizers use to formulate crucial conditional probabilities. These conditional beliefs can have substantial political consequences. Yet the decision to use one framework rather than another is sometimes itself a political consequence. Ideology influences politics; politics influences ideology. By understanding these political influences on ideology, we also get some analytic closure on our understanding of how decisions based on CEU maximization come to be made.

We are unable to achieve this closure generically, of course, but only within particular models of heresthetics. Still, the model developed here has a number of interesting political implications. Specifically, when the political environment of voters includes parties trying to shape their ideological judgments: (1) substantial ideological differences among voters may underlie the strategic positioning of parties on a public liberal-conservative continuum, (2) due to their reputations, parties in equilibrium generally will fail to converge along this continuum, (3) the possibility of party-induced ideological shifts will depend on the cognitive distance between different ideologies, (4) yet heresthetic moves will be more successful when preferences between ideologies are less sharp and policy preferences more polarized, (5) heresthetic opportunities are increased by alienation, (6) incumbency will be a disadvantage when ideological choice is volatile, and (7) party ambiguity need not be a handicap. In short, our model integrates ideological choice and manipulation into the calculations of voters and parties, specifying conditions under which heresthetic strategies do and do not work.

How do these general results, in turn, fit into political science's current understanding of public opinion? I suggest they be viewed as an attempt to respond to Stanley Feldman's (1988, 416) call:

> to uncover the *underlying principles* that lend some degree of consistency and meaningfulness to public opinion. Not too many years ago such attitudinal consistency was routinely attributed to the widespread existence of political ideology. However, a considerable amount of research, beginning with Converse's (1964) seminal paper on mass belief systems, has fairly conclusively shown that the political thinking of much of the public cannot be adequately described as ideological in the sense of deductive reasoning from an overarching set of integrated principles about politics and the social world (see Kinder, 1983, for a summary of much of this research). . . . As a result, we know more about how people do not think about politics than about how they do.

In one sense, the results developed here agree with Feldman's characterization of belief systems. Individuals do not generally deduce their opinions from an overarching set of principles because rational individuals are not purely deductive. Typically, there is too much learning from experience—too much induction—for an elaborate theory of the political world to remain completely stable, although we have seen how some rational ideologues can protect their bedrock beliefs (this protection, arguably, is the real test of their being bedrock). Although rational, moreover, learning may also lead to behavior that looks nonideological, in the traditional sense of the term, because it seems too dependent on individual history and circumstance.

Suppose, then, that ideology is part and parcel of rational inference and decision making and therefore that the rationality hypothesis is less vulnerable to objections based on experimental evidence for psychological framing effects or based on survey evidence for the volatility of individual opinion. If so, the immediate empirical question for students of ideology is no longer whether individuals behave as if they have an ideology but which ideology they behave as if they have.

By the same token, we cannot hope to rationalize the behavior of ideologues and the heresthetic maneuvers they provoke without recognizing some degree of ideological diversity at the level of basic categories. What separates the CEU maximizer from the EU maximizer is her willingness to exploit the social and political categories distinguishing her own group's behavior from the behavior of others. Pure homogeneity is uninformative. But if human populations are diverse, so too are ideological populations. Categories multiply not only because people are varied but because the frameworks for interpreting them vary as well. A CEU maximizer whose behavior is sensitive to categories will be sensitive to the possibility that alternative categories will do a better job. CEU maximizers are not only subject to ideology. They are subject to ideological change.

When we realize the centrifugal political forces operating on ideology, we realize how easy it is to mistake surface uniformity for ideological homogeneity. From this standpoint, terms like *liberal* and *conservative* may provide the coin of the realm for survey analysis and political discussion not because they are shared conceptual building blocks but because, as abstractions, they paste over the divergent ways in which individuals rationally form political hypotheses. Since individuals must translate this generic public terminology into their own varying ideologies, the sensitivity of their responses to context should not be surprising. On this view, the abstract principles mentioned by Feldman are not necessarily the sign of a common political culture. Perhaps they help us conduct political business in the absence of one.

CHAPTER 4

Selves and Self-Interest

To this point, we have focused CEU theory on some of the more celebrated problems in political science such as turnout and ideology. Yet ordinary human decency, honesty, and sacrifice also seem to defy the predictions of standard rational choice theory (Frank 1988). On a grander scale, there is for example evidence that presidents do try to honor their campaign commitments, notwithstanding the limits on their terms set by the Constitution. The threat of retaliation, it may be argued, keeps elected officials accountable. Yet why punish a president after disappointing results in the first term when only the second term now matters?

This is not to say that EU theorists have been unable to devise solutions to particular variants of these problems. As mentioned in chapter 3, if infinitely lived political parties control incumbents, a retrospective voting rule can promote accountability (Ferejohn 1986). But this solution, in turn, presupposes retrospective voting, which means that voters may desert a candidate who represents a superior choice for the future. Why do voters honor the commitment implicit in a retrospective rule? Important work by Kenneth Rogoff (1990) rationalizes retrospective voting by arguing that past policy can signal the special competence of the incumbent. Aside from questions about the place of differential competence in a rational choice model, I want to maintain our focus on the more general phenomenon of commitment. With that in mind, consider a setting somewhat analogous to one encountered by a political candidate facing voters over a fixed and finite number of elections. David Kreps and Robert Wilson (1982) analyze a chain store's willingness to fight entrants into its local markets when none of these fights is in its self-interest. Kreps and Wilson's solution, roughly speaking, depends on the possibility that potential entrants believe the chain store they face may be the odd sort of competitor that does prefer to fight. When the ordinary chainstore fights, then, it may earn the reputation justly belonging to the odd store and thereby deter potential predators. Here too, the solution relies on the existence of companies whose very nature is to engage in the sort of behavior the model is attempting to explain.

This chapter uses CEU theory to address the phenomenon of commitment or, more accurately, commitment behavior. The first section shows that CEU maximization can explain apparent violations of forward-looking self-interest by political actors. The second section examines more carefully what it means to be a forward-looking CEU maximizer, focusing particularly on the tendency of people to discount the future. The third and fourth sections continue this examination of future-oriented behavior by investigating the role long-term rules or principles might play in the strategies of forward-looking CEU maximizers. Section V briefly does the same for norms, sociology's favorite explanatory device and increasingly a crutch for rational choice theorists.

I

CEU maximizers, we have seen, treat their own behavior as evidentially on a par with the behavior of others. All behavior is a potential source of information relevant to the calculation of an act's CEU. In particular, the CEU maximizer treats her own behavior more impartially than does the Downsian, who strictly distinguishes the behavior he causes from the behavior others cause. Yet make no mistake. For all this, the CEU maximizer's behavior remains quite partial, maximizing one particular individual's utility. CEU theory's rationalization of turnout in mass elections, like its rationalization of group identity, exploits rather than disregards the self-interest assumption. Behavior in such cases may look ethical, but one is witnessing morality out of the barrel of self-interest.

In this respect, we have not adequately confronted a fundamental objection to rational choice theory, be it EU or CEU maximization. Both versions assume individuals who maximize their own future utility. Public spiritedness, honesty, and sacrifice seem to defy these forms of self-interested rational choice explanation (see, e.g., Mansbridge 1990; Monroe 1996; Wilson 1993). Similarly, the commonly observed inclination of travelers to leave tips at restaurants to which they will never return can usefully stand in for the many political acts, like voting for incumbents and keeping campaign promises, that often seem to ignore future utility by looking irrationally retrospective. Tipping out of town is a useful representative case since issues of long-term reputation or implicit logrolling with the waiter cannot enter the tipper's calculations. As noted previously, many instances of political revenge and credible retaliation pose the same kind of challenge to rational choice theory. Let us concentrate on acts of decency and trustworthiness, since these cases provide sufficient material for an evaluation of rational choice theory's potential.

How can it be rational to act decently when doing so demands sacrifice? To see the depth of the question, it is useful to dispose of some of the easier examples. Although a particularly profound violation of the egoistic notion of rational self-interest, parental sacrifice, for example, seems relatively easy to address. Genetic similarities between kin, such as those between parent and child, mean that the supposed sacrifice actually enhances the prospects for the genes of the "altruist." Hence relations of kinship can generate what then become rationally explicable sacrifices in the name of maximizing "inclusive fitness" (see, e.g., Becker 1976, 282–94).

True, the "self" in self-interest becomes reduced to the genetic composition of the individual, not its temporary corporeal embodiment. But the general outline of this biological explanation seems widely accepted. Indeed I think there is a general consensus that altruism based in biology and evolution challenges only the most legalistic versions of the rational choice hypothesis. Intuitions about the meaning of rationality aside, particular examples of altruism can be incorporated into rational choice theory once the special substantive goal of self-interest maximization is no longer automatically imputed to individuals.

More generally, mutations leading individuals away from the pursuit of strict genetic fitness toward genuine altruism can, under certain circumstances, become individually rationalizable in terms of interdependent utilities (Wilson 1993 calls this "affiliative behavior"). If so, there will be rational individuals who derive utility from the utility received by others. Although this claim is more speculative from the standpoint of biology, "socializing" mutations can become evolutionarily stable at the group level (e.g., Boyd and Richerson 1985).

In such cases, of course, critics of the rational choice hypothesis are bound to note the triviality or emptiness of models positing interdependent utilities to explain altruism. Do not such models simply redescribe the behavior they purport to explain? I prefer to characterize the hypothesis of interdependent utilities not as trivial but as promissory. How these utilities become established is a question for biologists and others. In the meantime, they can be formally registered within rational choice theory, which can proceed to characterize and explain the resulting social and political interactions. As Charles Plott (1987, 140–41) remarks, "Moral considerations might influence the shape and form of preferences, but that does not contradict the existence of preferences or choices based on them."

Moving to more concrete and politically relevant cases of decent behavior one finds, as in the case of voting, some specific explanatory fixes that, I will argue, the notion of maximizing CEU obviates or crucially supplements. One fix was already considered in chapter 2. Margolis (1984) argues that a generalized concern for the group, instilled by evolution, appears in the individual's decision making as a distinct, group-oriented self demanding its "fair share" of utility. As noted then, Margolis's analysis relies on a general interest in groups that are often diffuse and arbitrary. To that extent, their biological status, or a plausible extension of it, is unclear (although see Samuelson 1993). CEU maximization, we noted, does not share this problem since group members are calculating conditional probabilities of similar behavior rather than substantial economic or material homogeneity. For that matter, the agent need not have any concern for the group.

What of tipping in a restaurant out of town, when neither reputation nor interdependence counts for very much? Robert Frank (1988) has developed an ingenious and widely discussed explanation of human decency in these cases.

First consider a one-shot Prisoner's Dilemma game or alternatively a "supergame" in which the number of finite iterations of the dilemma and the rationality of the players are common knowledge. Standard rational choice theory recommends never cooperating with one's fellow prisoner, especially when the other prisoner is cooperating. Unfortunately, experimental evidence suggests that agents do not use the logic of "backward induction" motivating this recommendation (e.g., McKelvey and Palfrey 1992).

But suppose, Frank responds, some players are programmed through a genetic mutation to cooperate "irrationally" and being thus programmed or not is involuntarily signaled, perhaps by facial expressions. Under these circumstances, cooperators will chalk up individual benefits by choosing to play among themselves. Since individuals signal their disposition to cooperate, and these signals can be read by potential partners, cooperative individuals can guarantee mutual cooperation. From a self-interested standpoint, they will compete successfully with noncooperators. Noncooperators may be individually "rational" in each play and, unlike cooperators, will never be played for a sucker, but they are generally stuck with noncooperative partners and therefore realize an individually inferior outcome.

To use Frank's own example, suppose mutual cooperation nets four utils apiece, mutual defection nets two utils apiece, and defection when the other player cooperates nets six utils and zero utils for the cooperator. Finally, it costs individuals disposed to cooperate one util to determine the disposition of another potential player. If the proportion of cooperators exceeds 75 percent, the EU of their playing without scrutiny is higher than playing with scrutiny and therefore they will be inclined not to scrutinize. But when scrutiny is not employed, individuals disposed to defect are at a relative advantage, and the proportion of cooperators will decline. Conversely, when the proportion of cooperators drops below 75 percent, scrutiny now pays, defectors are at a relative disadvantage, and the proportion of cooperators increases. The population in the artificial example will stabilize at 75 percent cooperators.[1] Of course, your species' results may vary.

This rationalizes cooperation and shows why it is possible for cooperators to invade a population of defectors, but only up to a point. There are many cases in which decision situations are isolated enough to protect defectors against the consequences of their misdeeds. Thus consider the restaurant patron from out of town. He is not in partnership with the server. He cannot tip to bolster his reputation at home or to encourage future service. Nor, of course, can tipping raise the (C)EU of service that has already been provided. A truly optimal strategy in cases such as these is to defect, reserving cooperation for interdependent decision settings. Why then do travelers tip?

Frank offers this solution. Although agents may not have immediate control over the signals for decency they send, they can, in effect, develop their capacity to send them by being consistently the sort of people associated with them (1988, 16–19). In old-fashioned language, this is called character building. So, to finish the story, travelers tip in order to become the kind of people who later will seem honest and decent to those whose judgment does matter. In this manner Frank extends EU theory's notion of a causal agent to intertemporal decisions. The self-interested agent does decent things like tipping in order to cause a future change in character, which initially is biologically determined.

Frank's rationalization of the ostensibly irrational provides additional evidence that a priori restrictions on the scope of rational choice theory are more likely to become lines in the sand than permanent intellectual barriers. Granted, Frank rationalizes decency in the most obvious way by assuming the existence of individual preferences for decent behavior. Decent behavior then becomes rational because it maximizes EU. Yet he shows that these preferences are not ad hoc but can be derived from evolutionary biological considerations. Decency enhances long-term self-interest rightly understood. Moreover, by using the character-building process associated with tipping out of town and similar acts, agents can transcend the fate biology dealt them.

Frank need not assume, incidentally, that these evolutionary processes are optimal. Even if "evolutionary trajectories seldom if ever lead directly toward global optima" (Lumsden and Wilson 1981, 195), a biological explanation of the preferences we have is consistent with our rational pursuit of them once we have them.[2] Questioning their optimality using some standard or another is a perfectly respectable form of second-guessing. Indeed criticizing people for failing to have preferences coincident with their self-interest, like our apparently genetically dictated enjoyment of foods with high fat content, is a rather refined art, even if the notion of interest is not always clear. But the preferences we have are those that we, if rational, rationally pursue.

There is, in short, much to commend Frank's analysis. Still, there are two important objections to it. First, Frank's analysis does not adequately handle the "easier" case of mass elections that we have taken as paradigmatic for the public goods problem within political science. To put the objection simply, it is doubtful that behavioral signals of decency are subject to external monitoring sufficient to motivate the signaler who wants to be "known as the type of person who takes duty seriously" (Frank 1988, 231). In mass elections, anonymity is the rule, and the voter's reputation need not be at risk.[3]

The issue of anonymity also arises in another way. Using Bayesian considerations, Joseph Harrington (1989) shows that if the decent send noisy signals, they cannot invade a sufficiently large population of the nondecent since, in effect, the large numbers prevent the decent from adopting strategies based on the past behavior of the other party. The base rates for the nondecent dominate all calculations.

Conversely, Frank (1989) responds, in small group interactions, where our social instincts presumably were first wired, monitoring is possible; moreover, the potential gain from defection can, theoretically, be small enough to counteract a low base rate for the decent. In the latter case, of course, the value of the game may be correspondingly diminished, and therefore its players may not compete successfully against those who play large group, big-payoff games. If so, the anonymity of base rates remains a delicate issue for Frank's approach.[4]

For all these reasons, CEU theory provides needed support to his analysis when anonymity threatens the value or integrity of the signal. Both in small group interactions and in structured settings like institutions, where membership is fairly easily defined but potentially quite large, information from the agent's own behavior will be able to supplement the less than perfectly reliable signals she receives. Agents who maximize CEU are less dependent on contemporaneous signals from and to others since they can also rely on "signals" from their own behavior. The anonymity of the voting booth, in particular, becomes less problematic and the near-perfect reliability of signals less important.[5]

With this as background, we can now examine more formally the contrast between the treatment of noisy signals by EU and CEU theory. To begin, the EU for a cooperator to interact (I) with an agent sending a signal S of decency is calculated as

$$EU(I \mid S) = \text{prob}(H \mid S)(x_3) + (1 - \text{prob}(H \mid S))(x_1), \tag{4.1}$$

where $\text{prob}(H \mid S)$ is the probability of a decent agent given his signal of decency, $1 - \text{prob}(H \mid S)$ is the complementary probability of a nondecent agent given a decency signal, x_3 is the utility of mutual cooperation, and x_1 is the utility from cooperating with a nondecent agent; h denotes the proportion of decent agents in the population. Finally, the cooperator's uncertainty about S is represented by continuous probability density functions $f_H(S)$, positive for all S, concerning signals from decent agents and $f_D(S)$, also positive over the relevant S, concerning signals from nondecent (dishonest) agents, where the densities have the same support on the spectrum of signal strengths. So

$$\text{prob}(H \mid S) = hf_H(S)[hf_H(S) + (1 - h)f_D(S)]^{-1}. \tag{4.2}$$

For $0 < h < 1$, $0 < \text{prob}(H \mid S) < 1$: all signals are imperfect unless everyone is decent or everyone is not decent (in which case the signals are unnecessary).

Finally, let $\Lambda(h) = \{S : EU(I \mid S) \geq x_2\}$, where $EU(I \mid S)$ is the cooperator's EU from interaction with an agent signaling S and x_2 denotes the EU of not interacting, which is also the payoff to mutual defectors. Since $f_H(S)/f_D(S)$ is assumed to be increasing in S (an implicit assumption in Frank's analysis noted by Harrington), when $\Lambda(h)$ is not empty it is a closed interval in the signal spectrum whose minimal value S^* denotes the smallest signal for which an agent would find it worthwhile to interact. The value of this signal to the agent receiving it depends, as suggested earlier, on the probability the signaler is a decent agent and on the potential loss to the receiver when her inference is mistaken. To emphasize the distinction between CEU and EU, we focus on the former problem rather than on changes in the relative cost to a cooperator when she gets suckered.

We now have sufficient details to outline Harrington's objection, which we have seen complements Frank's more positive conclusions. Specifically, if S^* is a decreasing function of h, which it clearly is, then from equations (4.1) and (4.2), $EU(I \mid S)$ approaches zero as h approaches zero. More precisely, there is always an h sufficiently small so that $EU(I \mid S) < x_2$. In such cases, cooperators do not interact, which means their relative share of the population does not increase and, their cooperative dispositions notwithstanding, there is no cooperative behavior.

If, however, CEU theory is applied to the cooperator's problem, the relevant calculation involves not $EU(I \mid S)$ but $CEU(I \mid S$ and $H_C)$, where H_C denotes the cooperator's act of cooperating. The expression $CEU(I \mid S$ and $H_C)$ in turn reflects a change in $prob(H \mid S)$:

$$prob(H \mid S \text{ and } H_C) = hf_H(S \mid H_C)[hf_H(S \mid H_C) + (1 - h)f_D(S \mid H_C)]^{-1}. \tag{4.2'}$$

Insofar as $f_H(S \mid H_C) > f_H(S), f_D(S \mid H_C) < f_D(S)$, and $f_H(S)/f_D(S)$ is increasing in S, then if $\Lambda(h)$ is nonempty $S^{*\prime} > S^*$. This of course does not refute Harrington's argument. There is still an h' sufficiently small such that $CEU(I \mid S$ and $H_C) < x_2$. However, since $h' < h$, cooperators have more breathing room with CEU maximization.

Extra breathing room, not certainty, is really all any cooperator can expect. Even when cooperating with good friends or members of one's own family, absolute and certain identification—the case in which it is physically or logically impossible for the partner to be anyone other than the kind of person the cooperator has in mind—is too much to expect. Eyes and ears deceive, lighting conditions vary. In short, Harrington's formal concern can only be mitigated; it is unreasonable to think otherwise. There will still be an h such that cooperators will not interact.

The example of family and friends also leads to questions about the proper estimation of the base rate. Is the base rate defined as the proportion of friends in the population of a given city, in the population of the country as a whole, or in the world's population? One can easily imagine supplementary markers carried by potential interactors that serve not so much to indicate whether they are honest or dishonest, as in the case of the signal, but to indicate what the potential reference class or base rate is. Indeed we already explored this possibility in chapter 2 using the different language of ethnic group membership. The base rate in that case reflects the proportion of group members in the population rather than the aggregate population conceived homogeneously. Similarly, the perceived *disposition* to cooperate may have a strong contextual component.

The second important objection to Frank's proposal concerns his notion of character building.[6] Frank asks us to imagine less than perfectly decent individuals choosing to become more decent for self-interested reasons. These agents calculate that at some later stage they will, conditional on their increased decency, be more likely to send the appropriate signals, which in turn will increase any other decent player's willingness to cooperate with them. Unfortunately, the mechanism underlying this transformation is unclear.

Frank's central idea seems to be that by engaging in a series of decent acts, agents simply become trained, programmed, or habituated into decency, an idea going back at least to Aristotle. My problem with this venerable idea is as follows. In order to become habituated into decency, an agent must link her present habituating act to a future disposition to decency, since act A can reinforce act B only if the agent "sees" them as relevantly similar. Tipping, however, is quite different from the behavior the agent actually wants to encourage. After all, it would be pointless for the agent to tip just to ensure she will tip in the future. Rather, the agent will have to link her present tip and different future acts by means of their abstract character as decent.[7]

Yet when the act of tipping plays its habituating role, it is *not* a decent act and therefore is not appropriately linked to other decent acts. Rather, it is motivated by a strictly self-interested calculation concerning the future advantage of decency. Tipping becomes self-defeating. Agents will rationally tip only if they see it as a self-interested act, but if they correctly see it as a self-interested act it does not add to their decency.

This internal Catch-22 is particularly troubling since character building in this case is not manipulated by others, as in the training of children, but is rationally self-induced. We are considering, in other words, agents who are already rational and already harbor a full set of preferences and beliefs but who choose to modify their behavioral dispositions. It is a clearly defined self-interest they are pursuing.

Worse, suppose instrumental character building is commutative, in which case agents can destroy as well as build character. This possibility may lower the value of those hard-won signals of decency, since receivers believe that individuals who instrumentally create decency can, when the temptation is strong enough, instrumentally create their own opportunism. Perhaps like Shakespeare's Richard III, people can decide to become villains.[8]

Frank's conception of rationality, in short, does not easily encompass its two fundamental elements: willful character building and involuntary signals of a programmed disposition. The two work in opposite directions. In saying this, I do not question that in some situations individuals can precommit to send such signals. They may, for example, rationally choose to lift weights in order to send subsequent signals concerning their strength and determination. In Frank's analysis, however, adults are molding their actual dispositions, that is, the matrix of beliefs and preferences rationalizing their ensuing decent behavior. Molding the preferences of rational adults is different than molding their bodies. Bernard Williams's (1985, 38) observation about Aristotle's original notion of character building applies here: "He gives an account of moral development in terms of habituation and internalization that leaves little room for practical reason to alter radically the objectives that a grown-up person has acquired."

Of course, if molding the preferences of rational adults is not different than molding their bodies, my objection is weakened. Consider the individual who acts in ways *society* happens to regard as decent but, as far as he is concerned, are instrumentally self-interested. Suppose he still becomes more likely to create and signal a disposition to engage in decent acts generally, as judged by society. Then Frank's analysis does hold. Such an individual can rationally plan to transform himself through insincere acts. But this scenario weakens my objection because the notion of character building is so much less clear. For on this alternative construction of Frank's proposal, it is simply a brute fact, unmediated by clear mechanisms, that habituation produces the appropriate kind of decency even when the habituating acts are purely egoistic.

What generates a quandary for Frank's analysis, then, is the odd interaction of two ideas of rationality, one conceived in terms of agents who determine what things they choose to cause, including their future character, and one conceived as a fixed disposition. According to Frank, agents take advantage of their own anticipated rationality by developing good habits. They thereby hope to transform the nondecent act, which in their present sinful state is currently feasible for them, into an act that their acquired decency makes rationally infeasible. Trying, in effect, to fool Mother Nature, and lure social partners, they plan to become moral by practicing morality.

Knowledge of this welcome effect, I have argued, undermines the normative decency of this supposedly character-building act. Long-range self-interest is still self-interest. The principle of maximizing CEU, on the other hand, avoids this conundrum. With an eye on her CEU, an individual tips in remote restaurants not to influence or cause her transition from self-interestedness to decency.

She tips in good Calvinist fashion because decent behavior gives her evidence of the kind of person she is and will be in other situations calling for decency. The willingness to tip, for example, tells her something about the kind of person who will be playing and signaling in future Prisoner's Dilemma games.[9] A person gets to know herself by observing the way, so to speak, she is becoming herself in various settings. Her current decent behavior is a fact about her representing a corrigible summary of the kind of person she is. In this sense, a tip is the price of good news.

A reminder here may be appropriate. The agent is not actually choosing a future character in light of the information her decent behavior may provide. Rather, she is maximizing CEU under circumstances where her decent behavior happens to have implications for something she cares about, namely, her life in the future. Unlike the agent who should not worry about visiting doctors, here, as in the case of turnout, the agent is legitimately worried about the behavioral dispositions of others (her future selves) as indicated by her current dispositions. For her to stiff the waiter in order to take advantage of her newly discovered inclination to tip would give powerful evidence of her lack of decency with all that implies for a less satisfying future. Actions speak louder than words or, as we might now say, dispositions speak louder than deliberations. In short, when the agent tips in restaurants, it is just that she is, as a matter of fact, maximizing her CEU. This is no more problematic than saying wings solve a problem about flight even though birds do not actually consider alternative solutions.

CEU theory helps explain how altruism is implemented by showing how agents can generalize the implications of current behavior to the future. Yet this generalization assumes that agents care about the utility of their future selves. The concern is familiar, but the logic behind it is not as clear as one might think. Why, to put it bluntly, does a rational agent want to reduce present consumption (e.g., by tipping) in order to benefit a possibly very different later self? For as Derek Parfit (1984) has observed, it is by no means obvious why one should have special regard for one's own remote later selves as compared to one's current self or even as compared to one's contemporaries. In a less philosophical fashion, Richard Posner's (1995) rational choice analysis of aging has shown that intertemporal calculations over a changing self may be crucial to understanding key dimensions of life-cycle and intergenerational behavior.

Consider, then, the core problem of intertemporally bridging the various selves of an agent. In order for long-term sacrifice for future selves to make sense, the current self at time t must be reasonably sure that subsequent selves, say, at $t + 10$ seconds, will not abscond with all the benefits. True, the disutility from this short-circuiting will be mitigated to the extent the current self identifies much more closely with its $t + 10$ second future counterpart than with its

$t + 30$ year counterpart. But if that consideration were decisive, the current self could consume now and give the benefits to a self who is temporally and psychologically even closer to it. For that matter, it could consume now and hope, hypocritically, that the 10 second older self comes to its senses and begins sacrificing. In either case, the current self about to save rather than consume could use some assurance about the behavior of future selves in light of its own current behavior.

Identifying with its future selves gives it this assurance insofar as identity implies that future selves have a higher probability of saving (resp. consuming) given the current self's act of saving (resp. consuming). CEU maximizers exploit this conditional probability.[10] In this sense, saving does not simply transfer money to the future but transfers expectations. The continuity in a person's behavior over time gives evidence of a continuity of self. Actors who do not discount the future too heavily welcome this additional news about their own long-term behavioral dispositions.

I suggest, in sum, that the idea of identity developed in chapter 2 for social categories of agents applies to temporal conglomerations of selves, if anything in a more direct way. Insofar as a biological link from past to future (e.g., genes) provides a foundation for identification, our historically specific choices create the rest of the edifice. For our behavior does not merely manifest the identifications we inherit. Our current choices strengthen and define our intertemporal identity by giving evidence of the kind of person we are and will be, thereby further rationalizing the very concern for the future we are demonstrating through our behavior. If current selves care for their future selves, then they will wish to provide for them. For the same reason, they will welcome information that their more immediate future selves will do likewise. Trustworthy is as trustworthy does.

Intertemporal conglomerations of selves still constitute one person, and Robinson Crusoe's island remains an inadequate model of society and the altruism practiced within it. Nevertheless, the principle of CEU maximization may link both cases since the individual virtue of caring for one's future self can be a social virtue as well. Agents who care for their future when choosing in isolation are the same people choosing in social settings, and people observing them can draw appropriate inferences. For a person who does not discount the future too heavily out of concern for future selves is more likely, we have seen, to be trustworthy in the iterated Prisoner's Dilemma and principal-agent games that abound in social and political life (e.g., Taylor 1987). These players, who do not give in to the tempting antisocial strategy of getting the quick gain at the immediate expense of others, can be more successful in the long run. Even when players of this sort lose in individual encounters with the untrustworthy, they can prosper in an environment or ecological niche containing enough trustworthy players (see, e.g., Axelrod 1984).

In short, the decent who maximize CEU have, in comparison to the non-decent, increased sensitivity to the heterogeneity of their social context. In their calculations, heterogeneity reveals itself as different statistical dependencies for different group memberships and different institutional roles. As a consequence, CEU maximizers will also have a greater ability to behave appropriately in more anonymous settings such as the voting booth, and they will display greater ability to surmount problems of reliability. Their resulting acts of honesty, decency, and trustworthiness not only influence the judgments and expectations of other political participants, but they also provide the actors themselves with useful information about their future political behavior and prospects. We are used to the idea that introspection helps us gain self-knowledge. What one might call extrospection brings us knowledge as well.

Obviously, this analysis does not by itself rationalize those relatively rare but spectacular acts of heroism and self-sacrifice that, perhaps not accidently, prove in some troubling sense to be as enigmatic and alien as they are inspiring. Nevertheless, we have seen how our ordinary expectations about decency, reliability, and political commitment are anchored in a conception of self-creation in which one's own behavior has implications for oneself and one's interactions with others.

II

Individuals often attempt to build reputations as combatants who are peace loving, as leaders who will exact vengeance when their nations are attacked, as voters who will not let bygones be bygones, or as politicians who act out of principle. Some of them in fact want to be those sorts of people. Regardless of motivation, all face temptation every step of the way. Easy gains, cheap shots, opportunities to rise above principle, to move the line never to be crossed, to accept the bribe, to sell out, and to cash in are the stuff of political life. The self-interest assumption, of course, stands ready to pick up the pieces whenever the resolute prove themselves weak and the weak prove themselves consistent. But the self-interest assumption used without subtlety is too easy by half, too tempting one might say.

For one thing, when short-term gain involves sacrificing a much bigger long-term gain, then the implied discount rate for future benefits is absurdly high. Individuals in this case do not seem to be maximizing their self-interest in any obvious sense. Second, the phenomenology is wrong (see, e.g., Ainslie 1992, 14–23). Individuals in these situations do not seem to have executed a simple rational choice. Rather, they often experience the contrast between their long- and short-run good as a deep and troubling conflict. The same conflict grips those outside of politics who try to diet or exercise. True, this phenomenology per se is not overwhelmingly important for CEU theory, but such conflicts do seem to have behavioral manifestations. Third, individuals provide behavioral evidence of struggle, and, most important, some resist temptation, maybe not always but for substantial stretches of time. Some, more poignantly, will opt against the tempting alternative for a relatively long period, leading exemplary lives in the process, yet relent when the temptation approaches. When corrupt officials are caught, one wonders whether they have learned anything from the sad experience of others. Did they think they were specially immune from discovery? Ideally, the self-interest assumption ought to have something interesting to say about what determines alternative resolutions of the short-run versus long-run dilemma. Unlike Fisher's science fiction case of a common gene for smoking and cancer, the answer to this generic puzzle is unlikely to reside in genotypes or, harking back to chapter 1, in random preferences.

This section tackles the problem of intertemporal judgment and commitment by focusing on the sources of weakness over time. There is a rich political-economic literature on the topic of "time inconsistency," or what game theorists address under the title of subgame perfection. Briefly, as this literature recognizes, an intertemporal rule that is optimal initially may not be optimal when the reality of following the rule is faced. But in this literature, the agent's problem is not weakness per se but rather rational behavior when there is simply no technology for making a commitment that is credible to others. Here we take up the problem of consistency within an individual agent. This in part is because strong psychological evidence suggests that internal consistency or weakness of the will is a fundamental problem for agents generally; in part because to many observers this evidence (and personal experience) refutes rational choice theory generally (and CEU theory by implication); and in part, as we shall see, because CEU theory strengthens and legitimates some of the refinements necessary to reconcile rationality and the phenomenon of weakness of the will.[11]

In psychology, perhaps the best established characterization of the distribution of choices over time is derived from Richard Herrnstein's Matching Law (Herrnstein 1961). In the form given by Herrnstein and Dražen Prelec (1991), the Matching Law says that for a set of n repeatable alternatives chosen at rates $x_1, x_2, \ldots, x_n$ within a particular interval of time, each x_i having a value $v_i(\mathbf{x})$ to the agent, individuals will act to equate all values, so that $v_i(\mathbf{x}) = v_j(\mathbf{x})$ for $i,j = 1, 2, \ldots, n$, where $\mathbf{x}$ is the vector of alternatives. In other words, values are matched.

According to standard (C)EU theory, individuals focus on each alternative's marginal contribution to the overall utility, $U(\mathbf{x})$, resulting from the distribution of their choices over the x_i. An optimum utility is achieved when

$\partial U/\partial x_i = \partial U/\partial x_j$ for all i, j. Assuming $U(\mathbf{x}) = \sum_i x_i v_i(\mathbf{x})$, these marginal utilities are given by $\partial U/\partial x_i = v_i + \sum_j [x_j(\partial v_j(\mathbf{x})/\partial x_i)]$, with the second term measuring the indirect impact of a change in x_i on the agent's valuation of x_j.

Because individuals following the Matching Law concentrate exclusively on equating values, they ignore this second term that reflects the "cross effects" of their choices. For example, when excessive drinking by alcoholics diminishes their family life, it may register in their decisions only as a lower valuation of this alternative. They fail to recognize the role of their drinking in reducing this value. As a result, even though drinking is itself subject to diminishing valuation like any other activity, under the limited calculus of the Matching Law the desire to match values can lead to increased rates of alcohol consumption.

As Herrnstein and Prelec (1992, 248) put it, "the person is victim to an *externality*, but one that is internal to his or her own choices." Given their indifference to this externality, individuals obeying the Matching Law fail to consider fully the range of alternative distributions available to them, which $U(\mathbf{x})$ does capture. As a result, their utility will not in general be maximized, although the inefficiency of their choices will often be less apparent than it is in the case of addicts.

The Matching Law raises two distinct issues. One is whether individuals maximize utility or whether they are content to match values. Thus much of the debate over maximization versus matching concerns whether agents equate marginal utilities for different alternatives or average rates of return (e.g., Rachlin 1983; Prelec 1982, 1983). The other issue is how temporal discounting enters either the valuation or utility function. We shall now see, however, that one cannot evaluate the relative success of the Matching Law versus utility maximization without addressing the way these theories introduce temporal discounting. Utility theory is in trouble only if it insists on adhering to its traditional model of discounting. In order to see this, it is necessary to digress into an experimental finding illustrating utility theory's alleged difficulty. The resulting analysis not only will complement CEU theory with a better understanding of the individual's calculation of self-commitment or internal altruism, but it will also show how CEU theory further illuminates the empirical analysis of this calculation.

To take Prelec's (1982) example, suppose there are two alternative behaviors associated with two different reward schedules, one providing a reward with a constant probability of .03 and the other providing the same reward with a probability of .02. However, once the latter reward is realized by the probability mechanism, the reward mechanism is restarted. Under the second schedule, therefore, the subject perceives the probability of a reward at the first opportunity for choice as .02, the probability of a reward at the second opportunity as $1 - (1 - .02)^2 = .0396$, the probability for the third opportunity as approximately .0588, and so on, by the formula $1 - .98^n$, where the first option had been selected in the preceding $n - 1$ trials.[12]

Since the first schedule's average rate of return will be .03, subjects obeying the Matching Law will select the second alternative so as to produce a rate for it also equal to .03 (there is more than one way to accomplish this). By equating marginal utilities, utility maximizers on the other hand can garner an overall rate of return of .045. If there are 100 trials, they can accomplish this by patterning their selections so that the first option is chosen 12 times in a row and then the second option is chosen and repeating this pattern ad infinitum. In any case, Prelec argues that data from this experimental setup confirm the Matching Law.

Fortunately for utility theory, however, this is not the end of the story. For as Prelec (1983, 387) observes, "both matching and maximizing theories are defined with respect to molar [aggregate], long-run measures of responding and reinforcement. . . . [The marginal rate of reinforcement], for example, refers to a small change in the long-run rate of reinforcement that would be induced by a small change in the long-run rate of response and not to any local contingency." Prelec, then, views the previously discussed example as a decision problem about long-run behavior. On the initial trial the first alternative, which provides a .03 chance of reward, is a better bet than the second alternative, which provides a .02 chance of reward. By the second trial, the probabilities shift in favor of the second alternative. Yet the latter's probability keeps climbing. Subjects wishing to maximize their overall utility, therefore, must calculate how long to persist with the first alternative before cashing in the second alternative's greater likelihood of reward but thereby restarting the process if rewarded. They need to maximize utility over the optimal length n of the pattern as a pattern, where the first alternative is chosen $n - 1$ times and the second is chosen the nth. With $U = n^{-1}[(.03)(n - 1) + 1 - .98^n]$, U reaches a maximum when $n = 13$, which is Prelec's analytic result but not his experimental finding about the actual behavior of subjects.

Obviously, Prelec's analysis assumes stability in the long-run behavior of the EU maximizer. This is by no means an assumption Prelec has arbitrarily foisted on EU theory. Long-run stability or internal time consistency does indeed result from the standard discounted utility calculation used, for example, by Ferejohn (1986) in his discussion of political reputation (in the short run it was also implied by the dynamic programming approach to presidential policy making developed in chap. 3). In the standard intertemporal problem, the decision maker calculates the present value of a particular series of outcomes by multiplying the appropriate discount rate for future outcomes by their utility and summing over all future periods. Given a discount rate β, the discount for period t is β^t.[13]

Yet nothing about the rational choice assumption per se requires this exponential form of discounting. In fact, faced with the discrepancy between experimental findings and the results predicted by discounted utility theory, George Ainslie (1992) focuses precisely on the way the valuation functions incorporated in the Matching Law discount time. In order to rationalize the kinds of behavior involved in conflicts between short-term and long-term rewards, Ainslie argues, the exponential discounting function needs to be replaced by a hyperbolic function.[14] Ainslie offers this substitute (1992, 71):

$$v_i = x_i[Z + \Gamma(T - t)]^{-1}, \qquad\qquad\qquad (4.3)$$

where x_i is again the chosen rate of alternative i; $T - t$ is the delay between the time of the choice t and the time of the reward T; Z is an empirically determined parameter partly designed to prevent v_i from taking an infinite value when there is no delay (i.e., when $T = t$) and partly designed to represent the "integration" factor due to the delay in consumption of a reward even when there is "instant" gratification; and finally Γ is a parameter reflecting the subject's sensitivity to the delay. A more general formulation would of course replace x_i with $U[x_i(t)]$ and again integrate over time (see 276).

The crucial difference between exponential functions and hyperbolic functions like v_i can be stated quite simply. In the former case, the agent's position along the time line running from 0 to T does not change the impact of the discounting. We have already seen this for discrete time, where every additional period means discounting by a factor of β no matter how large t initially is. The same is true for continuous time: since $e^{t+n} = e^t e^n$, when a time of n elapses the discount e^t changes by e^n, which clearly is independent of t. In short, for exponential functions the change in the discount depends solely on the interval over which the change occurs.

This property, called stationarity, is not true of hyperbolic functions. One need only think of the case $t^{-(n+k)} = t^{-n}t^{-k}$. Since the discount t^{-n} changes by t^{-k}, the change clearly is not independent of t. The hyperbolic discounting function is nonstationary, in other words, because the impact of changes in the interval depends on the agent's position along the time line. Broadly speaking, hyperbolic discounting reflects a kind of path dependence, which we encountered in the case of ideology.

A standard example is the choice between the prospect of a large sum of money and a smaller sum when the smaller reward is delayed by t and the larger reward by $t + n$ ($n > 0$). The smaller reward might be a bribe to a politician and the larger reward the payoff for an honorable political career. For some k (which k depends on the agent), when $n = k$ the larger reward will be equivalent in utility to the smaller and for $k' < k$ will be preferred. Now to complete the example, suppose time elapses so the delay is now $t' < t$ for the smaller reward and analogously $t' + k'$ for the larger reward. The experimental evidence strongly suggests that typically there is a t' at which the agent will opt for the smaller reward. In street language this is called finally giving into temptation. The politician takes the bribe, an act that appears to be foolish in retrospect.

Insofar as discounting is stationary, as in the case of exponential functions, the relative utility positions of the two rewards should not change. In contrast, hyperbolic discount functions for the two rewards, Ainslie notes, will cross as t increases, leading to the preference reversal exhibited in experimental and nonexperimental settings. Agents using hyperbolic discounting functions have temporary preferences, a "weakness" revealed in behavior by their tendency to give into temptation when temptation gets within arm's length.

We see, by analogy, that an individual maximizing CEU with a hyperbolic discounting function will make long-run utility calculations in terms of marginal utilities, but, as the smaller reward approaches, the individual will switch tracks and opt for the immediate reward. This smaller reward will nonetheless have a smaller present value as calculated by the standard, exponential discounting function.

A CEU theory respecting the empirical evidence on discounting functions, therefore, cannot model only long-run behavior but must address the short-run local contingencies that occur when the individual's hyperbolic discount curves cross at specific points in time. Technically, of course, these marginal rates are still the mathematical limits of processes of change. They represent increments that are too "small" to engage real subjects. In the case of hyperbolic discounting, nonetheless, these marginal rates can also function as important *approximations* of the locally contingent behavior of subjects maximizing CEU with nonexponential discount functions. A model of long-run behavior alone is no longer adequate even for maximization theory.

Partly in recognition of this technical complication, Ainslie (1992, 66) argues that the length of delay in receiving a reward is more important to an agent than the rate at which it is received. Therefore his formulation of the Matching Law focuses on the former rather than on the contrast between matching and maximization per se. We will follow him in this respect.

Hyperbolic discounting can encourage the individual to yield to temptation against her apparent long-run interests.[15] Fortunately, if hyperbolic discounting explains why agents are tempted, it may also show in conjunction with CEU theory how some agents find ways to resolve their conflict in favor of the long run. They do so, presumably, by strengthening the subjective links between their present choices and their long-term future. As we see in the next section, CEU theory can elucidate why agents will be altruistic toward their own future selves, this time in the empirically more realistic setting of hyperbolic discounting.

III

Ainslie (1992) notes that many choices between a small reward and a delayed larger reward are not unique but occur as a sequence. Agents prospectively face the same choice, or the same kind of choice, many times. If, accordingly, agents collapse the associated set of choices into a single, *ex ante* decision called a policy, their choices along the sequence might be very different than the choices they would make if the choice at each point were made independently. According to Ainslie, then, agents often address the problem of temptation by invoking rules or principles (see also Prelec and Herrnstein 1991).

The reason is mathematical (cf. Ainslie 1992, 144–47). Suppose the agent's policy alternatives are either to take the smaller reward whenever it is offered or to take the larger delayed reward whenever it is offered. Under these circumstances, the agent can calculate the result of each policy, given discount functions of the form in equation (4.3), by summing over the times T in which the choices appear. In this summation, the successive values of the term $T - t$ in the denominator get larger and the utility of the choice is successively discounted more heavily. But $T + k$ for each delayed larger reward is greater than T for the counterpart smaller reward. Therefore, in later iterations of the choice, which lead to comparisons of $T + k + n$ with $T + n$, there will be less additional discounting associated with the larger than with the smaller reward.

If, for example, $T - t = 3$ and $k = 4$ for one of the choices, the relevant discount terms are $1/3$ and $1/7$ respectively. A second choice opportunity delivered one unit of time later will have comparative discounts of $1/4$ and $1/8$ respectively, the discount increasing by 25 percent for the smaller reward yet by only half as much for the larger reward.

The upshot is a decrease in the amount of delay in rewards necessary to motivate an agent to wait for the larger reward. In fact, at some point the sum of larger rewards will exceed the sum of smaller rewards, dictating a policy in favor of the larger delayed reward even though the smaller reward is immediately available and even though an agent making each choice individually will always choose the smaller reward when it becomes available.

Unfortunately, the benefits of summing over choices can be realized only if agents can choose policies instead of submitting to each of the temptations arising in the sequence. In Ainslie's terms, agents will obtain the benefits of summing if they adopt and adhere to a rule of behavior. What do agents accomplish by explicitly adopting such a rule rather than merely acting as if they follow it? One thing, Ainslie notes, is that by publicly declaring the rule or principle—be it "no more desserts for me," "any violation of the peace will be met by a full retaliatory response," or "read my lips, no new taxes"—agents make a side bet committing themselves to obey the principle at the risk of losing political capital, respect, cooperation, or perhaps something even more tangible.

As Ainslie recognizes, agents do not always honor the principles they declare. There are obvious explanations. Unforeseen opportunities arise, the cost of reneging is initially overestimated, or their public declarations were always eyewash. Yet these simple explanations reveal a deep problem with the concept of principles itself. If principles can be abandoned, if they are perpetually subject to opportunistic dereliction, what conceivable force for transcending immediate temptation do they represent? If they have no impact, they would always be incredible and therefore would not be worth expressing in the first place. If, on the other hand, agents always try to follow them, statements of principle would be very accurate predictions, while in real life they fall short of this mark.

Public expressions of principle may establish some kind of side bet, but the role of those principles is in the end no less mysterious than principles not receiving public expression but still affecting behavior. What is involved in binding oneself to a principle or a rule, and how does the binding work? It is not enough to say that principles and rules serve an evolutionarily useful purpose for organisms with hyperbolic utility functions, however unknown the means. These same organisms also violate principles, so the role of principles in a self-interested utility maximizing scheme is still a pressing issue. Nor does the language of private side bets explain the impact of this form of "mental bookkeeping," which, Ainslie (1992, 154) concedes, "seems somewhat magical."

CEU theory, I suggest, throws some light on how principles work. We start with chapter 3's focus on the role of ideological partitions in the assimilation of information. Partitions influence learning by biasing the kind of projections agents make from a body of evidence. If, for example, their partition includes *labor peace**, as this is defined in chapter 3, their rational inferences about the future will differ from those of *labor peace* users.

As we have seen in this chapter, agents do not confine their inferences to the behavior of others. They have a stake in predicting their own responses to future circumstances, which their current behavior may allow them to do. People do display a certain character, a personality, and particular dispositions. Some kinds of behavior signal a rosy future; other kinds of behavior do not. But nothing is certain, particularly for a subject with hyperbolic discount functions: "In situations where temporary preferences are likely, he is apt to be genuinely ignorant of what his own future choices will be. His best information is his knowledge of his past behavior under similar circumstances" (Ainslie 1992, 150). Indeed "people often must seek opportunities to see themselves behaving as if their beliefs were true, such as making a sacrifice to or for a god. . . . Without such a chance to establish his credit rating, the person may lose his expectation that he will follow his rule in this case, and thus be forced to abandon his particular leap of faith" (307).

The rub is having to determine which properties are to be used in judging whether current circumstances are similar to those arising in the future. As in the case of ideology, the basis for prediction—the partition—that agents choose will depend not only on which outcomes they most care about predicting but also on which partitions support the most accurate predictions. "Utilitarian theories heretofore have depicted choice-making organisms as analog computers, weighing the values of alternative rewards against each other. . . . [T]he more important tasks facing at least some organisms are digital tasks: People must construct sets of categorical requirements that will permit some kinds of weighings but not others" (Ainslie 1992, 199). Ainslie thinks the two modes of analysis are "somewhat incompatible." If the argument presented in chapter 3 is correct, they are fully complementary. CEU maximization puts the categories to work, while this work presupposes a categorical framework.

For CEU maximizers, the self-diagnostic use of their own concrete behavior presupposes categorizations of behavior on which those diagnoses are based. In this respect, to behave as if one is following a principle or rule is to behave as if one had selected one category linking one's behavior over time as opposed to some other category. To say "no new taxes" is to link one's current refusal to endorse a tax increase to future decisions. In the future there will be temptations to raise taxes in the interest of advancing some appealing purpose that can be billed as deficit reduction, an increase in user fees, the removal of a loophole, a measure respecting aggregate revenue neutrality, a long-term income increase due to "dynamic scoring" of the resulting additional investment in capital, or all of these. The rule "no new taxes" suggests how these potential decisions will be categorized given the many ways, legitimate and illegitimate, they could be categorized. The rule suggests one particular pattern of decision making in these circumstances not just to the agent's political audience but to the agent himself.

When agents abide by principles or rules, their behavior is coherent and predictable. In the absence of a rule, their behavior may still be coherent, but the coherence is harder to discover and therefore harder for the agent to exploit when using CEU maximization. A rule the agent follows in this sense is not necessarily ontologically different from a rule rationalizing previous conduct on an ad hoc basis. It is just more useful and therefore something that on utilitarian grounds the agent will feel worth honoring as a rule.

This is why, as Ainslie (1992, 152) suggests, people adhering to a diet—a rule about eating—will hesitate to have a piece of candy even though one piece has a negligible impact on their weight. People who give in to one small immediate reward may see themselves as setting a precedent for their future behavior in similar circumstances. If they follow the diet, they eventually will lose weight, but they can eventually lose weight only if they adopt a partition that links the circumstances of one occasion to eat with many other occasions. A rule signals this linkage. Without it, each small violation of the diet no longer figures in the summation of hyperbolically discounted utilities, and the larger reward of slimness and health remains unrealized. Sweat the small things, and the big things will take care of themselves.

What, then, is at stake in verbalizing or at least bringing the rule to consciousness for purely private use? If an agent following a rule behaves more predictably, then to state a rule is to offer a hypothesis about the agent's behavior. Agents will find such hypotheses to be valuable for the same reasons observers find them valuable, as guides to figuring out where their behavior will take them. In this sense, there should be no more mystery about agents declaring rules concerning their own behavior than about agents positing rules to characterize the behavior of others.

Yet self-description by means of rules appears to play a motivational role whereas, it may be argued, rule descriptions applied to others do not. Actually, I am not convinced this is necessarily true of agents who are aware of the descriptions that others have applied to their behavior, but for the sake of argument let us assume the distinction. Why the difference?

When an agent hypothesizes about her own behavior, I suggest, her hypothesis becomes somewhat self-validating. This is because the very formulation of it may highlight utility-relevant connections that motivate behavior in conformity to the rule the hypothesis marks. A golden rule hypothesis, for example, describes how other people should be treated, and, as an interpretation of the agent's own attitudes and behavior, it predicts how she will treat people in the future, given other more attractive possibilities. The statement of a rule is an act that like ordinary acts can signal the agent's future by highlighting some connections to that future as opposed to others.

An appropriate rule hypothesis, then, does not tell agents something they already know but identifies a rebuttable connection between their current behavior and their future course of action. It tells the agent "what" her behavior is and thereby what it portends for the future. Agents presumably confront an observer's rule hypothesis about their behavior as reflecting an alternative interpretation to their own. In this case, typically, agents already "know" what they are doing, and an observer's rival interpretation faces the unenviable task of disabusing them of this knowledge. In the case of autoprediction, on the other hand, the rule hypothesis helps establish that original interpretation.

Scientists who make use of typologies are used to this gray area between a categorization and a hypothesis. In one sense, of course, typologies are simply ways of sorting cases. But we all know that some ways are useful, sometimes very useful, and some are pointless. When a typology is useful, developing it is no longer the mindless filing of cases into conceptual boxes. A good typology, rather, helps orient good hypotheses. Rule hypotheses and systems of categorization similarly work hand in glove. In the language of chapter 3, rules and ideologies go together.

IV

Hyperbolic discounting imposes an interesting dynamic on individual decision making, allowing the trade-off between short-term and long-term considerations to change as time progresses. Extending Ainslie, I see this dynamic as providing a particularly strong motivation for CEU maximizers to behave according to rules and principles. I have not followed Ainslie in seeing this dynamic as reflecting a game theoretically–described "limited warfare" (1992, 153) between one's successive subselves or interests. Nor have I followed his view of the adoption of a rule itself as a specific, even magical, psychic occurrence having its own power against the lures of short-term pleasure. Explanations of forbearance that rely on the simple adoption of rules are unsatisfying. The very forces that rules are designed to fight are the forces that make the efficacy of simple adoption problematic.

In CEU theory, motives are captured by preferences, not by rules. From this perspective, rules are not self-validating or self-motivating. They must be integrated into an analysis whose building blocks are preferences and beliefs. This is what the CEU maximizer's self-diagnostic use of behavior is designed to do. The decision maker's interest in outcomes—long term and short term—provides her with desires. Rules provide her with cognitive links between her current behavior and her uncertain future by helping to inform her about what sort of behavior she is disposed to produce. Some of these rules are worth sacrificing for, but not for their own sake. Rules are worth maintaining for the sake of rewards whose conditional probabilities they raise.

Ironically, given their efficacy, rules can also enhance a sense of freedom in those who conform to them. For when rules help organize behavior, behavior appears neither random nor at the mercy of internal or external forces beyond the agent's control. In order to achieve this result, Ainslie (1992, 185–227) observes, agents must gain leverage over short-term impulses without letting their conformity to rules become compulsive.

When rules are too weak, individuals feel buffeted rather than oriented by their desires. When rules are too strong, their immediate desires seem almost irrelevant. A sense of freedom occurs in the middle ground between these two extremes, where conflict between the short term and long term is possible and the exact resolution of the conflict is difficult to predict on the basis of the rewards themselves. In this "balanced zone" (Ainslie 1992, 201), the decision to adhere to a rule can make a decisive and welcome difference in the agent's decision to opt for short-term or long-term rewards.

Of course, a sense of freedom is not freedom, so the principle of CEU maximization is not at stake here. But for those who worry about the extent to which this principle clashes with their introspective insights, it is useful to point out the extent to which our subjective sense of freedom is contingent in the way just described. "After all," Ainslie notes (1992, 201), "many behaviors are quite predictable in practice and still are experienced as free. What becomes crucial is the person's belief that a given choice depends on this self-prediction process."

The sense of freedom dissolves, on the other hand, when "a train of causality is seen to determine a choice reliably. . . . Thus, freedom has seemed to suffer from a paradox of definition, in that as soon as the author specifies the steps by which he imagines choice to proceed, he takes choice away from the self and thereby renders it unfree" (Ainslie 1992, 200). This is a paradox hounding Causal Decision Theory, which understandably has resorted to elaborate hierarchies of beliefs about beliefs about choices in order to float high above the track on which the train of causality is running.

In fact, Ainslie argues, autoprediction through rules "bridges the distinction between diagnostic and causal acts" (1992, 203). To use the famous example he invokes, when Calvinists do good works in order to reinforce their belief in their own predestined salvation, they are not necessarily fooling themselves: "if one can do good for any reason, that may be valid evidence of being among the saved; such a situation would not contradict predestination, but only provide another mechanism through which destiny might act" (203–4).[16]

V

The notion of principles and rules lies very close to the notion of social norms, another widely heralded source of information about behavior and prospects. Rational choice theory, which long defined itself in opposition to traditional sociology (e.g., Parsons 1968), increasingly finds itself incorporating or at least flirting with its rival's factotum (e.g., Koford and Miller 1991; Kreps 1990; Hardin 1995; Ostrom 1998).[17]

Historically, rational choice theory has been spooked by norms for a number of reasons. One is methodological. Rational choice theorists like Andrew Schotter (1981) and Michael Taylor (1987) have labored mightily to produce models in which rational individuals within a Hobbesian state of nature generate institutional order. Biological approaches such as Frank's similarly focus on the kinds of cooperative strategies that will be "evolutionarily stable" (Maynard Smith 1982)—hold their own—when competing with alternatives they encounter. But in sociology the Parsons school of institutional design accomplishes the same task simply by invoking shared norms. As Brian

Barry (1970) has observed, it is too easy to invoke norms to explain any pattern of behavior, including the existence of social order itself. Rational choice theory's historic suspicion of the ease with which norms explain social and political order is, in effect, its revenge for all the criticisms of its limited focus on strict self-interest models.

There is a related substantive reason rational choice theorists have been leery of norms. To the extent norms work by dictating a particular pattern of behavior, they also seem to prevent the actor whose behavior they are dictating from engaging in any kind of instrumental calculation of their worth. As a result, it becomes more difficult to understand the acceptance of norms over the alternatives and thus their genesis. In real life, moreover, there are trade-offs dictating partial conformity to norms (e.g., Hechter 1987). The problem of explaining this contingent conformity is reflected in the well-known crack that economics is the study of the choices people make and sociology is the study of how people do not have any choices to make.

A third problem with norms is more philosophical but is reflected in the preceding two concerns. It is by no means clear what norms are, what it means for them to exist.[18] We know it is important in general for norms to be internalized. What is their status before then, when they are "external"? Or is a naturalized theory of norms really a theory of patterns of behavior to which participants develop distinctive "normative" attitudes? If so, is the attitude responsible for the binding quality of norms rather than the norms themselves?

By way of illustrating these issues, consider Elinor Ostrom's (1998, 9) definition of a norm as an internal evaluation of an action beyond its objective cost. Following Barry, one must wonder how deep an explanation of behavior norms in this sense will provide. In regression analysis, after all, a norm would be called the residual. In the Downsian analysis of voting, it would be the notorious civic duty term. Similarly, Ostrom (9–10) defines a rule as a shared understanding concerning what actions will or will not be taken and the sanctions to be imposed on deviants. But as I have already asked, what is shared? If it exists prior to or independently of being shared, then the definition is incomplete. If the sharing constitutes the rule itself, then the definition is too complete, since the socializing of action and preference is precisely what needs to be explained.

The three classes of concern—methodological, substantive, and philosophical—account for rational choice theory's traditional reluctance to recognize norms. But this is no excuse for ignoring the behavior norms are asked to explain. The remainder of this section will note the contributions of CEU theory to the explanation of normative patterns of behavior. By "normative pattern" I do not mean to prejudge whether norms explain the behavior. Rather, it is a pattern that fans of normative explanation would reasonably want to explain by norms. At the very least, in such situations the existence of a pattern of behavior, or some rule describing it, will figure in individual decisions concerning behavior relevant to maintaining the pattern. Given a certain vagueness in the meaning of norms, then, characterizing norm-relevant patterns is by no means easy. So for this reason and others just noted, this section will not undertake a full-scale and serious analysis of norms, their status within rational choice theory, or the growing literature devoted to them. My much more limited aim is to highlight the natural connection between what I have called a normative style of behavior and CEU maximization. Specifically, CEU maximization has a quasi-normative character insofar as CEU maximizers are implicitly relating their own behavior to the behavior of the larger group, asking in effect what the consequences of everyone doing such and such would be, asking in other words what if that behavior reflected a rule governing the group's behavior. In this sense, they act as if subject to a norm.

Proponents of norm-based explanation (e.g., Majeski 1990) complain that models deriving cooperation directly from self-interested calculation pick targets that are altogether too easy. Behavioral patterns aspiring to the level of norms must be social rules internalized as constraints. In the truly troubling cases, therefore, there is bound to be a lingering discrepancy between what self-interest demands and what norms prescribe (see Brennan 1991). I will focus, then, on those cases in which obeying a norm is not obviously in the agent's self-interest. This sidesteps a large and growing literature on norms within a more directly instrumental rational choice perspective (e.g., Coleman 1990; Lewis 1969; Sugden 1986, 1989; Ullmann-Margalit 1977). Instead, we focus on what to Elster (1989b, 98–99; 1989c, 99, 104–5), as we saw in chapter 2, is a defining characteristic of norms, namely, that they are not outcome oriented: "I don't throw litter in the park, even when there is nobody around to observe me." One does not obey a norm in Elster's sense in order to secure even a long-term self-interested end.

Now it is worth remembering that even noninstrumental norms do not strictly challenge a purely formal rational choice theory. A term for civic duty, for example, can always be added in a formalization. In her careful review of Elster (1989b), Jean Hampton (1991) observes, "the . . . rational-choice theorist will argue that a person is still utility maximizing if she follows a norm to avoid costly painful *internal* feelings" (736). And insofar as rational choice theory accepts norm-related preferences (feelings, angers, embarrassments, pangs of conscience) as brute givens, its analysis is generally no worse off than its competitors', although its formulation is starker and therefore its infirmities are clearer. In this sense, rational choice theory only weakly dominates its competition. It is no better in some norm-related cases and better in others. Still, noninstrumental norms, in this analysis, become one of rational choice theory's more trivial empirical applications. Trivial, of course, does not mean false. But it does not mean deep or illuminating either.

The norms social scientists ultimately care about have systematic social and political consequences, even when the norms are not obeyed with these consequences in mind. Is the convergence of external norms and these internal sanctions purely a coincidence? Or can we restore sociopolitical content to individual calculations when direct sanctions are not the motivation for obedience? The answer, I suggest, is to assume that individuals maximize CEU. CEU calculations, we have seen, already incorporate a crucial social component to the extent agents recognize some statistical dependence between their behavior and the behavior of others. CEU maximization thus introduces what Elster calls "everyday Kantianism" (1989b, 123; 1989c, 101).

Everyday Kantianism, he claims, is non–outcome oriented since each practitioner focuses on the benefits to all from cooperation by all, not on the specific consequences of her own cooperation. He cites voting as one instance in which Kantian norms apparently motivate otherwise irrational behavior. Happily, this distinction between instrumental and noninstrumental action is blurred under CEU maximization, and thus the relevant cooperative behavior can be rationalized in the ordinary self-interested sense (see also Skyrms 1996, 61–62; for further questions about the distinction, see Hampton 1991, 733–34). The CEU maximizer asks in effect, "What if everyone (or some subgroup) did that?" and thus factors in the possible generalization of her own behavior.

Instead of discussing more of Elster's fascinating examples, I want to emphasize CEU maximization's principal virtue for the study of norms. CEU maximization introduces social generalization into the agent's rationally self-interested calculus without the necessity of invoking the clear and present danger of sanctions by other members of the group. The social significance of norms is still reflected in the motivations of the individual agent when she calculates the CEU of her actions.

For this reason, CEU maximization is also a rational choice version of the internalization of norms. Granted, in this case it may seem even less psychologically intuitive than the more traditional rationalization of norm-based behavior by means of an outright appeal to normative preferences. The explanatory gains, I suggest, are sufficient compensation.

VI

In this chapter, we have considered phenomena such as decent behavior, altruism, and commitment. Some people, even politicians, keep their word, exact revenge, and follow their plans, often at considerable cost. For their part, most rational choice theorists tip at restaurants, do not steal, and review manuscripts for little or no compensation. CEU theory, I have argued, helps explain this behavior as instrumentally rational. This explanation does not simply appeal to the better angels of our nature. The key is recognizing that an agent's behavior provides him with information about his future as well as current circumstances. Good news about rewards in the future is still good news.

To most agents, however, delayed rewards are not as good as immediate ones. And just as CEU theory need not posit internal rewards to explain altruism, so it need not posit extraordinarily high discounting to rationalize systematic weakness in the face of temptation. Instead, we showed how CEU theory's approach to temptation can be rescued by an alternative form of discounting imported from psychology, where it has been amply confirmed. In turn, we showed how CEU theory may illuminate the way agents can exploit or counteract this form of discounting. Finally, we have noted how CEU maximization can do some of the work of norms, the analytical device invoked by sociologists and some rational choice theorists to explain the apparent link between psychic rewards and socially responsible behavior.

CHAPTER 5

Political Causes

I start by imputing a couple of concessions to an otherwise skeptical reader of the preceding portion of the book. One, I imagine this reader conceding that the first chapter shows why reasonable people can disagree over the proper definition of rationality. Two, I imagine the reader conceding that chapters 2, 3, and 4 show that the CEU definition has some empirical power. There is a case for treating CEU maximization as a basis for rational choice theory.

This conciliatory attitude, I trust, also has its limits. No one needed an alternative definition of rationality, the skeptical reader might say, to create reasonable doubts about current rational choice theory. Existing experimental evidence is troubling enough. So if this evidence has not sufficiently motivated most rational choice theorists to change their working assumptions, doubts motivated by CEU theory certainly will not. Simply put, theory does not offer knockdown arguments and will certainly not be more persuasive than the facts.

In this chapter, I hope to show that the two central themes animating CEU theory—the problem of free-willed agency and the calculation of probabilities conditional on acts—are by no means artificial or imported. They arise naturally as important problems in settings where CEU theory is not explicitly at issue. Rational choice theory, in other words, cannot avoid the challenge CEU theory poses simply by ignoring CEU theory itself. The issues of free will and conditional expectation are encountered in practice. My illustration of how the problem of free will intrudes into ordinary research is drawn from the field of economic policy analysis. Policy analysis is particularly relevant insofar as analysts provide recommendations to policymakers based on predictions of economic outcomes conditional on alternative policies. The normative intent of this brand of policy analysis is clear yet is implemented at a much higher level of aggregation and importance than the microlevel normative versus empirical problems we have considered to this point.

The issue of conditional expectations is illustrated by George Tsebelis's (1990) detailed game theoretic study of European parliamentary systems. How do institutionalized cooperative arrangements affect political outcomes? Tsebelis asks. How, more fundamentally, are these institutional arrangements created on the basis of noncooperative relations, that is to say, relations in which partnerships or coalitions are not binding but exist at the sufferance of the participants? Tsebelis's substantive analysis, it turns out, produces empirically valuable results whose assumptions, if philosophically offensive to anyone, offend the restrictions demanded by proponents of EU theory.

This chapter, in short, is designed to reinforce the message of the preceding four chapters. CEU theory is a natural tool whose assumptions are important for empirically oriented rational choice analysis and sophisticated methodology. The deeper issues CEU theory raises can only be avoided in name. Put another way, the case for CEU theory does not require special philosophical leverage. Objections to it do.

I

An idealized illustration of policy advice guided by rational choice theory might proceed as follows.

> An elected official in political trouble seeks the advice of his policy adviser to determine how best to restore his standing for the next election. After being provided by the official with all the relevant information and informed of this policymaker's goals, she responds, "If you were rational . . ." and lays out a detailed economic strategy based on the solution to the policymaker's optimization problem. The official follows the new strategy to the letter and triumphs at the polls.

What is wrong with this parable? One obvious answer is that it overestimates those who give and receive advice. In order to develop the paradox of policy advice, I nonetheless assume the ideal rationality of all participants. In particular, all are assumed to have rational expectations, meaning they use information optimally based on a correct model of political-economic processes. But this assumption suggests a more important problem with the parable: the asymmetry implied by the existence of an irrational policy *ex ante* and a rational policy *ex post.* Would not a consistently rational official, who by stipulation has all the information her adviser has, avoid the kinds of problems advisers can fix and therefore eliminate the need for their advice? Conversely, does rational choice theory purchase its influence on policy at the expense of its own rationality assumption?

These are not invented questions. Explicit recognition of the paradox of policy advice historically developed in the context of new classical models of political economy (e.g., Lucas 1981; Sargent and Wallace 1981; Barro and Gordon 1983a,b). To understand the significance of this development, however, it will be necessary to review some of the theoretical background. To begin, new classical models exhumed an old hypothesis from classical economics that Keynes was supposed to have buried: roughly, when markets clear quickly enough, government economic policy is essentially ineffective. Government can neither push the economy out of recession nor cool it when it overheats. It can still increase or decrease inflation, but government cannot use this power countercyclically to exploit a systematic trade-off with output or unemployment. At best, policymakers can be consistent, thereby reducing noise in the environment in which agents are trying to make plans.

The attempt to improve the economy using Keynesian techniques assumes that economic agents behave mechanically. Their behavioral output therefore can be regulated by regulating the policy input, mostly in the form of changes in the supply of money available to consumers and producers. Increases in money, for example, will generate increased demand, which will generate increased output, which requires increased labor, which reduces unemployment. The new classicals, by contrast, argue that if economic agents know the parameters of the government's money-supply rule, or at least have an unbiased estimate of it, they will anticipate the consequences of the policy change—increased nominal demand leading to higher inflation—and will have no motive to adjust the real levels of output or employment. Monetary changes bring only increased economic volatility due to random elements in the policy process. In these models, therefore, economic policy is ineffective. Government can only make the economy worse.

In new classical models, doubts about the effectiveness of the policy adviser arise most directly as a corollary of claims about the ineffectiveness of policy itself. When policy is ineffective, policy advice is idle. Why, however, would the ineffectiveness of a consistent policy pursued within a fixed regime (i.e., with fixed parameters in the money-supply rule) represent a barrier to effective policy *innovation?* After all, when policy regimes change, the public's existing forecast models, which presuppose stable parameters, may prove inappropriate. Perhaps, critics have suggested (e.g., LeRoy 1995), the transition between regimes—when the old one is no longer in force and the new one is not yet a stable source of data—presents an opportunity for policy innovation and, in turn, policy advice.

This challenge led new classicals to grapple more deeply with the issue of policy advice. Thomas Sargent and Neil Wallace (1981, 211) noted that policy changes, like policies, do not come out of thin air: "Something would cause the change [in rules]—a change in administrations, new appointments, and so on. Moreover, if rational agents live in a world in which rules can be and are changed, their behavior should take into account such possibilities and should depend on the process governing the rule changes." A rational public's political-economic model, therefore, will incorporate any uncertainties about intra- and interadministration policy variation, and their economic predictions based on this model will be conditioned on the set of possible political outcomes. In effect, this is the approach to policy analysis associated with Christopher Sims (1982). Overlying a complex policy game involving presidents, presidential candidates, legislators, interest groups, bureaucracies, voters, and economic actors is a stochastic model relating inputs and outputs of the policy process based on the assumption that radical, out-of-the-blue political and economic changes are very infrequent.[1] Government policy, in short, is endogenous to the model.

Assuming policymakers cannot contradict the comprehensive model their behavior embodies, Sargent and Wallace are able to show formally that officials will be unable to choose any recommended policies deviating from the model. "In order for a model to have normative implications, it must contain some parameters whose values can be chosen by the policymaker. But if these can be chosen, rational agents will not view them as fixed and will make use of schemes for predicting their values. . . . [As a result] those parameters become endogenous variables" (Sargent and Wallace 1981, 213).[2] In sum, "complete rationality seems to rule out . . . freedom for the policymaker" (211).

The parameters of the public's model, then, represent the objective characteristics determining each policymaker's behavior, that is, the rich set of factors governing the policy process. As a result, policymakers are seen to embody a roll of the dice whose distributional characteristics are known to the public. Policymakers are no more free to decide how this stochastic process is realized than are the dice. Quoting Sargent and Wallace (1981, 212–13), "The persons . . . that constitute the authority 'matter' in the sense that they influence the prospects about policy and so are represented by [relevant parameters of the model]. But the authority has no freedom to influence the parameters of the [model], since the objective prospects that it will act wisely or foolishly are known to the public and are properly embedded in [the model]."

In principle, Sargent and Wallace (1981) argue, this result is the coup de grâce for rational policy advice. Alternative policy regimes are represented within an overarching model of the political process allowing a rational public to anticipate the objective probabilities of alternative policies to within some irreducible forecast error. Policymakers then execute their assigned role of realizing the true probability distribution to within the anticipated error.[3] The full and consistent implementation of rational choice theory, Sargent and Wallace conclude, removes any role for policy advice. More broadly, this ostensible theory of choice threatens the presumption that there are free choices for policymakers to make. Focusing on their particular model of monetary policy, Robert Barro and David Gordon (1983b, 608–9) are drawn to the same conclusion: "the economist has no useful advice to offer the monetary authority. If monetary institutions were set optimally, then the economist's counsel would also not enter at this level."

Some may still hope to reconcile new classical results and normative theory. For example, they will want to interpret the public's success in modeling the authority's behavior as implying nothing more ominous than the public's recognition that policymakers independently choose to follow their own preferences. To Sargent and Wallace, however, this interpretation is too complaisant. If the public's expectations are rational, they insist, policymakers are constrained to behave as the public's model dictates. Moreover, the expansion of this model to include a range of policy regimes does not alter these antinormative implications. A rational public parameterizes away all degrees of freedom that a policymaker on the cusp of a regime transition might hope to exploit and thereby deprives the policy adviser of useful advice to give. In short, the would-be policy adviser may invoke the possibility of regime change to weaken the policy advice paradox, but ultimately this tack is self-defeating.

These considerations also undermine the usual, practical solution to the policy paradox, which relies on asymmetric information between the adviser and policymaker: "An adviser has to know something the advisee doesn't know" (O'Flaherty and Bhagwati 1997, 215). According to this solution, advice can matter—change the behavior of the receiver—when the preferences of giver and receiver overlap and the giver has an informational advantage.[4] In this vein, game theoretic analyses of the effectiveness of lobbyists who possess private information have been very fruitful (e.g., Austen-Smith and Wright 1992). But for purposes of this chapter, it is not particularly relevant that actual policymakers have limited information processing skills, time, and other personal resources and therefore rely on advisers in order to behave rationally, in the substantive sense of best achieving their goals. These complications merely complicate the story. The complicated version now says that advisers have become part of the model instead of observers, and the lesson then applies to the policy-making system as a whole along with all its individual members. The advisers become endogenous. And surely the policymakers themselves do not become freer by virtue of being less informed, less accurate, less capable, and less self-sufficient generally. At any rate, our ultimate lesson concerns the problem of free will in a rational choice model, not the ins and outs of the actual policy process.

To be clear, the resulting deflation of the adviser's role is not a recommendation to quit giving advice. For one thing, there is no more point to my giving advice to an adviser than to an adviser's giving advice to a policymaker. More important, advisers who supply information make a difference in the policy process, just as television, books, newspapers, and life experiences make a difference. But such advisers and their advice are endogenous. Their freedom does not substitute for the policymaker's since there is nothing to substitute for. Like the policymaker, advisers will make their decisions in real time without consciously knowing in advance where they will wind up. This is true of all of us. We have no alternative but "to treat ourselves as exogenous in everything we do, including giving and seeking advice" (O'Flaherty and Bhagwati 1997,

214). But this perception does not make us exogenous to the policy process, let alone to our their own decision making process.

In one sense, then, Brendan O'Flaherty and Jagdish Bhagwati (1997, 214) are correct. "We might as well act as if we were free to choose." Yet the *as if* is crucial: metaphysics isn't physics. Fundamental assumptions about free will or exogenous free agency will still affect our analysis of our situation or the situation of others.

"Even if we could read the book of our lives we would have to decide whether to believe it—whence Newcomb's Problem" (O'Flaherty and Bhagwati 1997, 213). But our behavior, I have argued, reflects the logic of only one of the alternative solutions to Newcomb's Problem. It is the other solution that assumes there are decision makers who actually have free-willed decisions to make. The comfort of believing in free choice does not come gratis. It is, in my view, incompatible with the best theory of rational behavior.

Nor do the empirical limitations of the new classical approach provide much consolation to the defender of freedom. The rational expectations assumption, it is true, makes strong demands on the public generally or at least on the efficient operation of markets under limited or asymmetric information. Worse, the rational expectations assumption does not even deliver policy ineffectiveness on its own. Ineffectiveness depends on additional and often questionable economic assumptions. Still, the mere empirical possibility of policy ineffectiveness, which economists have taken very seriously, shows that something about the role of free rational choice in empirical models is very troublesome. A theory ostensibly incorporating free choice that nonetheless undermines free choice in one logically possible case is a theory in trouble in all cases. For we are pushing standard rational choice theory to an extreme not, as in the case of engineers, in order to test the load limits of a working theory but in order to expose crucial structural flaws that everyday use might not reveal.

II

The behavior of policymakers, say Sargent and Wallace, cannot be at variance with the facts. By "facts" they mean correct model predictions, which among other things take into account the (neutral) effect of a policy regime on society and the effect of econometric information on policymakers, as well as the probability distribution of alternative regimes. If the rational public's predictions are correct, the policymakers' behavior must confirm them. Their decisions are not exogenous to the system they hope to manipulate.

What is wrong with *this* story? There is one thing, even though I am inclined to agree with its bottom line about the absence of seriously free choice for policymakers. This story understates the extent to which the key to the policy advice paradox is the idea of rationality underlying the story, not the particular class of policy models discussed earlier. These particular models reflect the paradox; they do not explain it.

Sargent (1984, 412) does note that the paradox poses "philosophical difficulties," but he more or less leaves matters at that. Yet something is deeply wrong when a formal theory cannot be taken to its logical conclusion. Put another way, it would be a mistake, as I have noted, to brush aside the paradox by denying the empirical accuracy of the original policy ineffectiveness proposition or even the rational expectations assumption itself. Fortunately, we have seen, the problem of integrating the empirical dimension of rational choice theory into its normative analysis offers a clue as to the nature of the paradox.

Normative rational choice theory presupposes free agents. They behave one way prior to receiving advice but can choose to alter their behavior after receiving it. From the standpoint of empirical rational choice theory, the problem with this presupposition is clear. If agents are predictably rational, their behavior is determined by their existing beliefs and preferences. Accordingly, useful normative advice is precluded so long as the adviser does not have an informational advantage (in which case she is offering new information, not just advice). As Eric Leeper and Sims (1994, 91) observe, "for the systematic use of the [adviser's] model to eventually change the [parameters of the policy-maker's rules], it would have to be true both that users of the model had a strong impact on policy debates and that the use of the model changed their conclusions about good policy, rather than simply letting them reach those conclusions more quickly and cheaply."

The same point can be generalized in terms of our original parable. When the policy adviser introduces her advice with the phrase, "If you were rational . . . ," she undermines her own role. If the policymaker were rational he would do what the policy adviser prescribed regardless. If he is truly rational, irrational acts are simply infeasible for him. By definition, rational agents do not behave irrationally.

If rational choice theory is correct, rationality is a fact about people dictating the way they do and do not behave. Their behavior is completely determined up to the uniqueness of their optimal alternatives. They should still be glad, of course, to find out they are rational. But, as noted previously, this discovery is no more liberating than the pleasing discovery that they are good looking, intelligent, or able to carry a tune. Rationality and the behavior flowing from it remain conditioning characteristics of the decision maker, not objects of choice. Robert Aumann and Adam Brandenburger's (1995, 1174–75) understanding of the proper focus of game theory captures the same intuition: "Not *why* the players do what they do, not what *should* they do; just what *do* they do, what *do* they believe."

Not everyone accepts this restriction. Recognizing that different people have different preferences, according to Alan Blinder (1984, 418), is "more or less the same as saying that they have free will." He acknowledges the obvious objection: "Given the same endowments, choices, and preferences, the individual will always make the same decision—except for pure randomness." Blinder's glib rejoinder—"It's my utility function, and I don't have to maximize it if I don't want to"—fails. If a policymaker is rational, she has to maximize her utility function precisely because it is hers (cf. Buchanan 1979, 25–26). The constraint on the policymaker, in other words, is not external. Rather, if as a matter of fact she happens to be rational, then she happens to be the sort of person who behaves rationally. There are worse fates.

Blinder's observations correctly suggest, nonetheless, that the policy advice paradox goes to the core of the rationality assumption. The normative application of rational choice theory to situations where its empirical validity is assumed reveals difficulties built into the idea of rational choice. This does not mean that paradox is endemic to the rationality hypothesis per se. Rather, as we have seen, its appeal to the free choice of the policymaker is crucially rooted in one particular, albeit standard, definition of rationality that has been serving double duty in normative and positive theory. Fortunately, there is an alternative to EU theory lacking the paradoxical free-will component and having different and empirically more reasonable consequences.

The analogy between the problem of rational policy advice and the CEU-EU theory debate is, then, clear. The EU maximizer hopes to remain aloof from the statistical facts about his own behavior and its predictable connection to the behavior of others. The policymaker similarly hopes to remain outside the predictable statistical relation between the factors governing his policy choices and the public's behavior. By intervening with salutary advice, the policy adviser, in turn, hopes to exploit the alleged margin of freedom between the policymaker and the stochastic relations in which the policymaker is embedded. In effect, both policymakers and their advisers regard free will as a causal factor in its own right. For as Sims (1986, 3) recognizes, "one cannot analyze the choice of policy variables without cutting through the seamless web of a model in which all policy variables are determined inside the model." Unfortunately, cutting through the seamless web by recognizing the external force of free-willed agency would require a rethinking of our inventory of basic causal forces that is difficult to contemplate.

Put another way, the puzzle of rational policy advice becomes philosophical primarily because of the special metaphysical assumptions EU theory introduces, and it remains a puzzle only so long as these assumptions are maintained. Ken Binmore's (1993, 330) comment on the Aumann and Brandenburger (1995) model of rationality cited previously reflects this EU theory–induced puzzlement: "The model certainly cannot be prescriptive because there is no point in offering advice to players who 'just do what they happen to do' and 'believe what they happen to believe.' Nor can the model be descriptive of a world in which people make conscious choices after transferring their experience into subjective judgments about the way things are." The first claim is correct. The model, however, can be descriptive of a world lacking choices emanating from free agency, conscious or not.[5]

III

The elimination of free-willed agency removes the deepest motivation for postulating causally exogenous policymakers. The behavior of policymakers remains a topic of considerable interest of course, and the question arises how positive policy analysis might proceed under this changed dispensation. In two respects, Sims (1982) advances a nontraditional view of policy analysis consistent with (although not implied by) CEU theory. In the spirit of CEU theory, his approach is fundamentally statistical.[6]

First, in place of a system of structural equations with clearly defined exogenous and endogenous variables, Sims substitutes a nonstructural model (technically, a vector autoregression) that can be used to predict the consequences of alternative draws from the probability distribution governing the behavior of the policymaker. The resulting estimate of the distribution of economic outcomes conditional on policy choices is thus based on a single model encompassing a continuous policy history. This policy world has no "joints" at which the policymaker can cut the stochastic connections and freely intervene. Accordingly, the resulting analysis does not envision recommending an optimal policy for a new regime modeled by a new set of "structural" equations.[7] The analyst is nonetheless entitled to make predictions conditional on the kinds of behavior that may occur. After all, neither the analyst nor the actor has a vantage point from which the world's entire future is revealed, just as no one sees all of the ordinary three-dimensional world from a given vantage point.

Second, Sims evaluates the impact of alternative policies using the concept of Granger causation rather than a more traditional and metaphysical notion of causation involving so-called internal relations between objects or events. According to Clive W. Granger (1980), a random dated variable Y_n causes a random dated variable X_{n+1} if for some set of values A

$$\text{prob}(X_{n+1} \in A \mid \Omega_n) \neq \text{prob}(X_{n+1} \in A \mid \Omega_n - Y_n), \tag{5.1}$$

where Ω_n is all information available at time n and $\Omega_n - Y_n$ is that same information minus the information embodied in the Y_t series up to Yn.[8] In sum, Y_t causes X_t if "we are better able to predict X_t using all available [past] information than if the information apart from [past] Y_t had been used" (Granger 1969, 428).[9]

The case of voting illustrates the intuition behind equation (5.1). If everyone but a particular decision maker has voted by time n, so that these votes are incorporated in the background information Ω_n, then the causal impact is properly assessed as the increased probability of his candidate's winning at $n + 1$. If his vote creates a tie, the increase is $1/2$; if it breaks a tie, the increase is also $1/2$; and in all other cases the increase is 0. Thus Granger's criterion captures the causal relations associated with the voting example, showing that the decision maker has a causal impact only when making or breaking a tie vote.

As one might expect, Granger causation has been subject to all the objections raised against the general idea of interpreting causation statistically (e.g., Cooley and LeRoy 1985; Granato and Smith 1994; Holland 1986, 970; Mankiw 1986, 141). Although a full evaluation of these objections is beyond the scope of the present analysis, they revolve around the charge that Granger causation relies "on a sophisticated version of the post hoc ergo propter hoc principle" (Sims 1981, 391). The primary objection to Granger causation, then, is its alleged inability to distinguish between genuine cases of causation and mere statistical dependence.

Granger's formulation, of course, tries to distinguish the two operationally by conditioning the causal judgment defined by equation (5.1) on all events occurring by the time the judgment is made. The influence of any genuine and confounding causal variables will be represented. In real applications, however, neither Granger nor the policy adviser has all this information. Under these circumstances, it is not too difficult for anyone willing to postulate a "true" cause to devise a stochastic system that resists Granger's test (see Skyrms 1988, 60–61).

But this, again, assumes a priori access to the genuine cause, since a causal analysis undermining Granger causation will have to rely on postulated "causal" relations. "No causes in, no causes out" is Nancy Cartwright's (1989) terse summary of the required presuppositions (see also Leamer 1985). For his part, Granger is suspicious of causal notions that elude the most refined statistical tests. He is quite willing to trade metaphysical depth for scientific utility: "I think it is fair to say that the philosophers have not reached a consensus of opinion on the topic, have not found a definition that a majority can accept and, in particular, have not produced much that is useful to practising scientists" (1980, 331). Granger, therefore, sticks with equation (5.1) despite possible counterexamples, such as the case of a cancer/smoking gene (see chap. 1) in which a spurious correlation masks a genuine cause. He eschews approaches treating causation, in effect, as an "unanalyzed oomph" (Glymour et al. 1987, 21).

Chapter 1 castigated EU theory for injecting a special notion of (human) cause into a web of statistical interdependencies encompassing human behavior. Expanding this narrow point, Granger insists that statistical definitions of causation are not ways of mimicking genuine causation but all that causation amounts to. Granger dissolves the purported opposition between causation and probability by treating the former as a specialization of the latter.

While clearly sympathetic to a statistical conception of causation, the CEU theorist, by contrast, is officially agnostic about the proper definition. Rather than equating unconfounded statistical dependence with causation, he recognizes a possible difference between the two. Instead, the CEU theorist argues that both metaphysical cause and statistical dependence should be recognized by a rational decision maker when both alter conditional probabilities.

In practice, nevertheless, there is an intimate link between the issues raised by Granger causation and the role of free will within decision theory. We can demonstrate the link beginning with a prominent political-economic example discussed by critics of Granger's approach (e.g., Hoover 1988, 170–74; Jacobs, Leamer, and Ward 1979). Imagine, say the critics, two structural relations concerning changes in money supply (M_t), which are controlled by a monetary authority, and changes in gross national product (GNP) (Y_t):

$$M_t = \theta Y_t + \beta_{11}M_{t-1} + \beta_{12}Y_{t-1} + e_{1t}, \tag{5.2}$$

$$Y_t = \gamma M_t + \beta_{21}M_{t-1} + \beta_{22}Y_{t-1} + e_{2t}, \tag{5.3}$$

where the Greek letters are parameters, and e_{1t} and e_{2t} are mutually uncorrelated white noise processes.[10] The first equation defines the authority's feedback rule for controlling money, which this policymaker bases on the current change in GNP as well as the preceding period's changes in the money supply and GNP.[11] Money supply is also subject to a random shock. The second equation describes how GNP is determined and, through control of the money supply, manipulated. GNP too is subject to a random shock. The reduced form of this system is

$$M_t = \Pi_{11}M_{t-1} + \Pi_{12}Y_{t-1} + u_{1t}, \tag{5.4}$$

$$Y_t = \Pi_{21}M_{t-1} + \Pi_{22}Y_{t-1} + u_{2t}, \tag{5.5}$$

where the Π_{ij} and u_{it} are functions of the original parameters and, specifically, $\Pi_{21} = (\gamma\beta_{11} + \beta_{21})/(1 - \theta\gamma)$.[12]

Let us make the standard assumption that the monetary authority seeks to reduce the variance of GNP. One component of this variance, e_{2t}, is uncontrollable. Through control of money, however, the authority can seek to eliminate the nonrandom contribution to the variation in GNP. Thus the authority aims for $Y_t = \gamma M_t + \beta_{21}M_{t-1} + \beta_{22}Y_{t-1} = 0$, or

$$M_t = (-\beta_{21}/\gamma)M_{t-1} - (\beta_{22}/\gamma)Y_{t-1}. \tag{5.6}$$

Clearly, the authority can achieve equation (5.6) via the feedback rule (5.2) by setting $\theta = 0$, $\beta_{11} = -\beta_{21}/\gamma$, and $\beta_{12} = -\beta_{22}/\gamma$. Therefore, returning to the reduced form, $\Pi_{21} = [\gamma(-\beta_{21}/\gamma) + \beta_{21}]/(1 - \theta\gamma) = 0$, and the coefficient of M_{t-1} in equation (5.5) is eliminated as well. But this says that M_{t-1} does not help predict Y_t, in other words, that M_{t-1} does not Granger cause Y_t. This result, say critics, constitutes a reductio ad absurdum of Granger causality, since the absence of Granger causation between changes in money and changes in GNP occurs precisely because the policymaker has successfully exploited that causal relation.[13]

The critics are right in one respect. There is a reductio here. Yet its source is the initial interpretation of the equations as structural, not the Granger causality test. The "structural" equation (5.3) would have us believe that there is an invariant functional relation between current and lagged values of money and lagged GNP on the one hand and current GNP on the other. But it is a fact, for whatever reason, that the policymaker operates according to equation (5.6). When therefore the coefficients of equations (5.6) and (5.2) are equated and this result is plugged into equation (5.3), all terms but e_{2t} drop out. Thus equation (5.3) in its original form is misleading. When the policymaker's actual behavior is factored in, changes in money do not control, cause, or Granger cause changes in GNP, for the system of equations in its entirety describes the relations and behavior of the authority and the economy. If $\theta = 0$, $\beta_{11} = -\beta_{21}/\gamma$, and $\beta_{12} = -\beta_{22}/\gamma$, then these facts are also part of the structural relations.

It is illicit, in short, to treat equations (5.2) and (5.3) as structural and then to introduce from some imagined outside a behavioral fact about the policymaker, represented by equation (5.6), that the policymaker can choose to obey or not. Once the policymaker's decision making is embedded in the structural model, as the policy paradox analysis suggests it should be, the policymaker's freedom to undermine Granger causality is eliminated. The reductio ad absurdum alleged in the preceding rests on an impermissible conflation of the nontraditional concept of Granger causation and a traditional, agency-based concept of policy making. This example would represent a reductio of Granger causation if it exhibited an idea at odds with itself. Instead the implied ideas of control, agency, and manipulation are at odds with the idea of Granger causation.

Many other objections to Granger causation rely on a similar conflation of the two notions of causation. Turning to a more political example, suppose administrations have identical preferences concerning economic growth but differ randomly in their ability to increase it (Rogoff 1990).[14] Growth, then, moves around some independent "natural rate." Voters, in turn, use existing data on growth and incumbent performance to predict future growth for the incumbent's next two-period term. The net effect is that random shocks to growth influence voting, while voting does not influence these random shocks. Yet under these circumstances, according to critics, the Granger criterion's confusion between prediction and causation once again creates problems. To formulate their complaint precisely, let the growth process be described by

$$y_t = y^* + u_t + \delta u_{t-1} + e_t, \qquad 0 < \delta < 1,$$

where y_t is growth at time t, y^* is the constant natural rate of growth, u_t and e_t are independent white noise processes, and voters have current as well as past information on both these series; u_t is the incumbent administration's competency shock, whose diminishing impact lasts two periods. The vote (V_t) is determined by

$$V_t = E_t \sum_{j=1}^{2} \beta^j y_{t+j}, \qquad 0 < \beta < 1$$

with β the voters' discount parameter and E_t mathematical expectation based on information available at time t. The incumbent administration is reelected if $V_t > (\beta + \beta^2)y^*$, which is the present value of the next two periods of growth at the natural rate, and defeated when the inequality reverses, while equality produces a coin toss between the incumbent and the challenger. Since $E_t(y_{t+j})$ $= y^* + \delta u_t$ for $j=1$ and $E_t(y_{t+j}) = y^*$ for $j > 1$, $V_t = (\beta + \beta^2)y^* + \beta\delta u_t$. Thus the deviation of V_t from its mean is white noise. It cannot be predicted from the past vote or growth series, and therefore growth fails to Granger cause voting. More remarkable, $\delta u_t = \beta^{-1} [V_t - (\beta + \beta^2)y^*]$ is a function of V_t, which provides information about y_{t+1} beyond that provided by y_{t+1}'s own past. Therefore, V_t helps predict y_{t+1}, and voting Granger causes growth.

This doubly counterintuitive situation derives from two factors. First, although voting is a function of expected growth, these expectations are not based solely on past growth. Therefore additional information about competence can be recovered from the voting record, which in turn becomes useful for forecasting growth. Second, although only expectations about growth determine voting, this voting predates the (expected) future growth. Hence a prediction of future growth based on past voting preserves Granger's temporal format.

Critics of Granger, I suggest, underestimate the important mediating role of expectations, notwithstanding the enormous role the rational expectations assumption has played in discussions of Granger causation. We can see this by returning to CEU theory, where this mediating role has of course also been controversial. Some critics, let us recall, have argued that CEU theory is unable to distinguish between spurious correlations and true causation. The classic example is when the impact of a common cause creates a potentially misleading correlation between two of its effects. In the present case, the competency shock at t affects both the deviation of growth from trend ($y_{t+1} - y^*$) and the vote at time t. This common cause generates a potentially misleading statistical association between the vote and future growth, which due to the temporal structure Granger imposes on causation can only be causally interpreted one incorrect way.

Since the common cause scenarios typically considered in the context of CEU theory, such as the Fisher hypothesis about the cancer gene, are too speculative for clear intuitions, it will be more perspicuous to use a less exact but adequate analogy from our discussion of CEU theory, the case in which the statistical association between visits to the doctor and illness is alleged to discourage CEU maximizers from seeking medical treatment. Although it still involves the misleading association between visits and illness, this situation is simpler because the ultimate cause, illness, is funneled entirely through the patient's behavior and does not cause doctor visits on its own. As we might put it now, visits Granger cause the continued illness.

How does CEU theory confront this situation? As Eells (1982) and others have argued, once an agent appreciates the role of her expectations about illness in prompting her visit, the visit itself poses no further statistical threats. The association is screened off by the agent's decision to seek treatment. This approach to the problem is controversial in its original setting, where critics have questioned the validity of Eells's empirical assumption that agents always know their preferences and beliefs.[15] Here this problem does not arise since our concern is with the causal inferences drawn by observers who explicitly calculate the rational expectations of voters. What is at issue here, in other words, are voter expectations within the model, not what voters know about their own expectations.

In assessing Granger causation between growth and voting, we can consider growth (y_t) as analogous to symptoms, the stochastic process determining growth ($u_t + \delta u_{t-1}$) as analogous to illness, and voting (V_t) as analogous to visits. First, why does growth fail to Granger cause voting? Symptoms (viz. growth) Granger cause visits to the doctor (viz. voting) only if the crucial role of the decision to go to the doctor is ignored. Given the decision to see the doctor or, more precisely, the information that the decision has taken place, the statistical association dissolves and symptoms themselves fail to Granger cause the visits. It is, by analogy, entirely appropriate that growth fails to Granger cause voting when the process determining growth has been filtered through expectations. One must, in effect, control for these expectations.[16]

Second, visits (viz. voting) can be used to recover information on symptoms (viz. growth), and therefore, it is alleged, the visits Granger cause the symptoms along with the illness those symptoms reflect. This supposedly prevents the CEU maximizer from seeking treatment. Yet once the decision to seek treatment (viz. the formation of expectations about growth) is allowed to screen off this statistical relation, Granger causation is once again blocked. Properly understood, voting does not Granger cause growth since expectations, which cause voting, intervene in this direction as well. Voting itself provides no information beyond what the expectations themselves convey.

Voting, like seeing the doctor, is a function of expectations. Expectation formation, in turn, is a concrete event, like pulling a lever and other behavior eventually leading to the electoral outcome. This psychological act, therefore, must be recognized in calculations of expected utility conditional on acts. It must also be recognized in calculations of Granger causation. For as noted in equation (5.1), Granger causation is conditioned on all available information Ω_n, which in this case includes the information that appropriate expectations have been formed (as well as the u_t series, so expectations do not add additional information about y_{t+1}). The demonstration that voting Granger causes growth suppresses this filtering.

Granted, if one focuses solely on the mathematical value of the expectation, the comparison with CEU theory breaks down. However, the expectation embodied in the identity $V_t = (\beta + \beta^2)y^* + \beta\delta u_t$ is both psychological and mathematical. Confusion between expectations and their mathematical values is possible, unfortunately, given the ambiguous status of rational expectations as both imputed psychological forces—conditions of choice temporally prior to the expected event—and disembodied mathematical objects used by observers calculating Granger causation. If the latter are the causal factors, Granger causation indeed makes the wrong call. Yet it fails exactly when an ordinary physical notion of causation—states of the brain causing behavior—would fail as well. In other words, in a model of expectations as causes, the cause is not the mathematical value of the expectation but its mental or neurophysiological representation.

If physical causation is to be our benchmark, one might respond, it is best captured not by Granger causation but rather by Herbert Simon's (1957) seminal definition of causation in terms of invariance to interventions.[17] Simon's basic intuition is that causal relations are fixed or invariant and therefore are the appropriate instruments for experimenters or other actors wishing to manipulate their environment. Simon's approach, accordingly, is popular among econometricians interested in policy interventions. Nonetheless it faces some serious difficulties.

Specifically, there are two related problems with Simon's approach that echo issues from the CEU-EU debate (see Mackie 1980). One, his approach is suspiciously anthropomorphic. Intervention seems to require an intervener, whereas causation presumably can proceed anonymously.

Two, a definition of causality in terms of direct control or intervention is circular insofar as the latter are causal ideas. In part, this problem seems to be generic to any nonstatistical causal approach. As noted previously, Cartwright (1989) argues that even when scientists apply Simon's method within laboratory experiments, they must presuppose some causal relations in order to determine causation.[18] But circularity does mean that a Simon-based account of the purported causal efficacy of policymakers presupposes their causal capacities. In any case, scientists' intuitions about causation had better be strong ones since Simon's approach does not end their reliance on them (see Granger 1980, 335).

Given the analogy between policy intervention and experimental intervention that Simon's definition of causation suggests, the two problems of anthropomorphism and circularity take on special importance in light of our discussion of CEU theory's relation to the policy advice paradox. Policy advice assumes that policymakers have a causal role that, we have seen, assumes a causal role for free agency. Within Simon's definition, however, causation itself is seen as a form of agency. If agency has deep conceptual problems, then to the extent Simon's definition is modeled on agency it will inherit them as well. The natural inference is that his definition may be leading scientists precisely in the wrong direction.

In defense of Simon's method, Kevin Hoover (1990, 220–21) argues, "Economics is about *human* decisions; an anthropomorphic approach is then generally appropriate." Moreover, "For econometrics, it is enough to perform the thought experiment 'if we could directly control X, then . . . ,' to define a workable concept of cause and to use the analogy, as Simon suggests, of nature with an experimenter to glean information useful to causal inference." With regard to circularity, "For pragmatic econometrics, it is enough then to notice that propositions about direct control, which may be disputable in another context, may sometimes be taken to be indisputable in the process of inferring indirect causal orderings."

Apparently, these problems of definition are irrelevant to a workable concept of cause in economics since the researcher has clear intuitions about real or hypothetical (causal) control. Yet as we saw earlier, the sense in which policymakers control policies, let alone the sense in which individuals hypothetically control things out of their control, is by no means clear, particularly in the case of stochastic processes. Is there obvious agreement, for example, over what decision makers faced with Newcomb's Problem, or with the voters' lotteries, control? Moreover, does not the paradox of policy advice challenge any radical distinction between human causation and natural causation by deanthropomorphizing human beings rather than by anthropomorphizing nature?

What, then, remains of policy analysis? Policy analysis as a normative exercise remains fundamentally problematic. Telling a rational agent what is rational to do amounts to crashing through an open door. This caveat, once again, does not preclude a role for analysts who possess additional information, computer resources, or other appurtenances of scholarship, but my main point is theoretical, not practical.

Even in the theoretical realm, nevertheless, there is a role for empirical policy analysis as distinct from advice. Empirical policy analysis makes "probability statements about the consequences of alternative realizations of policy actions on the basis of the historically estimated probability structure" (Sargent 1984, 408). To extend an analogy employed earlier, given the different possible ways a pair of policy dice might be loaded (including the degenerate case of fair "loading"), observers can make accurate—in the long run very accurate—conditional forecasts about the outcome of rolling the dice. But observers cannot advise a particular pair of loaded dice about which faces it should land on.

IV

Both CEU theory and Granger causation rely on statistical dependencies in place of the causal relations central to EU theory. In the case of CEU theory, this reliance is based on two considerations. One, the probability distribution of utility-relevant states of affairs conditional on the agent's own behavior is sufficient for determining the relative desirability of her alternative courses of action. Two, the search for a causal lever permitting agents to transcend these conditional probabilities not only attributes a scientifically questionable causal power to free-willed agency but generates a paradox.

We see this paradox emerge in the traditional rational choice approach to policy advice. According to this approach, a conditional probability model, perhaps using Granger tests for causation, tends to be insufficiently "structural" to handle genuine rational choice. Real causal relations must be distinguished from spurious correlations and the like. Yet the advice-prone choice of policymakers turns out to be unstructured in its own way. It is subject to guidance from rational choice theory only because the official making the choice is (temporarily) irrational. By the same token, when officials seek to manipulate the behavior of private agents who *are* rational and able to model the policy process to which they are subject, the freedom of these officials to choose the policies recommended to them evaporates.

Some, no doubt, would relegate this paradox to the dustbin of intellectual curiosities. To them, the paradox has no implications for the formal structure of rationality. Instead, it indicates that rationality can be equally viewed as embodying either free will or "stochastic Calvinism" (Cooley 1985; Craine and Hardouvelis 1983). These rival views coexist because of a coincidence: freely chosen actions happen, on account of their rationality, to be fully predictable as well (Hoover 1988, 196). If so, these are two interpretations of the selfsame rational behavior, not two interpretations corresponding to two different phenomena. According to this evaluation, there is no fact of the matter to the disagreement (Lucas 1987, 8–9).

By interpreting the anti-free-will argument as a Calvinist gloss on unambiguously defined behavior, however, we fail to recognize the depth of the problem. For one thing, the principle of parsimony suggests that if the concept of free agency is doing no detectable work in the model of rationality it does not belong there. The Calvinist interpretation is therefore the superior interpretation. More important, free will is not in fact a nuisance term. As we have seen, it is built into the idea of EU maximization in a crucial way, where it generates exactly the same paradox-inducing problem of predictability versus free choice, and it has unfortunate empirical consequences. Insofar as free will is a crucial assumption for EU theory, the paradox of policy advice becomes, much more seriously, a contradiction.

Fortunately, the alternative notion of CEU maximization, which lacks the free-will component, has different and empirically more reasonable consequences. So the paradox of policy advice does not condemn rational choice theory to conceptual incoherence. To the contrary, it provides further motivation for a different rationality hypothesis with considerable empirical merit in its own right. CEU theory represents a kind of stochastic hyper-Calvinism in which predestined choices produce no puzzle about their character. CEU theory escapes these puzzles because it does not explain behavior by invoking choice, either of a predestined or undestined variety.

The empirical merit of CEU theory, of course, is only relative. The preceding analysis, in truth, has been unrealistic about the scope and accuracy of current rational choice models in either form. As a practical matter, one may therefore object, policymakers behave imperfectly, and agents do not have the predictive power the preceding argument presupposes. In the real world of government, there is plenty of room for normative intervention.

This objection encompasses two claims. One, rational choice theory currently lacks the requisite capacity to predict. Two, the rationality assumption does not accurately characterize human behavior. Yet if the overestimation of current rational choice theory is misleading, it is misleading in an ironic way. For it is precisely the potentially encompassing power of rational choice theory—its capacity to make accurate predictions—that gets it in trouble. Although rational choice theory's policy recommendations may seem less superfluous in the meantime, they too suffer from the theory's predictive weakness.

Furthermore, if the ultimate correct theory is choice free, the current weakness of rational choice theory only creates *apparent* room for free-willed choice. And normative advice using this weak theory will depend on our ignorance of a political theory of behavior that awaits discovery. Should our theories, rational choice or not, develop richer and more accurate models of policy incorporating the impact of the information conveyed by their own recommendations, we will find even the apparent room for free choice to have been illusory. Such is the price of success, as policy science becomes contemplative and theoretical rather than the active, practical form of engineering recommended by Peter Ordeshook (1996) among others.

This is not to deny that this chapter and the empirical analysis in the other chapters presuppose an excessively idealized conception of rationality. At the very least, the costs of calculating the logical consequences of a rational agent's beliefs will have to figure into any actual agent's epistemic economy. In plain language, rational agents will find certain implications of their beliefs not worth discovering. So a rational adviser can fill in when the agent's brain gives up. Advisers rush in where wise but cost-conscious agents fear to tread.

A more realistic rational choice theory will have to recognize these important psychological constraints. Some might find the introduction of calculating costs ad hoc, but it seems to be a reasonable accommodation for a rational choice theory aiming to explain the behavior of real human beings.[19] It has limited value, on the other hand, as a defense of normative analysis. For one thing, it does not address the extreme but logically forceful case of rational expectations. For another, the assistance provided by normative advice is, according to this view, roughly akin to the assistance provided by a more powerful computer, a good mathematics text, or a quiet room to think. If these are economically worthwhile to a rational agent, so too, I grant, is getting policy advice when the adviser has calculated further than the policymaker. All of these enhancements, therefore, can and should be figured into a complete model of policy formation. Yet they do not offer the enhanced rational policymaker any new measure of freedom or rational policy analysis any new opportunity for converting suboptimal into optimal behavior. From the start, the theory should treat the policymaker as behaving *and learning* optimally within a model incorporating policy advisers.

Past a certain point of sophistication and accuracy, then, an increasingly well-specified normative model begins to undermine its normative motivation. For the interaction between adviser and advisee is no longer sufficiently uncertain to sustain an old-fashioned interpretation of the advisee's actions in terms of free will and choice. Now the interaction between adviser and advisee is itself within the purview of the model. The odd conclusion is that the better the model, the less room in it for truly normative policy analysis.

Of course, CEU theory by no means precludes an external normative judgment about policies and their likelihood of producing appropriate, ethical, or just results. But this judgment is, to repeat, passive or contemplative. To make a judgment is not to substitute the judge's goal for the actual policy-maker's goal. It is not an intervention into the policy making process. Of course, an intervention to change the policymaker's goals is another tactic. If this intervention undermines the original policy model, the original model was misspecified.

Finally, those who question the empirical validity of rational choice theory are not necessarily exempt from this moral about normative theory. Suppose individuals for whatever reason fail to exhibit rationality, either with regard to the policies of an ongoing administration or, as is more likely, with regard to changes in policy regimes. By escaping the constraints of rational choice theory or the strict requirements associated with the rational expectations assumption (see Sargent 1993, 26–28), these individuals also seem to escape the implications of the policy advice paradox. Yet in the battle for free agency, this escape may represent a Pyrrhic victory. For as some have argued (e.g., Ainslie 1992, 185–227; Weber 1949), people feel most free, whether in their daily lives or in making policy, when they are deciding rationally. Neither Weber's nor Ainslie's conception of rationality is, of course, the one found in CEU theory. But their argument does offer a valuable warning nevertheless. To abandon the empirical rationality assumption, we now see, is not necessarily to reintroduce the possibility of free-willed policy choice. It may foreclose it in a different, even more direct way.

V

Our moral once again is that rational choice theorists can run from the philosophical issues surrounding decision theory, but they can't hide. They will invariably confront them albeit in different guises. If there is to be a genuine resolution of these issues, fundamental theoretical questions must be addressed and answered. CEU theory is one answer, EU theory is another.

Unfortunately, one response to this message may be that, contrary to my hopes, the example of the policy advice paradox debate merely substitutes one arcane and abstract discussion for another. Stylistically, econometricians are theoreticians and may be equally removed from sensible attempts to reason about evidence. To alleviate this concern I will consider one more example illustrating how fundamental questions involving decision theory inevitably reappear in new guises: George Tsebelis's (1990) influential empirical analysis of European legislatures. His widely praised comparative research will show how naturally CEU-style reasoning slips into theoretically self-conscious work designed to provide a careful empirical analysis of political behavior and institutional outcomes in a wide range of settings. This work reflects neither barefoot empiricism nor formal theory for its own sake. It seems a perfect example of the intuitive lure of CEU theory.

But first I should repeat a warning. Far from proving CEU theory's validity, this exercise does not even provide a shred of evidence for it. Rather, it shows that when our intuitions are diverted from the specific examples in which EU theory's way of seeing politics has been hammered in, as in the turnout puzzle, political scientists, like the lay public studied by cognitive psychologists, may revert to a form of reasoning congenial to CEU theory. It was the aim of chapter 1 to show that CEU theory is not wrong in the abstract. This section's brief dissection of Tsebelis's analysis makes a more concrete point. CEU theory is not necessarily wrong as a matter of gut instinct, theoretically educated though the instinct may be.

To see this, we return to the one-shot Prisoner's Dilemma where, it is widely maintained, the dominant equilibrium strategy for both players is not to cooperate even though this equilibrium is socially suboptimal. Suboptimality, of course, is what makes the Prisoner's Dilemma game a dilemma for EU theory.

In his analysis of this crucial game, Tsebelis (1990, 68–72) notes that the dilemma can be resolved when individuals develop contingent strategies. What is a contingent strategy? Depending on one's perspective, it can be one of two things. We will first consider the standard view. From the EU perspective, a contingent strategy in the Prisoner's Dilemma arises when a player chooses to make her decision to cooperate or defect depend on the preceding choices of the other player. When the decision of each agent is made contingent in this way, the originally dominant strategy of defection may prompt a negative reaction from the other player that is sufficient to deter it. This expansion of the strategy space, at any rate, is the usual idea behind the introduction of contingent strategies.

Yet in a one-shot game, a strategy to reward the other player's previous cooperation with cooperation and to retaliate in response to his previous defection is impossible. Such a strategy cannot be implemented. A second interpretation of contingency in one-shot games uses Robert Aumann's (1987) notion of correlated strategies. Formally, a correlated strategy is "a random variable whose values are n-tuples of actions" (3). More concretely, the strategies of players are associated with the shared observation of a random event like the throw of dice. Using this mechanism, different players can forgo the usual statistical independence assumed for their strategies and instead choose to correlate them.

In this way, cooperation from one player in the Prisoner's Dilemma can become positively correlated with cooperation from the other. The result is a statistical form of contingency. Since its formal inception, game theory has recognized the importance of and need for correlations in the strategies of a single player. Aumann has generalized this notion to include interplayer correlations.

Tsebelis's (1990, 68) version of contingent one-shot strategies apparently relies on Aumann's generalization. "Let us consider the following situation: two players play the prisoners' dilemma game; when the first (the row player) chooses to cooperate with probability p, the second chooses to cooperate with probability p. . . . Moreover, assume that once the row player chooses to defect, the column player chooses to defect with probability q." Finally, "players can develop contingent strategies if they can communicate, if they can write down contracts, *or* if they can enter into repeated interaction" (69; emphasis added). Tsebelis reserves a distinct section for the discussion of repeated games.

I quote Tsebelis in detail because, in addition to the direct citation of Aumann's work, his text gives one good reason to believe that the correlated strategies under discussion are those introduced by Aumann as appropriate for one-shot games. This means that correlated strategies are to be understood as a thoroughgoing EU generalization of the concept of strategy. For correlated strategies, like strategies generally, are chosen by players. If they are individually beneficial, they are adopted. If they are not beneficial, they are not adopted. Consistent with EU theory, adopting a correlated strategy—choosing to follow the "recommendation" of the device—is not a collective decision but one made individually.[20] This definition of correlated equilibrium parallels the Nash equilibrium, which it rationalizes in some cases.

Aumann (1987, 4) formally defines a correlated equilibrium in a game as a collection of correlated strategies, specifically, a random variable f such that for each player the expected payoff from f is at least as large as the expected payoff from any alternative collection of correlated strategies in which that player chooses some other strategy and the remaining players continue to follow f. "Equilibrium is achieved when no player can gain by deviating from the suggestions [represented by f], given that the others obey them."

Turning to the Prisoner's Dilemma, in one correlated strategy both players use a fair coin so that with probability 1/2 one player cooperates and the other defects and with probability 1/2 they reverse roles. If the relative rewards to unilateral defection are high enough, this strategy will maximize their payoffs. In other words, in this case each player finds the equal prospect of each player defecting against the other individually superior to the correlated strategy of mutual cooperation (i.e., cooperate if the coin comes up heads, cooperate if the coin comes up tails).

Yet neither correlated strategy, as Aumann (1987, 4) notes, is a correlated equilibrium. "Indeed, in the prisoner's dilemma, it is *always* worthwhile for Player 1 to play bottom [i.e., defect]."[21] Tsebelis, by contrast, believes a contingent strategy in the form of a correlated equilibrium can solve the Prisoner's Dilemma. In particular, let

EU(Defect) = $T(1 - q) + Pq$,

EU(Cooperate) = $Rp + S(1 - p)$,

where p and q are defined as before, T is the payoff to a player who unilaterally defects, P is the payoff from mutual defection, R is the payoff from mutual cooperation, and S is the payoff from unilateral cooperation. In the Prisoner's Dilemma, then, $T > R > P > S$. On Tsebelis's calculation, cooperation is rational if EU(Cooperate) > EU(Defect), and one can show by algebraic manipulation that this can occur, for given values of T, R, P, and S, when

$$(R - S)p + (T - P)q > T - S, \tag{5.7}$$

that is, so long as p and q are sufficiently high. In words, to the extent the correlation involving mutual defection and the correlation involving mutual cooperation are both high, cooperation is rewarded. Indeed for any values of the payoffs meeting the strict payoff inequalities, there are values of p and q capable of motivating cooperation, as can be seen by substituting $p = q = 1$ in equation (5.7) and noting that the result, $R - P > 0$, is true by construction.

What accounts for the discrepancy between Aumann's negative but mathematically correct conclusion about the Prisoner's Dilemma and Tsebelis's more optimistic result? Simply put, Tsebelis does not permit individuals to choose to accept or not accept the recommendations embodied in p and q, notwithstanding his terminology of "instruction" in describing p and "retaliation" in describing q. Evidently, in his scheme the values of p and q must be facts about the players that they can exploit but from which they cannot unilaterally deviate. In Aumann's world, individual defection will always destroy the cooperative correlated equilibria Tsebelis has identified. In Tsebelis's world, this individual defection does not make sense since it brings with it a sufficiently high probability of defection by the other player.

Further observations by Tsebelis provide additional evidence for this interpretation. Cooperative games, he suggests, permit players to make binding agreements, which preclude any other result than mutual cooperation or, in the event of violation, mutual defection. Here $p = q = 1$. Conversely, in non-cooperative games $p + q = 1$, "because each player determines his or her course of action independent of the other" (1990, 83). In turn, Tsebelis explains this characterization of independence as follows. "Statistical independence is defined as the case in which the conditional probability of cooperation (when the other cooperates) is equal to the unconditional probability of cooperation. However, because the unconditional probability of cooperation is the weighted average of the conditional probabilities of cooperation when the opponent cooperates and when the opponent defects, when these two probabilities are equal, their average (the unconditional probability) is also equal" (81–82).

The algebra underlying this last comment is, once again, straightforward. But the philosophical implications are not. As we saw in chapter 1, the independence posited in EU theory's version of noncooperative game theory is not statistical but causal. The conditional probabilities p and q can even equal 1 without violating this understanding of noncooperative games. Tsebelis apparently does not accept this very limited view of the implications that can be drawn from statistical facts about the players.

Finally, in the same vein Tsebelis also notes that different sets of payoff values are consistent with different degrees of correlation. Some values support many more combinations of p and q than others. Ideally, he notes, observers would have information about the distribution of p and q in different settings; but the relative *likelihood* of cooperation can, in general, be determined from the payoff values (1990, 84). Here too Tsebelis is treating the statistical dependencies as behavioral facts. For if p and q were chosen by the players, as Aumann envisions, no particular pair of values for these probabilities would be a priori more likely than any other, and the existence of one such pair capable of producing cooperation would be sufficient to create a correlated equilibrium, assuming the human mind can devise the appropriate randomizing devices. But if p and q are facts about players, not choices of players, then the distribution of p and q—the likelihood of the appropriate facts obtaining—becomes an entirely relevant consideration, and Tsebelis's intuition applies.

There is nothing wrong with this intuition. Granted, it does not square with Aumann's notion of correlated equilibrium, which, in turn, is based on EU theory. Tsebelis's intuition, however, does square perfectly well with CEU theory, and, as I have argued, there are worse fates (choosing two boxes in Newcomb's Problem being one). What we have seen, then, is that not only does CEU theory have strong theoretical arguments on its side, but when it is detached from the protective guidance of the Downsian, EU theory paradigm, it has strong conceptual and empirical intuitions behind it as well.

CHAPTER 6

Reduced Expectations

This concluding chapter begins by stressing the coherent message underlying the variegated analysis of the preceding five chapters. My aim is part summary and part reorganization. The chapter will also extend the analysis by confronting one of the awkward complaints about rational choice theory raised by Donald Green and Ian Shapiro (1994), namely, that its advocates do not really test the theory but tend to focus on favorable illustrations. Although the preceding analysis tackled some of the most troubling anomalies facing rational choice theory, including electoral mobilization and cooperation, and explored some important contemporary political phenomena, including ethnic politics, it too can be accused of selection bias. Clearly, I have picked the topics and examples about which I thought CEU theory has something interesting and worthwhile to say. For the most part, on the other hand, I have ignored many of the less directly political but persistent questions raised by cognitive psychologists about the appropriateness of the rationality assumption per se.

Although profoundly different in some respects, CEU and EU theory are formally similar in so many other respects—especially when viewed from the outside—that these questions may seem to apply equally to both approaches. After all, they are both versions of rational choice theory. Accordingly, the many alleged failures of EU theory as a generic account of rational decision making, the way it models the use of probabilities for example, will appear to be failures of CEU theory as well. Faced with attacks by psychologists, EU and CEU theory are in danger of winding up in the same foxhole. One task of this chapter is to separate them even further.

Prominent rational choice theorists like Anatol Rapoport (1966) and R. Duncan Luce and Howard Raiffa (1957) have argued that rational choice theory's failure as a realistic account of human psychology necessitates treating it as a normative theory. I have argued the converse. Rational choice theory's status as an empirical account of human behavior conflicts with its status as normative theory. Its empirical role preempts its normative role, which, given the place it assigns to choice, would be in trouble anyway.

The less weight put on CEU theory's value as a normative theory, of course, the greater the pressure put on it to produce as a scientific theory. I therefore return to our original focus, CEU theory's scientific accomplishments. It is in this context one encounters general empirical complaints about the rationality assumption, whether of the EU or CEU variety.

I

The specific empirical claims of CEU theory are of course still important. Using CEU theory, the first chapter rationalizes voting and similar political acts that are often taken to be paradigmatic for modern democratic societies. The second chapter examines ethnic identity. Individuals around the world use historically and culturally salient schemas for classifying friends, neighbors, and countrymen into groups. Theorists have underestimated the importance of these schemas by assuming that ethnic categories piggyback on more fundamental concepts of class or even species. Ethnic classifications, I countered in chapter 2, help agents package crucial information about their social and political environment. In this role, they are part of the fundamental ideological inventory of rational agents.

The third chapter develops a more general way to explore ideology and, in the process, engages those critics who question whether the rational choice assumption applies to the mass public. In so doing, this chapter challenges the common view that either nature or intersubjective agreement automatically specifies objects of choice as objects. Some ways of categorizing objects may be common to the species due to shared genes or sufficiently similar upbringing. But chapter 3's model of ideology emphasizes an agent-specific classification of objects. In this formulation, each classification establishes the categories out of which utility-relevant propositions are constructed. When evidence materializes concerning matters of interest to agents, they update their beliefs using the categories available to them. Yet different experiences, I hypothesize, lead not only to different conclusions within a category system but also prompt the varied elaboration and perhaps replacement of initial systems of categories, which at some level of abstraction and political relevance help constitute different ideologies. Using these divergent ideologies, rational agents continue to learn rationally. To the foreign observer, however, some of these agents will seem irrational. Historically, those with divergent ideologies have been dismissed as ideologues, nut cases, or both.

In sum, armed with a conception of ideology, CEU theory links the information processing techniques of rational agents to the actions emerging from their new beliefs. This link has special importance for moral or ethical behavior. For based on their ideologies, agents not only can use their own behavior to learn about the behavior of others, but they also can apply this same strategy closer to home as they learn about who, behaviorally speaking, they are. In the process, we saw in chapter 4, agents may behave as though they are ethically self-regulated, abjuring opportunism in their dealings with others. To

Frank (1988), this ultimately involves recognizing one's causal responsibility for one's future character. To the CEU theorist, however, the agent is recognizing that her actions provide information about the person responsible for them. In many situations, evidence of one's moral character is good news.

In principle, information about oneself gleaned from one's own behavior is of a piece with the kind of information that an ethnic or a religious identifier gets from her own behavior. Those who behave decently project across time; those who mobilize along ethnic and religious lines project across space. In both cases, the agent acts as if she is rationally exploiting her current behavior to give her insights into the behavior of someone who is a distance away. In both cases, CEU maximizers will act in light of this information.

Finally, the fifth chapter uses macrolevel policy analysis to exhibit the problem of individual free will writ large. In this case, the significance of a scientific, third-person perspective is difficult to overlook since in the policy world the public operates with a third-person model of policymakers and the policy adviser operates with a third-person model of policymakers and the public. At this level, I hope, it is easier to appreciate the deep modeling consequences of truly embedding agents in the stochastic process they inhabit. Chapter 5's analysis of Tsebelis's (1990) comparative political research, on the other hand, shows how this same insight is reapplied at the microlevel.

II

Although CEU maximizers act in light of information derived from their own behavior, EU maximizers do not. Their sources of information are more limited. Yet despite their differences over the proper genesis of expectations, both EU and CEU maximizers use expectations, once generated, in the same way. First, they update their probability beliefs according to Bayes's Rule. Second, the calculated CEU and EU are linear in probabilities: the probability of each relevant state or outcome is multiplied by the (conditional) probability of its occurring, and the sum of each of these terms is the agent's (conditional) expected utility.

This leads to an important empirical objection to rational choice theory. There is considerable evidence that agents do not act as if their utility functions are linear in probabilities.[1] Of course a case can still be made for linear functions. Most important, they are mathematically tractable. Indeed David Harless and Colin Camerer (1994), who otherwise offer a sophisticated and fairly negative empirical assessment of EU theory, note the value of its relative parsimony. Furthermore, even the substantial empirical evidence against (C)EU theory is not completely secure. Kip Viscusi (1989), for example, argues that many of the experimental findings against the linearity hypothesis are vitiated by a failure to factor in the way subjects perceive the probabilities experimenters present to them (see also Kadane 1992). And this last defense would seem an ad hoc act of desperation were not the idea that rational agents integrate new evidence into existing priors such a firm part of the Bayesian understanding of rationality. So (C)EU theory is by no means dead. But it is not too soon to make arrangements, as the funeral industry euphemistically puts it. Indeed, as Machina (1987) documents, alternatives to EU theory abound.

In the light of their empirical difficulties, one is prompted to wonder how deeply connected CEU and EU theory are. In sorting this issue out, it is important to keep in mind that experimental findings bring into question only the particular technical structure CEU and EU theory share, most important, the linear role of (conditional) probabilities. Strictly speaking, this technical issue is independent of CEU theory's more radical step of removing free choice from decision making, however operationalized. Choice-free actions neither imply nor are implied by the CEU theory's specific use of conditional probabilities. Accordingly, some decision theorists, as we have seen, employ CEU theory's technical apparatus without questioning EU theory's free choice assumption.

I have exploited the technical and substantive contrast between CEU and EU theory, of course, to play up CEU theory's advantages in the explanation of political phenomena that give EU theory trouble. Putting aside that advantage for the moment, I now want to explore whether CEU theory can likewise illuminate some of the important, albeit less directly political, experimental findings that have tempted researchers away from the EU hypothesis.

I shall concentrate on two related characteristics of decision making documented in experimental studies. One is the failure of the independence postulate, which is a critical part of the foundation of EU theory and is implied by the fact that EU calculations are linear in probabilities. The independence postulate holds that the lottery X_i is weakly preferred to (is at least as good as) X_j if and only if $p(X_i) + (1 - p)X_k$ is weakly preferred to $p(X_j) + (1 - p)X_k$ for any lottery X_k and any probability p $(0 < p \leq 1)$, where a lottery is a set of chance prospects such as the probability .3 of receiving $100 and the complementary probability .7 of receiving nothing. In other words, agents who adhere to this postulate are not deflected from their preferences among specific lotteries when the alternatives are the same in every other relevant (i.e., EU) respect. The independence axiom is not only empirically tenuous. There is a robust debate over its normative validity (see, e.g., Seidenfeld 1988; McClennen 1990).

The second empirical characteristic of decision making is the tendency of experimental subjects to use a reference point when calculating the value of alternatives (e.g., Kahneman and Tversky 1979).[2] In standard versions of EU theory, a decision maker does not compare the differences between each alternative outcome and the decision maker's situation at the time the decision is

made. Rather, he compares the final situation represented by each of the outcomes. Unfortunately for EU theory, this is not in fact the way decision makers
seem to behave. For example the fact that one outcome reflects a loss relative to
an agent's current position while another represents a gain often seems to have
a bearing on his preferences distinct from the values he attaches to the outcomes as such. Again, some believe this behavior is normatively defensible as
well. Thus Peter Fishburn (1988, 33–34) finds it quite reasonable for agents to
prefer a certain amount of wealth when it results from a financial gain as
compared to the same amount of wealth when it results from a loss. Because
these outcomes are the same in the straightforward sense that they represent the
same dollar amounts, standard EU theory expects decision makers to be indifferent between them.

We now turn to the first characteristic. Machina (1989, 1643) tries to
motivate violations of the independence postulate by arguing that normatively
rational decision making uses probabilities in a *nonlinear* fashion. He offers
this example among many others.[3] A mother must choose between giving a
thing of value to one of her two children, Abigail and Benjamin. Given her
indifference between the two outcomes, A and B respectively, it is quite reasonable for her to prefer a coin flip to determine who gets the item as opposed to
giving it to one of them outright. Yet these preferences violate the EU hypothesis, which can be demonstrated by a straightforward calculation relying on
EU's being linear in probabilities: since $U(A) = U(B)$, $1/2U(A) + 1/2U(B) =
1/2U(A) + 1/2U(A) = U(A)$, but by assumption $1/2U(A) + 1/2U(B) > U(A)$.
According to (C)EU theory, therefore, the mother's preferences are incoherent.
In choosing the lottery, the mother is effectively committed to giving the item
to the child the lottery selects. In doing so, she is demonstrating her preference
for an outcome she originally avoided.

As a technical but important point, the mother is actually making a comparison between *sub*lotteries, specifically, the sublottery between A and B that
occurs if she rejects an outright choice between them. Thus her initial preference between A and B is not independent of whether these are her sole alternatives or whether they are embedded in a larger set of choices encompassing the
later sublottery. The mother's willingness to abide by the sublottery's selection
of one of her children, let us say A, when she refused to choose that child
originally, "tells us that *conditional on having borne, but not realized, a 1/2
probability of B . . . she strictly prefers the outcome A to the lottery (A, 1/2; B,
1/2)*" (Machina 1989, 1644). Her preference, in other words, cannot be sepa-
rated from the encompassing set of alternatives, whereas (C)EU theory's independence axiom demands separability.

The alert reader may wonder why Machina's normative defense of the
mother's decisions cannot be dissolved by playing the following trick on her.
Instead of a choice among A, B, and a sublottery between them, why not

reconstruct her decision problem as a comprehensive choice among three lotteries, $(A, 1/2; B, 1/2)$, $(A, 1; B, 0)$, and $(A, 0; B, 1)$ and treat her alternate preference for both the first and second lotteries as a violation of (weak) stochastic dominance?[4] Indeed in this fashion one can reduce the entire tree involving sublotteries (and sub-sublotteries) to one-shot choices among lotteries. Readers familiar with the reduction of extensive form games to their normal form will be familiar with the operation. In normal form games, players make a single choice among strategies summarizing all the possible paths through the game's underlying extensive form. Here equivalently the alternative paths have been laid out in the form of lotteries.

Readers familiar with game theory will get the idea but also note a difficulty. Among game theorists there is enormous controversy over whether sidestepping the typically elaborate details of the extensive form entails a significant loss of information.[5] According to advocates of the extensive form, players would not only be interested in evaluating the outcomes that are possible from that point on, as though the history leading to that decision point had not occurred. They might also want to take into account an initially unexpected position within the extensive form precisely because it is unexpected.

Machina similarly refuses to allow a reduction of the mother's decision problem to a single decision since her preferences at one stage depend on her preferences at another. The mother has nonseparable preferences that are sensitive to information that is lost when her alternatives are reduced to a single static choice. According to Machina, it is perfectly legitimate for her particular position on the tree to affect her choices, since her position has implications for what paths were and were not taken. But this means that her comparison of sublotteries embedded in the larger decision tree will produce different choices than her decisions among those sublotteries considered in isolation or impounded within a one-shot choice. In particular, she views giving the prized item to Abigail differently after Abigail wins the lottery than before the realization of the lottery occurs.

At any rate, like the players in extensive form games who are influenced by what has already transpired, agents with nonseparable preferences, argues Machina, do not examine their position in the midst of the decision tree solely in terms of the options that remain, an approach reflecting a principle called *consequentialism* (Hammond 1988). They are concerned about how they got to that position.

I now want to suggest that the CEU maximizer has a similar concern for history notwithstanding CEU theory's conformity to the linearity assumption. Recall the CEU maximizer discussed in chapter 4. In forming her expectations, she considers the implications of her current and past behavior for the future signals she will send about her character. The information provided by her current behavior is presumably the most useful, but past decisions reflecting past preferences count as well. As a result, these preferences seem to be nonseparable, just as Machina's analysis suggests.

So far so good. Yet there is a difference between using current and past behavior to form expectations about the future and using past behavior to affect current preferences alone. The latter leads to nonseparable preferences, and nonseparable preferences by themselves remain problematic, even for a CEU maximizer. To see why, observe that the mother's CEU of a choice of A outright is $\text{prob}(A \mid A)U(A) + \text{prob}(B \mid A)U(B) = U(A)$, where by an abuse of notation A and B denote the mother's choice of A and B respectively as well as those outcomes. Similarly, the CEU of B outright is $\text{prob}(A \mid B)U(A) + \text{prob}(B \mid B)U(B) = U(B)$. However, by construction $U(A) = U(B) < \text{prob}(A \mid \text{lottery})U(A) + \text{prob}(B \mid \text{lottery})U(B) = 1/2U(A) + 1/2U(B) = U(A)$. As a CEU maximizer, the mother's selection of the lottery involves her in contradiction since of course CEU, like EU, is linear in probabilities.

There is, nonetheless, an important connection between CEU choices made in light of expectations about the future and CEU preferences concerned only with the present. In order to understand this connection it is important to remember why nonseparability is controversial in the first place. After all, the contradiction derived in the preceding paragraph has no bite against the assumption of nonseparability since the derivation assumes the very linearity at issue. As Machina (1989) emphasizes, nonseparability is controversial because it seems to lead to a dynamic inconsistency that can be exploited. To take his illustration, imagine the coin flip leads to A but Benjamin, invoking the mother's original preference for the lottery over A, insists that for the sake of consistency she flip the coin again rather than give his sister the prize. Or to frame this kind of exploitation of the mother in a more familiar way, someone could offer to repeat the lottery for some positive amount $\$\varepsilon$ such that $U(\$\varepsilon) < U(\text{lottery}) - U(A)$. If she is consistent, apparently, the mother will find herself facing her original decision yet $\$\varepsilon$ poorer. After n repetitions, she will find herself in the same situation but $\$n\varepsilon$ poorer.

Machina's answer, we know, is that due to the nonseparability of her preferences, the mother's comparison between the lottery and A is different after B already had its fair chance. The alternatives, he insists, have not changed; her evaluation of them has. But this is puzzling. As Samuelson (1952) has observed, to choose the lottery is not merely to choose $1/2A + 1/2B$. This mixture does not exist. Rather, as we saw in the case of the artificial voter's lottery discussed in chapter 1, to choose the lottery is to choose either A or B outright but at the time of the choice not to know which. "Within the stochastic realm, independence has a legitimacy that it does not have in the nonstochastic realm. Why? Because either heads *or* tails must come up: if one comes up, the other cannot" (672–73). What then accounts for the change in the mother's evaluation when, in the decision process, the lottery is nothing more substantial than a reflection of her own ignorance about its realization?

My point against Machina is not that an agent with nonseparable preferences really should have the same attitude toward the alternatives independent of context. Rather, insofar as the ostensibly repeated alternatives are the same as the originals—to use Samuelson's term, they are uncontaminated by preceding alternatives—there must be an explanation for this difference in attitude. In the nonstochastic realm, for example, complements can occur together in varying proportions. The mixtures are not representations of the agent's belief about the realization of mutually exclusive components but are themselves physically realized. Different attitudes toward the components in a mixture and the components taken separately reflect genuine differences in the alternatives. What differences are reflected in the complementarities built into nonseparable preferences over lotteries?

Machina tells us that the mother rejects Benjamin's entreaties because having borne, but not realized, a .5 probability of B she strictly prefers the outcome of the lottery, A, to redoing the lottery. By itself, this is not very helpful since it describes the mother's preferences without explaining them. Her own explanation can be inferred from her response to her son, "You had your chance" (Machina 1989, 1644). Yet perhaps Benjamin takes a personalist view of probability and insists he never had a chance in the sense the mother means. Temporary ignorance should not be equated with bliss or even .5 bliss (imagine the mother trying to explain *exactly* what randomness means to her in the case of the single flip of a specific physical object). The truth is, the mother wants to have the recipient of the prize selected by the coin flip, not by her directly, and in selecting the coin she has not avoided selecting one particular child but has selected one particular child as dictated by the coin. By a strict liability standard occasionally used in the law she chose Abigail in either case. But at the very least, I suggest, the most reasonable interpretation is that she views the two outcomes differently because in this case she individuates outcomes by including the process producing them. The mother maximizing (C)EU continues to reflect utility that is linear in probability, but the implicit way she defines the consequences of her decisions is more refined than is first apparent.

When a rational agent behaves differently toward two alternatives, his behavior must be explained by differences between the alternatives. This principle, which has been promoted by John Broome (1991a,b) and was exploited in chapter 3, is also Peter Hammond's (1988) way of saving EU theory in the face of the experimental and thought-experimental examples we have been discussing. We can see its application here by considering the certainty equivalent of the lottery the mother faces, that is, the certain outcome equal in utility to the CEU of choosing the lottery. Let us designate it as $EQ(1/2A + 1/2B)$. Since we are not dealing with a monetary prize, this equivalent is hard to specify, assuming one exists, without trial-and-error offers to the mother. But from the mother's strict preference we can restrict the possibilities in a small but important way since, we know, neither A nor B is the certainty equivalent:

$$\text{prob}(A^L \mid \text{lottery})U(A^L) + \text{prob}(B^L \mid \text{lottery})U(B^L) = U[EQ(1/2A + 1/2B] = U(A^L) = U(B^L) < U(A) = U(B),$$

where the superscripts indicate a lottery outcome and I have assumed that $U(A^L) = U(B^L)$ just as $U(A) = U(B)$. In other words, the need for superscripts is implied by the mother's distinction between the prelottery and postlottery alternatives, as reflected in her revealed preferences.

After the lottery is realized, the mother must still hand over the prize to Abigail. But suppose Benjamin persists. Should the mother once again pick a fair lottery instead of giving the prize to Abigail outright? To avoid this, must she reveal nonseparable preferences covering both current options and past events? Again, I prefer to stick with CEU theory. As we have seen, it is natural to insist that what her preference reveals is that the outcome of a second lottery is indeed different than the outcome of the first. Indeed, what better criterion for individuating alternatives is there? To put the matter from her perspective, choosing the first means choosing what *it* chooses, which means that in making her initial decision the mother chose the first lottery but did not choose a second.

We now can extend this principle for individuating alternatives by examining the mother's expectations conditional on the history she experiences. First imagine she innocently thinks the choice of a lottery is basically the last choice concerning the prize she will have to make. Her naive CEU for the coin flip is again

$$\text{prob}(A^L \mid \text{lottery})U(A^L) + \text{prob}(B^L \mid \text{lottery})U(B^L).$$

But now Benjamin attempts his scam. The CEU for this second coin flip, I suggest, is

$$\text{prob}(A^L \mid \text{lottery \#1 and lottery \#2})U(A^L) + \text{prob}(B^L \mid \text{lottery \#1 and lottery \#2})U(B^L) < U(A^L) = U(B^L),$$

since given the indecisiveness of the first lottery the mother can no longer view A^L and B^L as exhausting the possible outcomes. If Benjamin had his way after the first lottery, the loser of the second lottery may prevail as well. If so, the mother will prefer adhering to the outcome of the first lottery. Note the subtle possibility that while the mother does not want to choose A or B outright, it is still true that $U(A^L) \neq U(B^L)$, in which case the offer of \$ε to accede to a second lottery is more likely to work for one realization of the first lottery than for another.

In short, we have used CEU theory to define the appropriate alternatives from the mother's perspective. In turn, by redefining the consequences we preserve a CEU theory committed to a behavioral approach to rationality, what one might call revealed rationality. Hampton (1994) has argued strongly against this strategy.[6] Consider, she writes (1994, 232–35), any partition of an outcome space. The partition can be explicitly designed to define away any complementarities in the agent's preferences over outcomes. Now assume a choice between a multistage and a single stage lottery involving consequences of equal utility according to the partition. Although designed to produce equal utility, she concludes, the consequences of the two lotteries would nonetheless be distinguished by an agent who has specific attitudes toward gambling. These attitudes do not disappear just because the outcomes were partitioned to reflect them. Suppose, therefore, we repartition the outcomes in light of this newly revealed distinction. Although the new partition ostensibly creates equally valued consequences, they too become unequally valued in light of the agent's distinction between single and multistage lotteries. The redefinition stratagem, she concludes, unravels in an infinite regress.

I have two responses. First, technically speaking, the outcomes in Hampton's example could always be defined to satisfy the independence axiom. After all, the lotteries are always being redefined post hoc in her example. Second, and of more direct relevance to CEU theory, Hampton's analysis bifurcates each redefined consequence into attitudinal and objective components rather than treating it as a whole (as does Machina 1989, 1660–62). CEU theory, by contrast, incorporates acts into states of the world. Operationally both states and acts are represented by propositions, as opposed say to Savage's (1972) distinction between states of affairs and acts. So when outcomes are defined, they include the acts associated with them. Yet the natural way to incorporate acts is to include within them the acting decision makers themselves, since it is bizarre to abstract the acts from their physical reality, the behaving agent. When, therefore, acting agents enter decision problems as components of outcomes, they register their preceding decision experiences. These experiences may include lotteries they faced and prizes they lost or avoided. Since they survive in the agent and the agent is an ingredient of states of affairs, partitions defining outcomes can reflect any circumstances relevant to behavior.

To Hampton (1994, 235), EU theory—by implication, CEU theory—is "divided against itself." "While it is supposed to permit our preferences over actions to be partly a function of our attitudes toward risk, one of its central axioms [the independence postulate] requires that our preferences over actions be *purely* a function of our preferences over consequences." She is right in one respect. Samuelson's (1938) own revealed preference theory reflects the operational advantages of linking rationality with behaviorally expressed preferences over observable objects. But the objects themselves are not as natural, as obvious, or even as cleanly observable as one might like. Subjective probabilities and hence expectations, both of which reflect the agent's role in defining outcomes, already sacrifice tidiness in our model of agents in order to maintain tidiness in our definition of objects. This is not a case of a theory divided against itself. It is a case of a theory's making pragmatic judgments about introducing expectations in the same spirit as it introduced preferences.

On this view, the independence postulate is basically an accounting principle: define objects so preferences over acts can be derived from them. As we have seen, this principle can work for pure preferences even when lotteries are involved so long as outcomes are defined to extend far enough into the past to include the outcome-generating random process. When distinctions marked by probabilities cannot be easily treated as distinctions among processes, then it is much more straightforward to attribute them to ignorance, which means defining them in terms of degrees of belief anchoring expectations. Ultimately, lotteries themselves must, of course, be interpreted in terms of ignorance since, for reasons Benjamin certainly appreciates, lotteries in the end produce definite outcomes.

In sum, by recognizing the role of an agent's history in determining her expectations about current and future lotteries, we can begin to distinguish objects of choice that otherwise look indistinguishable. Nonseparable preferences give way to nonseparable histories, and linearity in probabilities does not give way at all.

III

We are now in a position to consider the role of reference points in decision making. Clearly, the experimental finding that behavior is influenced by reference points has significant political implications. If, for example, the status quo is an attractive reference point, then political actors will be more conservative, more resistant to change, than their abstract preferences would lead us to expect. At the very least, if agents are sensitive to the direction from which they encountered a particular outcome then, for example, hypotheses connecting revolution and rising expectations begin to make more sense.

According to (C)EU theory, decision makers ultimately care only about final outcomes, such as the decision maker's terminal level of wealth. Formally, this assumption of asset integration (Kahneman and Tversky 1979, 264) requires decision makers to prefer the lottery $(X_1, p_1; X_2, p_2; \ldots ; X_n, p_n)$ over their current position w^* so long as $U(w^* + X_1, p_1; w^* + X_2, p_2; \ldots; w^* + X_n, p_n) > U(w^*)$, where again U is utility, X_i is an outcome, and p_i is its probability. The experimental evidence suggests, however, that decision makers seem to care about whether the final amounts represent increases or decreases over initial wealth, in effect whether $U(X_1, p_1; X_2, p_2; \ldots; X_n, p_n) > U(0)$. Initial wealth constitutes a reference point relative to which final outcomes are assessed.

The idea of reference points, however, is not completely foreign to EU theory. Analyzing the behavior of individuals belonging to different income classes, Milton Friedman and Leonard Savage (1948) noted that many individuals approach gambles involving relative losses, such as house fires, differently than gambles involving relative gains, such as lotteries in the ordinary sense of the term. These subjects tend to be risk averse for losses and risk acceptant for gains. Friedman and Savage showed that this difference could be rationalized by a utility function that is increasing in wealth but composed of concave and convex segments, where the horizontal axis now represents *changes* in wealth or income. Thus alternative positions along this axis correspond to these different segments of the utility function. In general, members of the lower income class would find themselves "underneath" a concave segment, members of the upper class would find themselves underneath a much higher concave segment, and members of a largely transitional group would find themselves underneath an intermediate convex segment. The members of different classes, accordingly, are predicted to display different attitudes toward risk. Members of the numerically larger lower class, in particular, will pay a risk premium to avoid loss yet gamble on lotteries that with low odds will bring them into the upper class.

The Friedman-Savage approach establishes a theoretical association between risk attitudes and an objective monetary indicator (Kahneman and Tversky's 1979 study of monetary reference points does not supply income data). In fact, Friedman and Savage suggest that within a given population the dividing points between the different utility curve segments they posit should occur at roughly the same income levels for all individuals. Yet this strength of their scheme is also a weakness if, as Harry Markowitz (1952) suggested early on, particular attitudes toward risk are independent of current wealth or income. His revision of the Friedman-Savage analysis introduced a more complicated utility function and, more important for our purposes, one no longer anchored by absolute levels of wealth (or income) defined across all individuals. This common utility function, in other words, is relative to the individual, not to the individual's income. Again, we find that despite the danger of tautology researchers are driven to individualize the calculation of utility. Here it occurs with regard to risk attitudes, earlier in this chapter, and in chapter 3 it occurred with regard to the definition of outcomes.

Thus in focusing on changes in wealth rather then wealth itself, Friedman and Savage (1948) make free use of the power of (C)EU theory to individuate outcomes in whatever way proves to be empirically convenient. In principle, we see, the outcome space could be revised further à la Markowitz to mimic the more drastic relativization Kahneman and Tversky (1979) introduce into their Prospect Theory. These revisions may seem arbitrary. But to be fair, Kahneman and Tversky's attention to gains and losses does not seem to have any deeper theoretical motivation than their desire to accommodate the experimental evidence.[7]

Still, I admit, pointing out that its critics use the same strategy is a very defensive posture for (C)EU theory to take. Fortunately, there is a case for thinking that within CEU theory, at least, it is natural to give the agent's current wealth special consideration as her reference point. Making this case will require us to develop Jeffrey's (1983) version of CEU theory in somewhat more detail.

Recall once again that Jeffrey homogenizes states of affairs and acts. States of affairs, the agent's action on or within them, and, for that matter, her inaction are all represented as propositions. As we have noted, this is particularly appropriate for a choice-free approach because actions and states of the world are equally captured by descriptive statements available to actor and observer alike. Agents in general have a greater than average interest in determining which statements concerning their decision problems are true, but the news they receive when they find they have acted rationally is, in principle, no different than when the observer judges them to be acting rationally.

"To say that [outcome] A is ranked higher than B means that the agent would welcome the news that A is true more than he would the news that B is true" (Jeffrey 1983, 82). Specifically, the agent would welcome act A over B if the CEU of the former exceeded the latter. Yet for all this, Jeffrey is reluctant to abandon the traditional metaphysics of choice. Anticipating the objection that the decision maker in this scheme is "construed passively" (83), he counters that "where acts are characterized with sufficient accuracy by declarative sentences, we can conveniently identify the acts with the propositions that the sentences express. An act is then a proposition which is within the agent's power to make true if he pleases" (84). In Jeffrey's view the objection about passivity is only half correct. The idea of preference "is active as well as passive: it relates to acts as well as to news items."

The problem with Jeffrey's concession to the traditional metaphysics of choice is that acts, interpreted as propositions, should not be contrasted with news items since, as far as the observer and decision maker are concerned, they *are* news items. If acts are characterized with truly sufficient accuracy, the agent's power to make them true, decision to make them true, effort to make them true, his being pleased to make them true, and so on, are all incorporated in the appropriate declarative sentence. This declarative sentence, in turn, is news.

To clarify this point, consider the case of "true passivity." On Jeffrey's reading, the implicit action of "deliberate inaction" is appropriately represented by the unique logically necessary proposition or tautology ($A \vee \neg A \equiv B \vee \neg B \equiv C \vee \neg C$, etc., where $\vee$ is the logical *or*). This proposition, designated by T, represents inaction since it amounts to "letting what will be, be" (1983, 84). In other terms, T stands for "noninterference with the status quo." Accordingly, since the agent does not act she receives no new information, which is what a tautology provides. Does T play a similarly distinguished role in a choice-free world? Certainly, Jeffrey's interpretation of this distinguished role has to go. *Que sera, sera* is a truism whether or not the agent acts. The necessary proposition is true in every possible world, not just the status quo.

Still, if one associates action with a change in the conditional probability of alternative outcomes, then inaction can be associated with the absence of change. In particular, suppose the agent's decision problem involves three mutually exclusive alternatives, X, Y, and Z. Given the possibility of inaction, designated by I, what can be expected to happen is X, Y, or Z weighted by their prior probabilities. So the desirability of inaction is

$$U(I) = \text{prob}(X \mid I)U(X) + \text{prob}(Y \mid I)U(Y) + \text{prob}(Z \mid I)U(Z),$$

where $\text{prob}(X \mid I)$ is the agent's prior degree of belief in X and similarly for Y and Z. Equating $\neg X$ with $Y \vee Z$, this formula reduces to

$$U(I) = \text{prob}(X \mid I)U(X) + \text{prob}(\neg X \mid I)U(\neg X) \equiv U(T),$$

which parallels Jeffrey's (1983, 81) formula for the desirability of T, the tautology/status quo in his scheme. Assuming the alternatives in question are neither certain nor impossible, so $0 < \text{prob}(X \mid I), \text{prob}(Y \mid I), \text{prob}(Z \mid I) < 1$, the utility associated with the status quo is a weighted average of each proposition and its logical complement. As Jeffrey (82) notes, the status quo value associated with inaction is therefore strictly between the value of any proposition and its negation (unless they are equally valued, in which case each equals the value of T).

With this as background, we are now in a position to appreciate T as a reference point for CEU maximizers. Since $T = A \vee \neg A$, the necessary proposition is in effect a gamble on A whose gain, in terms of utility, is $U(A) - U(T)$ and whose loss, again in terms of utility, is $U(T) - U(\neg A)$. Therefore, "it is appropriate to say that A is *good, bad, or indifferent accordingly as A is ranked above, below, or with T*" (Jeffrey 1983, 82). Arbitrarily setting $T = 0$, A is good, bad, or indifferent as its utility is positive, negative, or zero.

The net effect is to justify the agent-relative status quo as a reference point in the agent's decision making. Of course, the particular functional form taken by the utility function for outcomes below or above that reference point becomes an empirical matter. Kahneman and Tversky (1979) posit one particularly simple form, but judging from our brief survey of the literature, the issue is not fully resolved. The important point is that another of the empirical weaknesses of EU theory turns out to be more easily accommodated within CEU theory. In the case of status quo bias, the political implications are immediate.

IV

The status quo is not only a reference point for decision makers, some have argued, but is a positive attraction. In a number of experiments, William Samuelson and Richard Zeckhauser (1988) have documented a variety of decision situations in which agents are biased toward the status quo for its own sake. As noted earlier, the implications of this result for politics are obvious. For example, an extrapolation from their findings suggests that in a race between two candidates who otherwise would be equally popular, the incumbent wins by a margin of 59 percent to 41 percent (1988, 9). This status quo bias, of course, could even have an impact when citizens vote prospectively since they will give the incumbent the nod so long as the incumbent's expected performance is "close enough" to the challenger's.

For our purposes, the immediate question is how, if at all, a status quo bias can be rationalized. Samuelson and Zeckhauser (1988, 33–35) reject as inadequate some obvious explanations, such as the transition costs involved with changing one's mind. In some of their experiments, at least, transition costs and uncertainty do not seem to play an essential role. They also reject explanations appealing to the role of the status quo in framing the subject's perception of relative gains and losses (37–38). Some of their examples, like choosing car colors, are hard to interpret in terms of gains and losses in Kahneman and Tversky's sense, nor were these choices of car colors framed in those terms.

Two other explanations surveyed by Samuelson and Zeckhauser (1988, 38–40) seem particularly relevant to CEU theory. According to cognitive dissonance theory (Festinger 1957), individuals will suppress, reevaluate, or misinterpret new information in order to maintain consistency with existing beliefs. Accordingly, they will strive to maintain consistency in decision making in the face of conflicting evidence.

As we have seen, however, there is a fine line between stubborn consistency and inductive rationality. Chapter 3's discussion of ideology shows that rational agents can behave as if they are abiding by the maxims of cognitive dissonance theory, all the while revising their beliefs in a perfectly rational manner. Marxist ideologues, to take chapter 3's example, act as revolutionaries yet seem to exhibit an extraordinary bias toward the cognitive status quo. When this bias influences people in power, it can survive evidence of enormous policy failure. In these cases, institutional sclerosis may not be the sole reason for the resilience of seemingly outmoded policies. Ideology can affect even the most opportunistic and self-interested decisions.

A second explanation for status quo bias cited in Samuelson and Zeck-hauser's survey, Daryl Bem's (1978) self-perception theory, also has a natural affinity with CEU theory. According to Bem (222), "Individuals come to 'know' their own attitudes, emotions, and other internal states partially by inferring them from observations of their own overt behavior and/or the circumstances in which the behavior occurs. Thus, to the extent that internal cues are weak, ambiguous, or uninterpretable, the individual is functionally in the same position as the outside observer." Past decisions will guide current choices because past decisions help determine the agent's reading of her current preferences. Or in Samuelson and Zeckhauser's dramatic re-creation of the agent's reasoning, "If it was good enough for me then, it is (must be) good enough for me now."

An experiment by Leon Festinger and James M. Carlsmith (1959), cited by Bem (1978, 227) and Samuelson and Zeckhauser (1988, 40), shows how far this construction of preference can go. After being required to perform long and tedious individual tasks, subjects were paid either $1 or $20 to tell a waiting student that the tasks were really interesting and enjoyable. In later sessions with the researchers, subjects who were paid the higher amount described the tasks as much less enjoyable than those paid the lower amount. According to self-perception theory, subjects who infer their true preferences from their own prior actions conclude that since the smaller sum seems too little to prompt a positive evaluation of the tasks, they must have been genuinely rewarding; since the higher sum does provide sufficient incentive to misrepresent preferences, genuine enjoyment cannot be inferred in this case. Even though the tasks were not chosen but imposed on the subjects, they continue to reconstruct their behavior into a rational pattern.

Compare Bem's analysis to the preceding discussion of altruism. Individuals, I argue in chapter 4, often will need to discover their own beliefs and desires in the same manner as do more disinterested observers. If past decisions help them find out who they themselves are, one constraint on their discoveries, if they are rational, is the transitivity of their preferences: whatever they discover about their preferences concerning X, Y, and Z, their preferences will not imply, for example, $U(X) > U(Y) > U(Z) > U(X)$. As with the observer, transitivity will be a norm of rationality for them. Indeed conformity to transitivity—a form of consistency—is as much a criterion for concluding people have preferences as it is a key to inferring what those preferences might be. For as defenders of the transitivity assumption have long noted, subjects with intransitive preferences are not merely having trouble making up their minds; it is less than clear they have minds to make up.

Behaviorally, the result of this attention to the implications of past behavior may look like dutiful conformity to cognitive dissonance theory: "With his or her self-image as a serious and able decision maker comes a need to justify current and past decisions, whether or not they proved successful" (Samuelson and Zeckhauser 1988, 39). But success is relative to a set of preferences, and consistent rationality is the way to satisfy those preferences, a way to make sense of there being well-defined preferences. If agents see their past behavior as part of the continuing behavior pattern of a rational agent, then agents will be inclined to find success in that pattern. In this sense, rationality not only leads to success but helps define it.

Rational agents, one is often told, learn from mistakes. At the same time, as rational expectations theorists insist, rational agents do not make *systematic* mistakes. If so, the rational agent is inclined to discover that her previous decision making was successful. With relative equanimity, the rational agent will find her past to be prologue.

If self-perception theory and this application of CEU theory are correct, subjects are not undergoing an internal struggle over dissonant beliefs and attitudes so much as engaging in a process in which they discover their attitudes. There is some additional experimental confirmation of this reading of the Festinger and Carlsmith experiment. For example, when the initial attitudes of subjects are made more salient, ostensibly increasing their cognitive dissonance, they exhibit less attitude change, not more change as cognitive dissonance theory suggests (Bem 1978, 251). This too makes sense in rational choice terms. Since initial attitudes or preferences are now more firmly planted, behavior as a basis for attributing attitudes is less credible and informative. In terms of rational choice theory, the tighter the priors, the less the change. What results are ideologues in the usual, pejorative sense of the term.

Finally, the most important political expression of the status quo bias— the concept of private property—may have a special relation with CEU theory. Evidently individuals evaluate goods differently when the goods are theirs (Kahneman, Knetsch, and Thaler 1987). Goods one owns are viewed as intrinsically more valuable. The connection between this finding and CEU theory applied to games, Skyrms (1996, 78) observes, is that this "bourgeois strategy" constitutes "one of the correlated equilibria that arises when the symmetry of hawk-dove is broken by correlation" (i.e., the correlation that occurs when doves swerve and hawks do not in the game of Chicken). More generally, when correlations in behavior develop in games in nature, optimal strategies are calculated according to CEU.

V

The idea of choice-free rationality is the spiritual heir to Paul Samuelson's (1938) suggestion that a rational individual's preference among alternatives should be defined by her actual choice behavior, not by the way she psychologically compares the utilities associated with those alternatives. With the link drawn between this principle and self-perception theory, we come full circle. Indeed as (William) Samuelson and Zeckhauser (1988, 39) observe, the idea that individuals must infer their preferences from their own behavior simply takes revealed preference theory to its logical conclusion: "The economist will identify this notion as an instance of revealed preference applied to one's own, presumably uncertain, preferences."

In the end, however, Samuelson and Zeckhauser are unwilling to concede that this self-revelation is rational. "It is difficult to disprove the hypothesis that adherence to the status quo may constitute rational behavior. Nonetheless, the psychological evidence on self-perception suggests the opposite conclusion. Experiments have shown that even where initial choices are *imposed,* subjects will create inferences suggesting that the original choice was appropriate. . . . In drawing inferences from past behavior, individuals fail to discriminate to some degree between imposed actions, random events, and choices voluntarily (and thoughtfully) undertaken" (1988, 39–40).

Based on a traditional view of rational action, Samuelson and Zeckhauser interpret the failure of experimental subjects to discriminate fully among imposed actions, random events, and choices voluntarily and thoughtfully undertaken as a symptom of irrationality. To an adherent of choice-free rationality, this psychological evidence carries a different message. Such evidence is not only consistent with choice-free rationality's presumption that only a fine line separates these elements that are so distinct on the traditional view. It also provides some comfort to adherents of choice-free rationality as they swim against the tide of collective wisdom about what introspection, intuition, and language tell us about the power, significance, and pervasiveness of free choice.

The psychological evidence suggests irrationality to those who adhere to a choice-laden view of rationality. In this traditional view, agents not only have clearly defined preferences but know what these preferences are because they are displayed before the mind's eye of each agent. Indeed they are validated as the agent's preferences precisely because they appear before his mind's eye. Just as agency itself is clear and known to the agent through "direct experience" (Price 1991, 173), so too are its instruments, namely, preference and belief.

Our behavior, it turns out, does not always honor the distinctions made through our language, introspections, and intuitions. In fact, I am not convinced our intuitions and introspections always honor these distinctions. When actions speak louder than words, is it always because the actor was engaged in conscious deception? When we claim to know an author better than he knows himself, is this pure hubris on our part? Are all attempts to discover one's identity—who one is—ultimately nonsensical or redundant? Should the explanation for indecision, "I don't know what I like," always be seen as an embarrassing admission?

A choice-free world is not as strange or foreign as it may first appear. I do not mean to say that the absence of choice is simply not strange or foreign to ordinary intuition or common-sense wisdom. Except in the rarefied universe of natural science, and perhaps some social science, the natural attitude is to see ourselves as largely free, within some clear external constraints and absent some gross psychological maladies. Accordingly, the natural attitude is to see our behavior as chosen in the full sense of the term and to see a choice-free world as a horror. Still, as my litany of questions is meant to suggest, there are inklings from time to time that the choice model fits our behavior and our lives only crudely.

After all, we live in a post-Freudian world where the notion of internal compulsions, of forces our very choices manifest, is not too foreign to us either. This post-Freudian world is a scientific world in which the tension between individual responsibility and the biological, economic, political, and cultural causes of behavior has become so explicit it is now fully politicized. In recognition of this tension, for example, the use of experts to guide trial attorneys' selection of juries may someday be banned, or tests for certain behavioral dispositions may be prohibited. But laws or regulations cannot banish what this expert knowledge represents: a challenge to the ideal of autonomous rational choice.

In the arena of social science, the residue of the autonomy ideal, as I would accept it, is simply the hypothesis that our actions are rational. If this hypothesis is correct, the role of emotions and urges is structured by the rational economy of the agent. Or put more negatively, actions are generally not influenced, let alone dictated, via cognitive or emotive gaps in the internal rational processes leading to actions. In David Pears's (1984, 181) nice phrase, "actions always go through the narrow gate of reason." In this respect, I am one with Price (1991) and Eells (1982) in treating the rationality assumption as seamless, although their interests are primarily normative.

By recognizing the role of emotions, biology, and physiology in dictating ostensibly free choice, then, I by no means wish to question the comprehensiveness of the rationality hypothesis. The issue rather is how these undeniable influences on behavior should be integrated into the rationality hypothesis. Ainslie (1992, 24–53) is particularly valuable in this regard, pointing out and documenting the difference between recognizing these subrational elements and explaining how they affect behavior. Genes, drives, operant and classical conditioning, and cognitive mistakes will all play a role in any comprehensive theory of human behavior. Yet based on experimental evidence and conceptual considerations, Ainslie argues strongly that human behavior cannot be explained by these forces alone. Decision making must mediate between them. What these forces call into question, therefore, is the choice-based autonomy associated with traditional rational choice theory, not the rationality assumption itself. Insofar as intuition and broader philosophical considerations recognize these forces—and how in the end could they not?—they may yet lead us from freedom of choice to intellectual freedom from choice.

Nevertheless, to conclude by appealing to common-sense intuitions or philosophical speculation is to go out with a whimper. Choice-free rationality, for the time being, is still largely counterintuitive and perhaps even offensive. It must stand or fall as a scientific hypothesis about behavior. The weakening of common-sense intuitions may allow the hypothesis to get its foot in the door, but it should not get the job unless it can get the job done.

APPENDIX A

Supplement to Chapter 2

The proofs of propositions 1 and 2 parallel Ledyard (1984) except for the multiple group setting with conflicting intragroup interests.

PROPOSITION 1: *There is an equilibrium.*

PROOF OF PROPOSITION 1: We define the functions:

$$\mathbf{P}_\theta = F_\theta(\mathbf{P}_\theta, \mathbf{P}_\psi) = \xi_\theta[t(P_\theta, \ldots, P_{n\theta}, g_{1\theta}, \ldots, g_{n\theta}, h_{1\theta}, \ldots, h_{n\theta}),$$
$$f_{V\theta 1}, \ldots, f_{V\theta n}, f_{A\theta 1}, \ldots, f_{A\theta n}; t(P_{1\psi}, \ldots, P_{n\psi},$$
$$g_{1\psi}, \ldots, g_{n\psi}, h_{1\psi}, \ldots, h_{n\psi}), f_{V\psi 1}, \ldots, f_{V\psi n},$$
$$f_{A\psi 1}, \ldots, f_{A\psi n}]$$

$$\mathbf{P}_\psi = F_\psi(\mathbf{P}_\theta, \mathbf{P}_\psi) = \xi_\psi[t(P_{1\psi}, \ldots, P_{n\psi}, g_{1\psi}, \ldots, g_{n\psi}, h_{1\psi}, \ldots, h_{n\psi}),$$
$$f_{V\psi 1}, \ldots, f_{V\psi n}, f_{A\psi 1}, \ldots, f_{A\psi n}; t(P_{1\theta}, \ldots,$$
$$P_{n\theta}, g_{1\theta}, \ldots, g_{n\theta}, h_{1\theta}, \ldots, h_{n\theta}), f_{V\theta 1}, \ldots,$$
$$f_{V\theta n}, f_{A\theta 1}, \ldots, f_{A\theta n}],$$

where $\mathbf{P}_\theta$ and $\mathbf{P}_\psi$ stand for $(P_{1\theta}, \ldots, P_{n\theta})$ and $(P_{1\psi}, \ldots, P_{n\psi})$ respectively. Ledyard's fixed point proof now follows, showing there is a $(\mathbf{P}_\theta^*, \mathbf{P}_\psi^*)$ generating (Q_θ^*, Q_ψ^*), which in turn generates $(\mathbf{P}_\theta^*, \mathbf{P}_\psi^*)$. Hence $(\mathbf{P}_\theta^*, \mathbf{P}_\psi^*, Q_\theta^*, Q_\psi^*)$ is an equilibrium. ■

The alternative tie-break rule using a coin toss does not alter this result.

PROPOSITION 2: *If for some $1 \leq q \leq n$, $H_{q\theta}(c) > 0$ for $c > 0$, then there is positive turnout at equilibrium.*

PROOF OF PROPOSITION 2: Assume there is not positive turnout at equilibrium, that is, $Q_\theta = Q_\psi = 0$. Therefore, since $f_{Vq\theta}(Q_{\theta q}) \geq 0$, $P_{q\theta} > 0$ for all q. If $P_{q\theta} > 0$, then from $H_{q\theta}(c) > 0$, equations (2.4) and (2.8), $Q_\theta \neq 0$, contradicting the assumption. ■

COROLLARY: *If there are k and m $(1 \leq k, m \leq n)$, and $o = \theta, \psi$; $p = \psi, \theta$, such that $f_{Vko}(Q_{ok}) > f_{Vko}(Q_{pk})$; $f_{Vmp}(Q_{pm}) > f_{Vmp}(Q_{om})$; $H_{ko}(c)$, $H_{kp}(c)$, $H_{mp}(c)$,*

$H_{mo}(c) > 0$ *for all* $c_{ko}, c_{kp}, c_{mo}, c_{mp} > 0$; *and* $[Q_{o\backslash k} + Q_{o\backslash m} + f_{Vko}(Q_{ok}) + f_{Vko}(Q_{pk})], [Q_{p\backslash m} + Q_{p\backslash k} + f_{Vmp}(Q_{pm}) + f_{Vmp}(Q_{om})] < 1$, *then* Q_o, $Q_p > 0$.

PROOF OF COROLLARY: Again assume there is not positive turnout at equilibrium, that is, $Q_\theta = Q_\psi = 0$. If $[Q_{\theta\backslash k} + Q_{\psi\backslash m} + f_{Vk\theta}(Q_{\theta k}) + f_{Vk\theta}(Q_{\psi k})] < 1$, then $P_{k\theta} > 0$; by the reasoning used in proving proposition 2, this implies $Q_\theta > 0$. Note that $f_{Vk\theta}(Q_{\theta k}) > f_{Vk\theta}(Q_{\psi k})$ produces a tilt in favor of participation when the coin toss tie break is used. There is a parallel argument for $Q_\psi > 0$. ∎

PROPOSITION 3: *If for some k* $[f_{Vko}(Q_{ok}) + Q_{o\backslash k}] > [Q_{p\backslash k} + f_{Vko}(Q_{pk})]$ *and* $[f_{Ako}(Q_{ok}) + Q_{o\backslash k}] \leq [Q_{p\backslash k} + f_{Ako}(Q_{pk})]$; *or* $[f_{Vko}(Q_{ok}) + Q_{o\backslash k}] = [Q_{p\backslash k} + f_{Vko}(Q_{pk})]$ *and* $[f_{Ako}(Q_{ok}) + Q_{o\backslash k}] < [Q_{p\backslash k} + f_{Ako}(Q_{pk})]$, $1 \leq k \leq n$ *and* $o = \Theta, \Psi$; $p = \Psi, \Theta$, *then the equilibrium turnout does not limit to 0 as* $N \to \infty$.

PROOF OF PROPOSITION 3: Proposition 2 shows that positive turnout at equilibrium can limit to 0 only if $P_{q\theta}$ and $P_{q\psi}$ limit to 0 for all groups q. We therefore investigate the behavior of the $P_{q\theta}$ and $P_{q\psi}$. Denoting the sum of the first series in equation (2.5) for a representative of group k as Σ_k^V and the sum of this representative's second series as Σ_k^A, we take up the two tie-break rules.

(a) Coin toss tie break

Σ_k^V $(1 \leq k \leq n)$ for candidate Θ is

$$\sum_{s=0}^{\|N/2\|} \sum_{t=1}^{N-2s} \frac{N!}{(s+t)! s! (N-2s-t)!} [f_{Vk\theta}(Q_{\theta k}) + Q_{\theta\backslash k}]^{s+t} [Q_{\psi\backslash k} + f_{Vk\theta}(Q_{\psi k})]^s$$

$$\times [1 - [f_{Vk\theta}(Q_{\theta k}) + Q_{\theta\backslash k} + Q_{\psi\backslash k} + f_{Vk\theta}(Q_{\psi k})]]^{N-2s-t}$$

$$+ 1/2 \sum_{s=0}^{\|N/2\|} \sum_{t=0}^{1} \frac{N!}{(s!(s+t)!(N-2s-t)!} [f_{Vk\theta}(Q_{\theta k}) + Q_{\theta\backslash k}]^s$$

$$+ [Q_{\psi\backslash k} + f_{Vk\theta}(Q_{\psi k})]^{s+t}$$

$$\times [1 - [f_{Vk\theta}(Q_{\theta k}) + Q_{\theta\backslash k} + Q_{\psi\backslash k} + f_{Vk\theta}(Q_{\psi k})]]^{N-2s-t}.$$

Σ_k^A for candidate Θ is

$$\sum_{s=0}^{\|N/2\|} \sum_{t=1}^{N-2s} \frac{N!}{(s+t)! s! (N-2s-t)!} [f_{Ak\theta}(Q_{\theta k}) + Q_{\theta\backslash k}]^{s+t} [Q_{\psi\backslash k} + f_{Ak\theta}(Q_{\psi k})]^s$$

$$\times [1 - [f_{Ak\theta}(Q_{\theta k}) + Q_{\theta\backslash k} + Q_{\psi\backslash k} + f_{Ak\theta}(Q_{\psi k})]]^{N-2s-t}$$

$$+ 1/2 \sum_{s=0}^{\|N/2\|} \frac{N!}{s! s! (N-2s)!} [f_{Ak\theta}(Q_{\theta k}) + Q_{\theta\backslash k}]^s [Q_{\psi\backslash k} + f_{Ak\theta}(Q_{\psi k})]^s$$

$$\times \, [1 - [f_{Ak\theta}(Q_{\theta k}) + Q_{\theta\backslash k} + Q_{\psi\backslash k} + f_{Ak\theta}(Q_{\psi k})]]^{N-2s}.$$

For candidate Ψ, Σ_m^V $(1 \le m \le n)$ becomes

$$\sum_{s=0}^{\|N/2\|} \sum_{t=1}^{N-2s} \frac{N!}{s!(s+t)!(N-2s-t)!} [Q_{\theta\backslash m} + f_{Vm\psi}(Q_{\theta m})]^s$$

$$\times \, [f_{Vm\psi}(Q_{\psi m}) + Q_{\psi\backslash m}]^{s+t}$$

$$\times \, [1 - [Q_{\theta\backslash m} + Q_{\psi\backslash m} + f_{Vm\psi}(Q_{\psi m}) + f_{Vm\psi}(Q_{\theta m})]]^{N-2s-t}$$

$$+ \, 1/2 \sum_{s=0}^{\|N/2\|} \sum_{t=0}^{1} \frac{N!}{s!(s+t)!(N-2s-t)!} [Q_{\theta\backslash m} + f_{Vm\psi}(Q_{\theta m})]^{s+t}$$

$$\times \, [f_{Vm\psi}(Q_{\psi m}) + Q_{\psi\backslash m}]^s$$

$$\times \, [1 - [Q_{\theta\backslash m} + Q_{\psi\backslash m} + f_{Vm\psi}(Q_{\psi m}) + f_{Vm\psi}(Q_{\theta m})]]^{N-2s-t}.$$

And for Σ_m^A:

$$\sum_{s=0}^{\|N/2\|} \sum_{t=1}^{N-2s} \frac{N!}{s!(s+t)!(N-2s-t)!} [Q_{\theta\backslash m} + f_{Am\psi}(Q_{\theta m})]^s$$

$$\times \, [f_{Am\psi}(Q_{\psi m}) + Q_{\psi\backslash m}]^{s+t}$$

$$\times \, [1 - [Q_{\theta\backslash m} + Q_{\psi\backslash m} + f_{Am\psi}(Q_{\theta m}) + f_{Am\psi}(Q_{\psi m})]]^{N-2s-t}$$

$$+ \, 1/2 \sum_{s=0}^{\|N/2\|} \frac{N!}{s!s!(N-2s-t)!} [Q_{\theta\backslash m} + f_{Am\psi}(Q_{\theta m})]^s$$

$$\times \, [f_{Am\psi}(Q_{\psi m}) + Q_{\psi\backslash m}]^s$$

$$\times \, [1 - [Q_{\theta\backslash m} + Q_{\psi\backslash m} + f_{Am\psi}(Q_{\theta m}) + f_{Am\psi}(Q_{\psi m})]]^{N-2s}.$$

Theorem 3 of Palfrey and Rosenthal (1985) allows us to disregard the preceding terms that are multiplied by 1/2, since they limit to 0 as N approaches ∞. The Strong Law of Large Numbers (see Ledyard 1984, 20–21) implies that when N approaches infinity, then for some G_k and candidate Θ (given the tie-break rule, the distinction no longer matters):

$$\lim_{N \to \infty} \Sigma_k^V = \begin{cases} 1 \text{ when} & [f_{Vk\theta}(Q_{\theta k}) + Q_{\theta\backslash k}] > [Q_{\psi\backslash k} + f_{Vk\theta}(Q_{\psi k})] \\ 0 \text{ when} & [f_{Vk\theta}(Q_{\theta k}) + Q_{\theta\backslash k}] < [Q_{\psi\backslash k} + f_{Vk\theta}(Q_{\psi k})] \\ 1/2 \text{ when} & [f_{Vk\theta}(Q_{\theta k}) + Q_{\theta\backslash k}] = [Q_{\psi\backslash k} + f_{Vk\theta}(Q_{\psi k})]. \end{cases}$$

Likewise,

$$\lim_{N\to\infty} \Sigma_k^A = \begin{cases} 1 \text{ when} & [f_{Ak\theta}(Q_{\theta k}) + Q_{\theta\backslash k}] > [Q_{\psi\backslash k} + f_{Ak\theta}(Q_{\psi k})] \\ 0 \text{ when} & [f_{Ak\theta}(Q_{\theta k}) + Q_{\theta\backslash k}] < [Q_{\psi\backslash k} + f_{Ak\theta}(Q_{\psi k})] \\ 1/2 \text{ when} & [f_{Ak\theta}(Q_{\theta k}) + Q_{\theta\backslash k}] = [Q_{\psi\backslash k} + f_{Ak\theta}(Q_{\psi k})]. \end{cases}$$

So:

$$\lim_{N\to\infty}(\Sigma_k^V - \Sigma_k^A) > 0 \quad \text{when } [f_{Vk\theta}(Q_{\theta k}) + Q_{\theta\backslash k}] > [Q_{\psi|k} + f_{Vk\theta}(Q_{\psi k})] \quad \text{and}$$
$$[f_{Ak\theta}(Q_{\theta k}) + Q_{\theta\backslash k}] \leq [Q_{\psi\backslash k} + f_{Ak\theta}(Q_{\psi k})]; \quad \text{or}$$
$$[f_{Vk\theta}(Q_{\theta k}) + Q_{\theta\backslash k}] = [Q_{\psi|k} + f_{Vk\theta}(Q_{\psi k})] \quad \text{and}$$
$$[f_{Ak\theta}(Q_{\theta k}) + Q_{\theta\backslash k}] < [Q_{\psi|k} + f_{Ak\theta}(Q_{\psi k})].$$

(b) Ψ wins when there is a tie.
Compared to (a):

1. Σ_k^V and Σ_m^A for Θ and Ψ respectively are increased by 1/2 the probability of a tie vote when there are N voters in the respective calculations;
2. Σ_m^V and Σ_k^A for Ψ and Θ respectively are decreased by 1/2 the probability of a tie vote when there are N voters in the respective calculations;
3. Σ_k^V for Θ is decreased by 1/2 the probability of k's creating a tie;
4. Σ_m^V for Ψ is increased by 1/2 the probability of m's creating a tie.

Again from Palfrey and Rosenthal's (1985) theorem 3, it is immediate that all probabilities in (1)–(4) limit to 0 as $N \to \infty$. Therefore the limits described for case (a) also apply in case (b). ∎

Supplement to Chapter 3

Proofs of Propositions Presented in Chapter 3

PROPOSITION 1: *If* $\sigma_{k\Theta}^2 = \sigma_{m\Theta}^2 = \sigma_{k\psi}^2 \sigma_{m\psi}^2 = 0$, $\text{prob}_t(\mathbf{I}_k)/\text{prob}_t(\mathbf{I}_m) > v^2$, *and* $y_{rk}^* \neq y_{sk}^*$ *for some voters* r,s, *then the unique Stackelberg equilibrium party announcements are* $\pi_{ik}^* = (\text{argmax}_{yki} \, \text{EU}_k^{M_k})/a_{ki}$, *where* M_k *is the set of voters with the median ideal point in k. If* $\text{prob}_t(\mathbf{I}_k)/\text{prob}_t(\mathbf{I}_m) < v^2$, *the unique equilibrium announcements for the parties are* $\pi_{im}^* = (\text{argmax}_{ymi} \, \text{EU}_k^{M_m})/a_{mi}$, *where* M_m *is the set of voters with the median ideal point in m.*

PROOF: Since for all position announcements and ideal points, $vy_k = y_m$, by equation (3.7) $v^2\text{EU}_k^j = \text{EU}_m^j$; and if $\bar{y}_{ki} = y_{jk}^*$, then $\bar{y}_{mi} = y_{jm}^*$. Accordingly, by equation (3.8) all j for whom $y_{ki} \neq y_{jk}^*$, $i = \Theta, \Psi$, use ideology $\mathbf{I}_k$ if $|\text{EU}_k^j(y_{k\Theta}) - \text{EU}_k^j(y_{k\psi})| > v^2 \, |\text{EU}_k^j(y_{k\Theta}) - \text{EU}_k^j(y_{k\psi})|$, which becomes $\text{prob}_t(\mathbf{I}_k)/\text{prob}_t(\mathbf{I}_m) > v^2$ by way of equations (3.8) and (3.10) and some algebraic manipulation. Voters j for whom $\bar{y}_{ki} = y_{jk}^*$, $i = \Theta, \Psi$ flip a coin between ideologies by virtue of the condition placed on equation (3.8) in case of equality. Thus if the parties adopt positions that translate into distinct $\bar{y}_{ki}$, all voters use ideology $\mathbf{I}_k$, and, by standard arguments, there is a unique median ideological position and Θ wins by adopting it. If both parties adopt the relevant π_{ik}^*, they both stand an equal chance of winning voters with and without ideal points y_{Mk}^*. An analogous argument proves the sufficiency of the strict inequality in the opposite direction. ∎

COROLLARY 1A: *If the assumptions of proposition 1 obtain except that* $\text{prob}_t(\mathbf{I}_k)/\text{prob}_t(\mathbf{I}_m) = v^2$, *then there are equilibrium position announcements* $\pi_i^* = (\text{argmax}_{y'i} \, \text{EU}_k^{M_{y'}})/a_{ki}$.

PROOF: When the assumed equality holds, voters not only are indifferent between ideologies but, again by equations (3.7) and (3.8), find that ideological translation does not affect their evaluation of the relative merits of party positions. This means that positions in the two ideologies can be measured on a common dimension. Specifically, we define the line y' such that $y' = y_k = y_m/v$ along with measures $\mu(y_k)$ and $\mu(y_m)$ such that $\mu(y_j) = 1/2 \times$ the number of voters with ideal points at y_j. This induces a measure $\mu(y') = \mu(y_k) + \mu(y_m/v)$. Since $\sum_j \mu(y_j') = 4N + 2$, there will, in general, be a closed interval of median points (see Enelow and Hinich 1984, 8–12). In any event, given median points $M_{y'}$ candidates will take equilibrium positions $\pi_i^* = (\text{argmax}_{y'ki}\ \text{EU}_k^{M_{y'}})/a_{ki}$. ∎

COROLLARY 1C: *For any mix of voters satisfying the assumptions of proposition 1, corollary 1A, and corollary 1B, there are equilibrium position announcements* $\pi_i^* = (\text{argmax}_{y'ki}\ \text{EU}_k^{M_{y'}})/a_{ki}$.

PROOF: For those voters satisfying the assumptions of corollary 1A or 1B, the construction of y' and $\mu(y')$ follows directly. For those voters satisfying the assumptions of proposition 1, we apply $2\mu(y_k)$ or $2\mu(y_m)$ as appropriate. ∎

PROPOSITION 2: *The optimal candidate strategies are determined for any finite number of ideologies.*

PROOF: Since preferences over ideologies are determined by expected utility numbers, from proposition 1 and its corollaries each voter has a preference ranking—technically, a weak ordering—over ideologies that is independent of particular party position announcements. For each voter who has a uniquely preferred ideology I_k, we apply $2\mu(y_k)$ as in corollary 1C. For each voter who has a preferred set of n ideologies I_k for which the assumptions of corollary 1A hold, we apply $\mu(y') = \sum_j \mu(y_j)/n$. The results of corollary 1C follow. ∎

PROPOSITION 3: *If* $\sigma_{k\theta}^2 = \sigma_{m\theta}^2 = \sigma_{k\psi}^2 = \sigma_{m\psi}^2 = 0$, $y_{rk}^* \neq y_{sk}^*$ *for some voters* r,s, *and* $\text{prob}_{(t-1)}(I_k)/\text{prob}_{(t-1)}(I_m) > v^2$, *then Stackelberg equilibrium candidate announcements are* (π_{ik}^*, k), *where* $\pi_{ik}^* = (\text{argmax}_{yki}\ \text{EU}_k^{M_k})/a_{ki}$.

PROOF: Clearly, Θ is not ill served by making ideological and position announcements that are consistent. If Θ makes announcement $(\pi_{\theta k}^*, k)$, then Ψ can announce $(\pi_{\psi k}^*, k)$ or $(\pi_{\psi m}^*, m)$. In the former case, the algebra of Bayesian updating confirms that Ψ merely reinforces Θ's choice; in the latter case the algebra confirms that $\text{prob}_{(t-1)}(I_k)/\text{prob}_{(t-1)}(I_m) = \text{prob}_t(I_k)/\text{prob}_t(I_m)$, also confirming Θ's choice. On the other hand, with an announcement of $(\pi_{\theta m}^*, m)$, Θ can at best equal its results with $(\pi_{\theta k}^*, k)$. ∎

COROLLARY 3A: *If the assumptions of proposition 3 obtain except that* $\text{prob}_{(t-1)}(I_k)/\text{prob}_{(t-1)}(I_m) = v^2$ *and (1) there does not exist a* $\pi_{\theta k}^* = (\text{argmax}_{yk\theta}\ \text{EU}_k^{M_k})/a_{k\theta}$ *such that* $\pi_{\theta k}^* \in (\text{argmax}_{y'}\ \text{EU}_k^{M_{y'}})/a_{k\theta}$ *or (2) there does not exist a* $\pi_{\theta m}^* = (\text{argmax}_{ym\theta}\ \text{EU}_m^{M_m})/a_{m\theta}$ *such that* $\pi_{\theta m}^* \in (\text{argmax}_{y'}\ \text{EU}_m^{M_{y'}})/a_{m\theta}$, *then the incumbent* Θ *loses.*

PROOF: In response to announcement $(\pi_{\theta k}^*, k)$, $k = 1, 2$, Ψ announces $(\pi_{\psi m}^*, m)$, $\pi_{\psi m}^* \in (\text{argmax}_{ym\psi}\ EU_m^{M_y})/a_{m\psi}$, $m \neq k$ and wins by uniquely adopting the unique median in $\mathbf{I}_m$. The announcement of $(\pi_{\theta m}^*, m)$, $m = 1, 2$ provokes a parallel response. In response to announcement $(\pi_{\theta k}^*, m)$, $k = 1, 2$ and $k \neq m$, Ψ announces (π_ψ^*, m), $\pi_\psi^* \in (\text{argmax}_{y'}\ EU_y^{M_{y'}})/a_{k\psi}$ and by restoring the initial equality with v^2 wins by uniquely adopting a median along y'. Finally, in response to any announcement $(*, k)$, $k = 0$, Ψ can, by appropriately adopting one of the two preceding announcements, uniquely capture a median of y' or of $\mathbf{I}_m$, $m \neq k$. ∎

PROPOSITION 4: *If the assumptions of proposition 3 hold except* $\sigma_{k\psi}^2 = \sigma_{m\psi}^2 > 0$, *then* Θ *wins with announcement* (π_{Mk}, k).

PROOF: It is immediate from equation (3.7) that $\partial EU_k^j/\partial \sigma_{ik}^2 < 0$ for all k. Therefore, regardless of ψ's ideological announcement, all voters vote for Θ when candidates announce positions $\pi_{ik}^* = (\text{argmax}_{yki}\ EU_k^{M_k})/a_{ki}$. Other position announcements by Ψ only change the plurality. ∎

COROLLARY 4A: *If the assumptions of corollary* 3A *hold except* $\sigma_{k\psi}^2 = \sigma_{m\psi}^2 > 0$ *and neither* $(\bar{y}_{\theta k} - y^{*\prime}) > 2\sigma^2$ *nor* $(\bar{y}_{\theta m} - y^{*\prime}) > 2\sigma^2$, *with* $\bar{y}_{\theta k}$ *and* $\bar{y}_{\theta m}$ *the counterparts in* y' *of* Θ's *announcements of* $\pi_{\theta k}^*$ *and* $\pi_{\theta m}^*$ *respectively and* $y^{*\prime}$ *the closest of* $M_{y'}$'s *ideal points,* Ψ *wins.*

PROOF: Suppose Θ announces $(\pi_{\theta k}^*, k)$, with $\bar{y}_\theta'$ its counterpart. If Ψ restores the equality between ideologies by announcing $(\pi_{\psi m}^*, m)$, $\pi_{\psi m}^* \in (\text{argmax}_{ym\psi}\ EU_m^{M_y})/a_{m\psi}$, $m \neq k$, Ψ can be expected to win if, by equation (3.8), $-\text{prob}_t(\mathbf{I})\sigma^2 > -\text{prob}_t(\mathbf{I})(\bar{y}_{\theta k} - y^{*\prime})^2$, that is, $(\bar{y}_{\theta k} - y^{*\prime}) > \sigma^2$, where $\mathbf{I}$ is $M_{y'}$'s ideology (or expected ideology for multiple median voters). Since, by assumption, $(\bar{y}_{\theta k} - y^{*\prime}) > 2\sigma^2$, Θ cannot move close enough toward $y^{*\prime}$ without allowing Ψ to win by announcing $(\pi_{\theta k}^*, k)$. Note also that since $\partial^2 EU/\partial(y^{*\prime})^2 < 0$, voters with ideal points on the side of $y^{*\prime}$ opposite that of $\bar{y}_{\theta k}'$ will experience greater reduction in Θ's expected utility than in Ψ's. A parallel proof applies to Θ's announcement of $(\pi_{\theta y^{*\prime}}^*, k)$ or $(\pi_{\theta m}^*, m)$. ∎

Model of Heresthetics with Weaker Information Assumptions

In the preceding analysis, parties were provided with unrealistically detailed information about voter beliefs. While our generosity nicely highlights the structure of heresthetic maneuvers, it is worth considering a weakening of this information requirement in order to develop a more realistic assessment of how parties influence the conceptual schemes CEU maximizers use. Accordingly, we conclude this discussion of heresthetics by modifying our assumptions about the parties, which are now fitted with probabilistic beliefs—priors—concerning the distribution of ideological frameworks among the voters.

Building on Hinich (1977), we assume that the parties share twice differentiable probability functions (suppressing time indices), $P_{jk} \doteq P_{jk}(\mathrm{EU}_k^j(y_{k\theta}) - \mathrm{EU}_k^j(y_{k\psi}))$, each giving the conditional probability that a voter with j's ideal point in $\mathbf{I}_k$ uses $\mathbf{I}_k$ and votes for Θ. (This is actually a specialization of Enelow and Hinich's [1989] model which can include inter alia a probability distribution on ideal points. Enelow [1992] generalizes the model further to include parties or candidates with mixed motives [i.e., winning and policy implementation].) Thus θ's total expected vote is

$$EV_\theta = \sum_{j=1}^{2N+1} \sum_{k=1}^{n} P_{jk}(\mathrm{prob}_j(\mathbf{I}_k) f_j(y_{k\theta}, y_{k\psi})), \tag{B.1}$$

where $f_j(y_{k\theta}, y_{k\psi}) = (a_{k\theta}\pi_\theta + b_{k\theta} - y_{jk}^*)^2 + \sigma_{\theta k}^2 - ((a_{k\psi}\pi_\psi + b_{k\psi} - y_{jk}^*)^2 + \sigma_{\psi k}^2)$ and Ψ's total expected vote is $2N + 1 - EV_\psi$. The first-order conditions for maximizing expected vote are

$$\pi_\theta^* = \frac{\displaystyle\sum_{j=1}^{2N+1} \sum_{k=1}^{n} (a_{k\theta})(y_{jk}^* - b_{k\theta}) P'_{jk}(\mathrm{prob}_j(\mathbf{I}_k) f_j(y_{k\theta}, y_{k\psi}))}{\displaystyle\sum_{j=1}^{2N+1} \sum_{k=1}^{n} (a_{k\theta})^2 P'_{jk}(\mathrm{prob}_j(\mathbf{I}_k) f_j(y_{k\theta}, y_{k\psi}))}, \tag{B.2a}$$

$$\pi_\psi^* = \frac{\displaystyle\sum_{j=1}^{2N+1} \sum_{k=1}^{n} (a_{k\psi})(y_{jk}^* - b_{k\psi}) P'_{jk}(\mathrm{prob}_j(\mathbf{I}_k) f_j(y_{k\theta}, y_{k\psi}))}{\displaystyle\sum_{j=1}^{2N+1} \sum_{k=1}^{n} (a_{k\psi})^2 P'_{jk}(\mathrm{prob}_j(\mathbf{I}_k) f_j(y_{k\theta}, y_{k\psi}))} \tag{B.2b}$$

with of course π_θ^* and π_ψ^* substituting in $f_j(y_{k\theta}, y_{k\psi})$ for π_θ and π_ψ respectively. Continuing the adaptation of Hinich (1977), assume there is a $\delta > 0$ such that for all j,k

$$P'_{jk}(y) = \mathrm{prob}_j(\mathbf{I}_k)/2n\delta, \tag{B.3}$$

where $|y| \leq \delta$; equation (B.2) then simplifies to

$$\pi_\theta^* = \frac{\displaystyle\sum_{j=1}^{2N+1}\sum_{k=1}^{n}(a_{k\theta})(y_{jk}^* - b_{k\theta})\text{prob}_j(\mathbf{I}_k)}{\displaystyle\sum_{j=1}^{2N+1}\sum_{k=1}^{n}(a_{k\theta})^2\text{prob}_j(\mathbf{I}_k)},$$ (B4.a)

$$\pi_\psi^* = \frac{\displaystyle\sum_{j=1}^{2N+1}\sum_{k=1}^{n}(a_{k\psi})(y_{jk}^* - b_{k\psi})\text{prob}_j(\mathbf{I}_k)}{\displaystyle\sum_{j=1}^{2N+1}\sum_{k=1}^{n}(a_{k\psi})^2\text{prob}_j(\mathbf{I}_k)}.$$ (B4.b)

Since $P''_{jk}(y) = 0$, $\partial^2 EV_\theta/\partial\pi_\theta^2$, $\partial^2 EV_\psi/\partial\pi_\psi^2 < 0$. Therefore equation (B.4) defines a local equilibrium at $\pi_\theta = \pi_\theta^*$, $\pi_\psi = \pi_\psi^*$. We now establish equation (B.4) as a global equilibrium (the proofs of the following propositions are at the end of the appendix).

PROPOSITION B.1: $\pi_\theta = \pi_\theta^*$, $\pi_\psi = \pi_\psi^*$ *is the pure strategy solution to the electoral game with fixed voter priors on frameworks.*

As the characterization of the optimal party strategies makes clear, θ and ψ will not typically converge in their public positions despite their lack of interest in policy. Once again, differences in the historical relation between public announcements and policies generate different party reputations that, in turn, dictate different optimal positions.

Turning to the heresthetic stage, Θ will be said to be *vulnerable* to an announcement $m \geq 1$ (denoted by $\mathbf{I}_m$) if $EV_\psi \mid \mathbf{I}_m > EV_\psi$. Thus given position announcements $\pi_\theta^* = \pi_\psi^*$ and in light of equation (B.4b), Θ is vulnerable if

$$\sum_{j=1}^{2N+1}\sum_{k=1}^{n}\text{prob}_{j(t-1)}(\mathbf{I}_k)[\text{prob}_{j(t-1)}(\mathbf{I}_m \mid \mathbf{I}_k)(\sum_{k=1}^{n}\text{prob}_{j(t-1)}(\mathbf{I}_k)$$
$$\times\;\text{prob}_{j(t-1)}(\mathbf{I}_m \mid \mathbf{I}_k))^{-1} - 1]f_j(y_{k\theta},y_{k\psi}) > 0.$$ (B.5)

This leads to the following result.

PROPOSITION B.2: *The electoral game with a heresthetic announcement by the challenger has a Nash equilibrium.*

We note without proof the following.

COROLLARY: *If there is a heresthetic announcement k such that $EV_\psi \mid \mathbf{I}_k >$ $EV_\psi \mid \mathbf{I}_m$, $m \neq k$, the Nash equilibrium is unique.*

In combination with proposition B.2, the formula for Θ's vulnerability suggests three things. First, heresthetics depends on the relative distances between each j's ideal point and π_ψ^* and π_θ^* as interpreted in each $\mathbf{I}_k$. *Ceteris paribus* the greater the positive difference in distances, the more useful is an increase in the associated $\mathrm{prob}(\mathbf{I}_k)$. As noted regarding the model in chapter 3, *to the extent j is "alienated" from Θ, Ψ has an opportunity to change j's likely interpretation of their positions.*

Second, the greater the positive difference between $\sigma_{\theta k}^2$ and $\sigma_{\psi k}^2$, the more useful is an increase in the associated $\mathrm{prob}(\mathbf{I}_k)$ and therefore the more likely there will be an election involving heresthetics. Again, this is consistent with the standard finding that ambiguity can weaken a political contender. In contrast to the standard result, we see again, *the more ambiguous party may not suffer* due to compensating adjustments in other $\mathrm{prob}(\mathbf{I}_m)$, $m \neq k$.

Third, by equation (B.4b) the higher j's prior on $\mathbf{I}_k$, the less likely is a heresthetic announcement to change it, and, therefore, the less likely is Θ to be vulnerable. We have assumed a certain stubbornness in the voters' use of their basic frameworks of interpretation and consequently a resistance to changes induced by heresthetic announcements. *Sometimes heresthetic maneuvers will work. It is also important to recognize that many times they will not: voters continue to judge the parties the way they have historically judged the parties.*

Proofs of Propositions

PROPOSITION B.1: $\pi_\theta = \pi_\theta^*$, $\pi_\psi = \pi_\psi^*$ *is the pure strategy solution to the electoral game with fixed voter priors on frameworks.*

PROOF: Integrate equation (B.3) and sum over the n ideologies to yield $P_j = \sum_k [\mathrm{prob}_j(\mathbf{I}_k)y/2\delta] + K$. However, $K = 1/2$, since when $y = 0$, $P_j = 1 - P_j$. Thus each voter j supports Ψ with probability $P_j = (1/2\delta) \times \sum_k \mathrm{prob}_j(\mathbf{I}_k)[(a_{k\theta}\pi_\theta + b_{k\theta} - y_j^*)^2 + \sigma_{\theta k}^2 - ((a_{k\psi}\pi_\psi + b_{k\psi} - y_j^*)^2 + \sigma_{\psi k}^2)] + 1/2$. The term P_j is continuous and strictly concave in π_ψ for any π_θ and strictly convex in π_θ. The sum of concave functions, EV_ψ, is also concave, and thus EV_θ is convex. Therefore, the game has a saddle point (see, e.g., Owen 1982, 78).   ∎

PROPOSITION B.2: *The electoral game with a heresthetic announcement by the challenger has a Nash equilibrium.*

PROOF: For any set of voter probabilities on the $\mathbf{I}_k$ there is, by proposition B.1, a unique pair of optimal positions π_θ^*, π_ψ^*. Therefore, if Θ is not vulnerable given the initial probabilities on $\mathbf{I}_k$, it announces $\pi_{\theta 0}^*$ and Ψ announces $(\pi_{\psi 0}^*,$ 0), where $\pi_{\theta 0}^*$ and $\pi_{\psi 0}^{**}$ are the optimal positions given the voter probabilities consequent to heresthetic announcement $m = 0$. Suppose, then, Θ is vulnerable to at least one $m \geq 1$. If Ψ announces $(\pi_{\psi k}^*, k)$, where $EV_\psi \mid \mathbf{I}_k \geq EV_\psi \mid \mathbf{I}_m, m \neq k$, then Θ will optimally announce $\pi_{\theta k}^*$ producing a combination of announcements from which neither party has an incentive to deviate. Finally, Θ cannot mitigate the impact of heresthetic announcements by Ψ since, given any anticipatory position change, an announcement of $(\pi_{\psi 0}^*, 0)$ or $(\pi_{\psi k}^*, k)$ will lead to an inferior result for Θ. ■

Notes

Introduction

1. Chapter 1 will consider various ad hoc remedies within expected utility theory, such as assuming voters participate out of a sense of civic duty even though they recognize that their vote makes a negligible contribution to whatever it is they feel so loyal.

Chapter 1

1. In order to generate positive turnout, Riker and Ordeshook (1968) essentially follow Downs (1957) in adding a "citizen duty" term to the voter's calculus. John Ferejohn and Morris Fiorina (1974), on the other hand, hypothesize that voters vote in fear that they will miss an opportunity to change the election's outcome. Both attempts have provoked essentially the same rebuke: as nongeneric solutions tailored to the case at hand, these explanations border on the tautological (see, e.g., Barry 1970 and Beck 1975 respectively). Aside from the issue of empirical emptiness, there are other empirical considerations to accommodate, such as the sensitivity of turnout to costs and to the closeness of the election.

2. The reason for introducing some more terminology is that some Causal Decision theorists do not subscribe to—or at minimum expand on—the technical requirements of EU theory, with its particular approach to risk and probability. Moreover, Causal Decision theorists sometimes contrast their position with EU theory on the grounds that expectation, as a statistical concept, is indifferent to the pertinent causal distinctions. Since Downsians model the voter as an EU maximizer and build into their analysis restrictions based on causal considerations, I believe it is not seriously misleading in the context of this analysis to equate EU theory with Causal Decision Theory and CEU theory with a broader statistical approach. William Harper (1993) provides further support for this equation.

3. I have adapted an example of Isaac Levi's (1982), which represents an important twist on the famous Newcomb's Problem (see Campbell and Sowden 1985), which is considered in section V.

4. Cf. Daniel Dennett's (1984, 120–21) collapsing of the distinction between "real" lotteries whose drawings occur after tickets are bought and the "YOU MAY HAVE ALREADY WON!" lotteries people clearly take seriously.

5. Henry Kyburg (1988) attempts to reconcile the two positions by recognizing an inside view for the decision maker distinct from the "evidential" view adopted by the

observer. Robert Nozick's (1993, 41–50) reconciliation, in contrast, uses a weighted average of the two decision rules in order to respect the divergent intuitions decision makers are supposed to have across cases. It is not clear, however, that Nozick's illustration, which seems to rely on the intuitive pull of what psychologists call the certainty effect, actually counts against maximizing CEU across the board.

6. For a discussion of some of the more complex and generic philosophical issues surrounding the idea of freedom of choice or free will largely compatible with the position advanced here see Dennett 1984.

7. The interpretation of predictive powers in terms of predictions conditional on acts not only fits the CEU maximization scheme but in fact is necessary to render the relevant probabilities in the decision problem uncontroversially determinate (see Levi 1975).

8. For technical reasons not bearing directly on the issue at hand, Levi is neither a Causal Decision theorist nor a CEU maximizer. In the interest of simplicity I will identify him as a CEU maximizer.

9. Section VI addresses the problem of common causes as generators of spurious correlations.

10. A referee writes, "One also finds in physics no fundamental particles which consume, reproduce, or love—but humans undeniably do these things." Nor are any fundamental particles hard or soft, porous or impermeable, but physics has not developed a new ontology to accommodate these concepts. True characteristics of things are not necessarily things themselves with their own distinct causal role.

11. Citing Howard Sobel, Nozick (1993, 43) argues that, unlike Causal Decision theorists, CEU advocates have failed to diagnose deep errors in the opposing argument. I count as such an error the special, nonscientific status Causal Decision theorists give to human action and the duality of mind and nature that notion presupposes.

12. Once the focus is on the decision making process, rather than the decision itself, another distinction between EU and CEU theory breaks down: EU maximizers can also internally monitor their own decisions for indications of causal relations between acts and outcomes (e.g., Skyrms 1990).

13. It is interesting to note that Levi (1992, 15) also questions whether agents can assign unconditional probabilities to their own acts since, he argues, doing so eliminates any real notion of choice. He likewise argues that unconditional probabilities are necessary for EU theory as well, which runs contrary to its commitment to the strong distinction between first-person and third-person analysis.

14. The notion of mixed act is analogous to the notion of mixed strategy in game theory. Some early students of game theory were puzzled over the meaning of a mixed strategy or the reasonableness of deciding by chance. It is now widely agreed that strategies themselves are unmixed; mixing refers to other players' ignorance about the strategy chosen, whether or not this is induced by the player. Thus there is no tension between the idea that any strategy is ultimately realized as a pure action and the idea that the strategy is mixed.

15. As Jeffrey (1993) notes, it is generally the case that $0 < \text{prob}(A) < 1$ even when $\text{prob}(C) = 0$ or $\text{prob}(C) = 1$.

16. The analysis in the text fixes beliefs but allows preferences to deviate from

those established by the original decision problem. What if the original preferences were fixed as well? My answer is that this is not possible since the preferences and behavior are incompatible. I would have the same reaction if someone were described as preferring vanilla over chocolate frozen yogurt yet always choosing chocolate. What does the preference for vanilla mean in this case?

17. Jeffrey (1993, 150) develops an analogous point when characterizing probabilities conditional on having the smoking gene even when the unconditional probability of the gene is 0. The formula for conditional probability is indeterminate under such conditions, but Jeffrey insists that the relevant formula is not what "defines" the conditional probability. Similarly, see Field's (1977, 381) argument in favor of Karl Popper's idea of taking conditional probability as primitive.

18. The connection between the probabilistic interpretation of causation and CEU theory is developed in chapter 5's discussion of the econometrics of policy analysis. For now, observe that Jeffrey's rigidity condition is analogous to the econometric notion of super exogeneity (Engle, Hendry, and Richard 1983), which, roughly, applies to models in which the parameters of interest are invariant to changes in the probability distribution of the exogenous (e.g., decision) variables. It is striking that, consistent with the assumptions of EU theory, Robert Engle, David Hendry, and Jean-Francois Richard (1983, 285) argue that super exogeneity is conjectural because, in part, "nothing precludes agents from changing their behavior at a certain instant." Their appeal to individual freedom or perversity seems to sit ill with their attempt to connect super exogeneity to a nonstatistical notion of causation: "When derived from a well-articulated theory, a [model] with z_t super exogenous seems to satisfy the requirement for Zellner causality [Zellner 1979] of 'predictability according to law'" (1983, 285). Freedom sits ill with Zellner's definition of causation because, presumably, a scientific law cannot be broken. Since it brooks no deviations, it precludes agents from "changing their behavior at a certain instant."

19. Chapter 3 includes a more formal presentation of Samuelson-style discounting; chapter 4 considers a different form.

Chapter 2

1. Michael Banton (1983) distinguishes race, which he argues is defined by exclusion, from ethnicity, which he views as being defined by inclusion. With the weight of the rational choice literature devoted to the former, the discussion of groups in chapter 2 concentrates on inclusion.

2. This problem, one might object, does not really reflect a particular difficulty with the instrumental analysis of group identity so much as weaknesses in rational choice theory's more general account of the supply of public goods. As chapter 1 suggests, I find merit in this complaint, yet I also follow Howard Margolis (1984) in viewing the problem of turnout and the question of group identity as deeply linked.

3. For other rational choice analyses recognizing the importance of choosing group identity see Lichbach 1996 and Gartner and Segura 1997.

4. For a more technical discussion of Bayesian theory see, for example, DeGroot 1970.

5. The impact of identification is symmetric. It allows agents to predict the choices of other group members based on their own, the relation captured by expression (2.1), but also allows them to predict their own choices based on the choices of other members. As discussed in chapter 1, the latter result is what worries Jeffrey (1993). Chapter 4 takes up a third case, the prediction of an agent's future choices from her present choices.

6. Richard Nadeau, Richard Niemi, and Timothy Amato (1994, 374) argue that party identifiers who switch their preferences form expectations based on the inference that other identifiers will behave the same way. Further, they argue this is genuine expectation formation and not simple projection.

7. Obviously, this normalization assumes a perceived difference between Θ and Ψ, which I believe is a reasonable empirical assumption (e.g., Wittman 1983, 145). Endogenous strategies for Θ and Ψ are considered briefly in section VIII. The fact that Θ and Ψ do not in general converge is also an implication of the model of ideology developed in chapter 3.

8. Proposition 3 requires of course that the relevant group k not reduce to a zero proportion of the population as the population increases. This assumption is reasonable so long as population growth is not associated with a general decline in groups.

9. By the same token, this independence is not obtained without cost. As the size of the electorate increases, for example, it becomes increasingly certain that anyone for whom $c < 1$ will be voting, which, like zero turnout, is extremely unrealistic. One way to achieve greater realism is to introduce a greater dose of realism into our assumptions about voters' knowledge. Voters, for example, will not in general be certain about the functions f_v and f_A, which the present model assumes. This uncertainty weakens the certainty of turnout. For a more formal discussion of this point, see Grafstein 1991 (1001–2).

10. The only complication qualifying this inference is that the advantage of participation also reflects the level of a group's identity in comparison to others.

11. A model in which the population is strictly partitioned into groups is itself unrealistic. Groups in real populations often have overlapping memberships. Multiple memberships can have a positive cumulative effect on turnout, attenuate it, or have no net effect at all. It depends on the relative strengths of the group identities and the degree to which politically relevant interests and group membership coincide. Formally, how-ever, the treatment of multiple memberships is reasonably straightforward. Essentially, each individual's calculation of the statistical impact of his participation and abstention is represented as the sum of $f_v s$ and $f_A s$ respectively for each of the subgroups to which he belongs. A model reflecting this modification should confirm our general intuitions about the influence of group membership. To the extent individuals who prefer Θ are connected to groups oriented toward Θ, the likelihood of their participation should increase. Conversely, to the extent individuals who prefer Θ are connected to groups oriented toward Ψ, the likelihood of their participation should decrease due to crosscut-ting cleavages.

12. The developmental model relies on class interest as the basis of mobilization, while the CEU model focuses on beliefs rather than preferences. If agents had a class

identity on a par with ethnic identity, then class-based mobilization would no longer be problematic. Roderick Kiewiet (1983, 19), however, questions the importance of class identification insofar as it implies more than the similarity of interests and experiences classes reflect. If these similarities do not generate the statistical dependencies necessary for the CEU model to apply, then class does not explain mobilization. The theoretical controversy over class identity is discussed in section VIII.

13. We have however already recognized a countervailing consideration, the natural affinity between a group and a particular policy preference: $f_{Vq\theta}(Q_{\theta q}) > f_{Vq\theta}(Q_{\psi q})$.

14. Chapter 4 offers a somewhat more detailed discussion of norms.

15. For a more sanguine analysis of second-order free riding see Heckathorn 1989.

16. For an interesting assessment of the role and fate of minorities according to formal spatial theory, see Miller 1996.

17. The emphasis on appropriate circumstances, once again, distinguishes the CEU approach from attempts to solve the collective action problem by appealing to a subjective and perhaps deluded sense of personal efficacy (e.g., Finkel, Muller, and Opp 1989).

18. One version of this reasoning from unconditional probabilities deserves special mention. Anatol Rapoport (1966, 141–42) and Douglas Hofstadter (1983) have argued that players in a Prisoner's Dilemma who believe each other to be rational should realize that their symmetric situation will produce an outcome in which either both defect or both cooperate. Since joint cooperation is preferable to joint defection, it should be chosen. As Brian Skyrms (1990, 13–14) observes, this reasoning takes on special interest since it is closely related to von Neumann and Morgenstern's (1953, 148) "transcendental argument" for the attraction of game theoretic equilibria. From the standpoint of CEU theory, the argument rests on the assumption that players do not act according to conditional probabilities but instead use the common unconditional probabilities of common action to limit their alternatives. As a result, players are not constrained by probabilities attached to their behavior so much as by the somehow independently defined meaning of rationality in this game.

19. Claus Offe (1974, 33–34) disputes the notion of a parallel capitalist class consciousness, but in arguing for the special problems faced by workers interested in collective action, Offe and Helmut Wiesenthal (1985) seem to be less sure. Obviously, nothing in the CEU model prevents a more universal ascription of class consciousness.

20. Przeworski and Wallerstein (1982, 221) indicate that they are not persuaded by the first three solutions mentioned in the text.

21. There is a related question about the role of leaders in solving the public goods dilemma prior to the existence of the goods (Elster 1985a, 366–67; Buchanan 1982, 92–94). Also, see Taylor 1988 (85–90) for questions about noninstrumental, "expressive" solutions to the dilemma. As we have seen, Margolis (1984) would offer still another solution by positing the existence of two selves within the worker, one oriented toward class benefits and one oriented toward individual benefits.

Chapter 3

1. Cf. North 1990 (23): "By ideology I mean the subjective perceptions (models, theories) all people possess to explain the world around them." North, however, treats these perceptions as a consequence of the limited cognitive capacities of people and not as characteristics of rational decision making itself.

2. Elster (1985c, 141–66) specifically links ideology to biased beliefs. Although I cannot fully address his complex discussion here, one alleged source of bias is the ideologue's use of "incorrect" theories to produce mistaken inferences. Section II touches on this. Alleged bias from the interaction of preference and belief is an even more difficult issue, but see section V.

3. This ideological theory, in other words, can be a theory in an ideal sense: a set of beliefs closed under implication and subject to revision. Granted, ideologies in practice may simplify reality a great deal, but it is odd for theorists (e.g., Higgs 1987, 37–38), particularly rational choice theorists (e.g., Hinich and Munger 1992, 14), to distinguish science and ideology on the basis of simplification. By the same token, as noted earlier, the present formulation takes no stand on the level of conceptualization appropriate to an ideologue.

4. This follows a parallel defensive move by Goodman (1983).

5. For a fuller defense of the approach to induction underlying this treatment of ideology, particularly against Bayesian criticisms, see Grafstein 1992 (135–40).

6. Technically, the convergence of probability measures representing degrees of belief does not imply their uniform convergence (Savage 1962, 14), so there is room for noticeable differences.

7. It has been found that when agents with rational expectations efficiently extract information from equilibrium prices in financial markets, they will not trade since no information asymmetries develop. As Thomas Sargent (1993, 25) observes, "it has proved very difficult to produce a compelling rational expectations model that breaks the no-trade theorem." The rational expectations assumption is used and discussed more fully subsequently.

8. Cf. Downs 1957 (96): "We define an ideology as a verbal image of the good society and of the chief means of constructing such a society."

9. To be clear, the notion of rational ideologies does not necessarily resolve all anomalies discovered by experimental psychologists. Rather, framing effects per se are consistent with rationality.

10. In view of the social dimension of ideology, it is worth mentioning Michael Bacharach's (1993) introduction of variable conceptual schemes into the game theoretic analysis of coordination.

11. This is a continuing problem for supporters of Converse's position; see, e.g., Jennings 1992 (435–36).

12. The analysis is based on Grafstein 1997a.

13. Charles Schultz (1989) makes an interesting observation connecting party divergence to the theme of ideology: parties may diverge because they have different economic models rather than different preferences. They would thus be in a position similar to that of the voters modeled in section V. John Roemer (1994) considers parties

that offer voters theories of how their positions translate into utility-relevant outcomes, but the parties in general do not believe their own theories.

14. This technique for shifting policy may create a link between public opinion and the president's actual policy, measured by the ideological position of the president's supporters in the legislature (Stimson, MacKuen, and Erikson 1995, 550).

15. In order to remain consistent with the established model we assume the two component functions for each voter are weighted so that the loss due to the deviation of an actual policy from that voter's ideal always exceeds the loss due to the deviation of the legislator's ideal.

16. Alesina and Cukierman (1990) examine the case in which voters also have incomplete information about party preferences. In this game, incumbent parties revert to ideological type in the second period but moderate their policies in the first. Thus the policy swing survives in this model. Many of our qualitative conclusions would likewise remain unchanged if voters have adaptive expectations based on past experience with the party's performance (e.g., Fiorina 1981; Hibbs 1987).

17. Since the strategy spaces of the voters and the executive are compact and convex, and each player's payoff is concave and continuous in the player's strategy, the technical preconditions for this result are satisfied.

18. This cost can introduce complicated game theoretic issues between the political parties (e.g., Persson and Tabellini 1990, 154–65).

19. Although they develop this idea much differently, George Rabinowitz and Elaine Stuart Macdonald (1989) posit an implied reference point with respect to which candidate positions are judged to lie in the right or wrong direction. In their language, the typical moderate voter would find the party positions posited in the text to be beyond the "region of acceptability." In Wlezien's (1995) "thermostatic model," the public prefers more or less of a policy based on the difference between an imputed ideal policy and actual policy, both of which can change over time. In Stimson's (1991, 18–23) different construction, when the policy variation induced by the electoral cycle is sufficiently outside the public's "zone of acquiescence," individual opinions shift.

20. John Zaller (1992) and Zaller and Feldman (1992), important exceptions, attribute volatility to the fact that different political considerations are elicited in different contexts. On their view, there is no simple attitude for survey research to recover since individuals have multiple and conflicting opinions. From a rational choice perspective, which assumes that respondents have coherent preferences and know the deductive consequences of their beliefs, it is difficult to imagine firm tests distinguishing the case in which a respondent is ascribed conflicting beliefs or preferences from the case in which the respondent lacks serious beliefs or preferences to elicit. Perhaps the conflicting responses cast doubt on the observer's original imputation of values.

21. For the association between ideology and inflation policy see, e.g., Hibbs 1987, Alesina and Sachs 1988, and Grier 1991.

22. Discussing Henry Chappell and William Keech's (1985) model of voter reactions to inflation, Nathaniel Beck (1991) argues that changes in utility-relevant outcomes are more important than their levels. One possible explanation for this finding is that stable outcomes, whether high or low, are more likely to have neutral economic

effects, so the public will be particularly sensitive to deviations from the status quo or, in a more sophisticated fashion, deviations from trend.

23. If instability were associated with unconstrained political thinking, one would expect it to covary inversely with education, a widely accepted proxy for cognitive sophistication. Interestingly, although Paul Sniderman, Richard Brody, and Philip Tetlock (1991) report an association between ideological level of thinking and education, Converse (1975, 103–4) finds that education's impact on the stability of opinion is "quite trifling" (but cf. Zaller 1992, 65).

24. More precisely, the restriction on d in the text rules out the possibility of exploding preferences so long as the exogenously determined value of P_{t-1} cooperates. A constrained policy environment is certainly consistent with context dependence. Incidentally, the implicit ideal point could easily be adjusted away from 0.

25. Returning to the preceding analysis, President Eisenhower's action in Little Rock may have placed him in a more extreme position relative to the electorate as a whole, thereby promoting the conditions for an attempted policy swing via a change in the legislature.

26. The parallel would be stronger if voter ideal points were normally rather than uniformly distributed, producing an even smaller proportion of stable opinions.

27. In order to highlight differences with the Downsian approach, I continue to ignore the costs of obtaining this information. Also, there may be a trade-off between success in prediction and the significance, in utility terms, of the ideology's categorizations. In this respect, all predictive comparisons discussed in the text carry an implicit ceteris paribus clause.

28. Cf. Converse 1966b (197): "it may be surmised that such perceptions instead of being interpreted as a function of a complex space which all voters perceive in the same way, may be interpreted as a function of simpler perceptions within spaces which differ from voter to voter." Moreover, Sartori (1976, 337) notes, "evidence that dimensions x, y and z are needed to account for a particular batch of preference orders does not assure that any of the actors are seeing in more than one dimension."

29. A more fully game theoretic approach would formalize the conditions under which a given party will reveal its true policy identity or type. The complications attending this analysis, not to mention the absence of a consensus among game theorists concerning the appropriate solution to these kinds of problems, suggest the approach taken in the text.

30. There is an alternative and important literature on reputation in which voters vote based on the incumbent's performance, which, in turn, is influenced by a trade-off between the advantages of holding office and the advantages of pursuing a policy the incumbent actually prefers (e.g., Ferejohn 1986). In Ferejohn's model, however, voters do not actually learn from this history; they judge in each period whether that period's performance has reached a particular level. It is interesting with regard to CEU theory that Ferejohn finds that when voters are heterogeneous, they can be exploited by politicians unless they vote sociotropically, that is, vote as if they are concerned with aggregate rather than individual outcomes.

31. Obviously, the ability to send either an accurate or an inaccurate signal introduces complicated game theoretic issues. But the problems are somewhat reduced

in the text insofar as the sender is only looking ahead one period in purely opportunistic fashion and the receiver judges the present announcement only in terms of its credibility given the entire history of past policies. Senders pay a penalty for making out-of-character announcements.

32. This use of R^2 is, of course, debatable, particularly given the distinct, albeit related, dependent variables; for a Bayesian analysis see Zellner 1971 (306–12).

33. This is why Bayes's Rule is not properly Bayes's Theorem: $\text{prob}(H \mid E) = \text{prob}(E \mid H)\text{prob}(H)/(\sum_i \text{prob}(E \mid H_i)\text{prob}(H_i))$ is a theorem, but $\text{prob}_{t+1}(H) = \text{prob}_t(H \mid E)$ is not.

Chapter 4

1. With 75 percent cooperators, cooperators and defectors do not receive equal utility. However, any resulting deviation from 75 percent tends to be corrected for reasons summarized in the text.

2. The optimality of evolutionary "invisible-hand" processes is a matter of debate (see, e.g., Dennett 1987, 1988).

3. Some group-oriented models of voter turnout however take precisely this tact (e.g., Uhlaner 1989a,b).

4. Another, more pragmatic problem for Frank's response is that when there is an iterated, small-scale game, the ordinary game theoretic analysis of supergames may suffice to deliver his results (e.g., Taylor 1987).

5. The role of ethnic and other group distinctions noted in chapter 2 may also play a role here. Kenneth Koford (1991) suggests the importance of cultural factors and heterogeneity generally in encouraging stability in the processes Frank (1988) models.

6. For character building in a rational choice context, see the work of Elster (1985c, 1984), who is more skeptical about the process than is Frank. For concerns about Elster's approach and the issue of character building generally, see also McClennen 1990 (231–38).

7. See Williams 1985 (36) for doubts about the underlying Aristotelian notion that moral virtue is not compartmentalized.

8. Frank, of course, may deny this possibility since a person with character, rather than an opportunist, is now making these calculations. Nevertheless, he also emphasizes the intuitive reasonableness of his approach, and for Margolis (1984), among others, intuition suggests a constant tug-of-war between even a good person's two natures.

9. Another way of putting this is that when playing those subsequent Prisoner's Dilemma games, agents need not ignore their earlier choices about tipping in deciding anew between cooperation and noncooperation. Thus as we will see in chapter 6 there is a connection between this form of strategic thinking over intertemporal choices and arguments by Machina (1989) and McClennen (1990) against the "consequentialist" assumptions underlying EU theory.

10. A self guided by causal EU considerations could make a decision-relevant prediction that future selves will save, but presumably it will not incorporate its own

behavior into its prediction unless that behavior causally influences future decisions. With respect to causal influence, one would think that current saving would, if anything, reduce future saving.

11. For empirical analysis, time plays a role even when uncertainty is apparently eliminated and there is only the direct maximization of a utility function U continuous in its arguments. As Howard Rachlin (1983, 377) observes, an agent's utility function with respect to actual behavior is always "integrated" over time when time is expended in consummating a choice. Technically, observers and subjects alike never witness the agent's acquisition of $U(x)$ outright but something more like $\int_b^a U[x(t)]dt$, where a is the time of consummation and b is the time of initiation and $a > b$. An individual waiting on line to vote, for example, has not actually voted.

12. I have corrected what is evidently a typo in Prelec's (1982) presentation of the probabilities in this example.

13. This form of intertemporal decision making is a specification of the general discounted utility model first developed by Samuelson (1937). The continuous version of this model for a choice made at time 0 for a stream of rewards $U(x)$ delivered through time T is $\int_0^T U[x(t)]e^{-\beta t}dt$, where $\beta > 0$ is the agent's discount parameter. Clearly one can set $x(t) = 0$ for periods representing a delay in the reward.

14. Under reasonable assumptions there is only the stark choice between exponential and hyperbolic discount functions (see Loewenstein and Prelec 1992, 125–26).

15. Ainslie (1992, 85–88) argues nonetheless that hyperbolic discounting is not necessarily less substantively rational than exponential discounting. When the agent's environment changes rapidly and therefore is difficult to predict, the "myopia" engendered by hyperbolic discounting can save the agent from excessive risk taking. By the same token, this same hyperbolic discounting will provide the agent in a relatively predictable environment with a more "objective" perception of long-term rewards, since hyperbolic functions eventually flatten out, leaving the utility of discounted rewards proportional to their undiscounted utility. Hyperbolic discounting, he concludes, may be an excellent compromise for an organism in an environment that is changing unpredictably in some respects and predictably in others.

16. One source Ainslie cites for the charge that diagnostic behavior is irrational, Quattrone and Tversky 1986, specifically analyzes the interagent "voters' illusion."

17. Albert S. Yee (1997) judges this attempt to be unsuccessful; for a broad response and defense of rational choice theory's original skepticism about norms see my 1997b.

18. I have attempted (1992) to answer related existential questions about rules.

Chapter 5

1. This qualification trades on the alleged distinction between risk, in which alternative states of the world are assigned specific probabilities, and uncertainty, in which probabilities cannot be assigned. Bayesians and others who deny this distinction would find this qualification unnecessary.

2. The policymaker chooses parameters rather than shocks because of the assumption that information is symmetric; alternatively one can think of policymakers as choosing the mean value of the policy output.

3. Commenting on the proper interpretation of mixed strategies, Ken Binmore (1988, 31) observes, "Jokes about game theory's recommending that finance ministers toss coins to decide precisely when to devalue are therefore misplaced: finance ministers can achieve exactly the same effect precisely as they always have—i.e., by using a committee of economic and financial experts."

4. William Roberds (1995) usefully characterizes the original policy ineffectiveness problem in terms of information structures. For Lucas, Sargent, and Wallace, the information set of private economic agents encompasses the information sets of the policymakers in both the pre- and posttransition regimes, while for critics (e.g., LeRoy 1995) the second group of policymakers has the informational advantage of knowing the specific realizations of the random variables on which economic agents have formed expectations. Yet the latter information structure does not place policymakers above the random processes that their own behavior realizes, so we must still confront the role of free choice in rational choice.

5. The most natural game theoretic counterpart to the issue raised in the text arises when considering whether players (e.g., policymakers) who are modeled as rational can nonetheless play irrationally, that is, play in ways the theory of the game assigns zero probability. If, on the one hand, this irrationality takes the form of unavoidable mistakes or "trembles," it can easily be incorporated in policy equations (e.g., money-supply rules) since these typically include random disturbances. In any event, the idea of mistakes raises no deep complications for the analysis in the text. Policymakers who make mistakes as well as policy are violating either their own instructions or those of their advisers. Indeed, Sargent and Wallace, as already noted, refer to the possibility that policymakers will behave "foolishly." If, on the other hand, ostensibly irrational behavior can be chosen, perhaps to signal future actions, these signals are part of the strategic character of the game accessible to all; they do not seem to create a special opportunity for advisers (see Roberds 1995 for the unclear relation between game theory and the policy paradox). Nevertheless, Binmore (1988, 1993) among others argues that this second interpretation reflects very profound problems with the definition of rationality and our ability to decide whether we or others satisfy it.

6. From our perspective the emphasis on statistics is also useful because CEU theory trivially reduces to EU theory under conditions of certainty, and, as Blinder's comments discussed previously suggest, some would find the true opportunities for free agency in uncertainty and even unpredictability (e.g., Jacobi 1993).

7. As Sargent (1984) notes, Sims disputes this characterization of his own position, taking a more optimistic view of "interventionist" policy analysis by assuming boundedly rational policymakers, not to mention causal "seams" in the policy model (e.g., 1986, 1987). Leeper and Sims (1994) also argue for optimism but partly by moving toward more structural models. Also, Sims does not rule out rare regime changes that are unpredictable using a historically estimated model. For present purposes, Sims's actual opinions are less important than having in place the stylized and, I believe, more consistent position Sargent attributes to him.

8. The formulation in terms of inequality rather than "greater than" reflects the possibility that Y_n may inhibit X_n rather than "produce" it.

9. For a clear introduction to Granger causality from a political science perspective, see Freeman 1983.

10. A white noise process is a set of serially uncorrelated zero-mean random variables with constant variance.

11. Kevin Hoover (personal communication) notes that this example does not necessarily bear on the policy ineffectiveness debate, since Y_t could represent nominal GNP without changing the (alleged) point of the example.

12. In a reduced form, no endogenous variables appear on the right-hand side of the equations.

13. The same issue is raised in a related way by Sargent (1981); Buiter (1984) addresses the case of suboptimal policy. Granger (1988) responds to both by questioning the realism of the assumptions leading to "Granger ineffectiveness."

14. James Hamilton (1994, 306–7) develops the following kind of illustration in the context of financial markets.

15. Recall from chapter 1 that, instead of Eells 1982, we follow Jeffrey's (1993) translation of causal conditions into rigid probability relations, which directly handles those cases in which causes operate entirely on the agent's actions. As noted in that chapter, the existence of a genuine common cause, by contrast, does create difficult complications.

16. Expectations may not be directly observable, but my point is analytical. Rational expectations do not require psychological introspection but, as shown earlier, are specified from the model and data assumed in the example.

17. See also Strotz and Wold 1960 (418). An alternative definition is predictability according to law (Zellner 1979), although "Everything depends on what 'predictability' and 'law' mean, and these two terms are at least as ambiguous . . . as is 'causality'" (Sims 1979, 105).

18. Simon (1957, 26) recognizes that these presuppositions lie behind the so-called zero restrictions his approach places on certain coefficients in the relevant system of equations.

19. Robert Stalnaker (1984) defends the possibility of inconsistency by allowing rational agents to have different, compartmentalized belief systems each of which is internally consistent. Stalnaker's proposal, however, has been strongly criticized by Hartry Field (1986, 442–47); cf. also the discussion of belief systems in chapter 3.

20. Thus see Tsebelis's (1990, 68) characterization of the probabilities in terms of "instruction" and "retaliation."

21. Some descriptions of the Prisoner's Dilemma incorporate payoffs that preclude the strategy of taking turns playing the role of sucker, but as we see this extra step is unnecessary.

Chapter 6

1. The citations are legion; see, e.g., Machina 1987.

2. As we saw in chapter 3, Rabinowitz and Macdonald (1989) also use reference points in their directional theory of voting.

3. This example, in turn, is a dramatic rendering of one invented by Peter Diamond (1967). For a more recent discussion of it, see Simon Grant (1995).

4. Roughly, one lottery stochastically dominates another when the probabilities of the former place greater weight on more preferred outcomes (for a formal definition see, e.g., Laffont 1989, 32–33). Machina wants to justify the nonlinearity of the mother's calculus without permitting her to make a stochastically dominated choice since the latter is not a particularly controversial requirement; Teddy Seidenfeld (1988), for example, treats the choice of stochastically dominated prospects as tantamount to incoherence. On the other hand, in order to prevent the agent from violating stochastic dominance under Prospect Theory, a well-known alternative to EU theory, Daniel Kahneman and Amos Tversky (1979) are forced simply to stipulate that agents eliminate "transparent" violations (1987, 79–81).

5. For example, what if a player winds up on a branch of the extensive form to which the theory of the game governing his play in the normal form assigns zero probability? Since this outcome, zero prior probability notwithstanding, has implications for the preceding choices made by other players it may also have implications for his expectations about their subsequent play.

6. The general strategy of redefining consequences to rationalize the agent's different treatment of them has been a lightning rod for critics, who see it as the royal road to tautology (Samuelson 1952). Donald Davidson (1980, 268–75) provides an important response: although behavior is the resultant of both the agent's utility function and beliefs, utility and belief, in turn, must be jointly imputed to the agent on the basis of behavior. Therefore, they cannot in general be independently confirmed by the behavior. This lesson, I hope, is driven home by chapter 3, which attempts to transcend an ongoing debate on ideology in which both sides assume there is a clear fact of the matter in specifying an agent's conceptual scheme.

7. The emphasis on gains and losses is, of course, not the sole difference between Prospect Theory and (C)EU theory. Chapter 3 offers a CEU rationalization of framing effects, which Prospect Theory also emphasizes, while section II of the present chapter discusses nonlinearity in probabilities, still another important component.

References

Achen, Christopher H. 1975. "Mass Political Attitudes and the Survey Response." *American Political Science Review* 69:1218–31.

Achen, Christopher H. 1992. "Social Psychology, Demographic Variables, and Linear Regression: Breaking the Iron Triangle in Voting Research." *Political Behavior* 14:195–211.

Ainslie, George. 1992. *Picoeconomics.* Cambridge: Cambridge University Press.

Ainsworth, Scott, and Itai Sened. 1993. "The Role of Lobbyists: Entrepreneurs with Two Audiences." *American Journal of Political Science* 37:834–66.

Alesina, Alberto, and Alex Cukierman. 1990. "The Politics of Ambiguity." *Quarterly Journal of Economics* 105:829–50.

Alesina, Alberto, and Howard Rosenthal. 1995. *Partisan Politics, Divided Government, and the Economy.* Cambridge: Cambridge University Press.

Alesina, Alberto, and Jeffrey Sachs. 1988. "Political Parties and the Business Cycle in the United States, 1948–1984." *Journal of Money, Credit and Banking* 20:63–87.

Althusser, Louis. 1971. *Lenin and Philosophy and Other Essays.* New York: Monthly Review Press.

Aumann, Robert. 1976. "Agreeing to Disagree." *Annals of Statistics* 4:1236–39.

Aumann, Robert. 1987. "Correlated Equilibrium as an Expression of Bayesian Rationality." *Econometrica* 55:1–18.

Aumann, Robert, and Adam Brandenburger. 1995. "Epistemic Conditions for Nash Equilibrium." *Econometrica* 63:1161–80.

Austen-Smith, David, and Jack Wright. 1992. "Competitive Lobbying for a Legislator's Vote." *Social Choice and Welfare* 9:229–57.

Axelrod, Robert. 1984. *The Evolution of Cooperation.* New York: Basic Books.

Bacharach, Michael. 1993. "Variable Universe Games." In *Frontiers of Game Theory,* ed. Ken Binmore, Alan Kirman, and Piero Tani. Cambridge: MIT Press.

Banton, Michael. 1983. *Racial and Ethnic Competition.* Cambridge: Cambridge University Press.

Barro, Robert J., and David B. Gordon. 1983a. "Rules, Discretion and Reputation in a Model of Monetary Policy." *Journal of Monetary Economics* 12:101–21.

Barro, Robert J., and David B. Gordon. 1983b. "A Positive Theory of Monetary Policy in a Natural Rate Model." *Journal of Political Economy* 91:589–610.

Barry, Brian M. 1970. *Sociologists, Economists and Democracy.* London: Macmillan.

Bates, Robert H. 1974. "Ethnic Competition and Modernization in Contemporary Africa." *Comparative Political Studies* 6:457–84.

Beck, Nathaniel. 1975. "The Paradox of Minimax Regret." *American Political Science Review* 69:918.

Beck, Nathaniel. 1991. "The Economy and Presidential Approval: An Information Theoretic Perspective." In *Economics and Politics,* ed. Helmut Norpoth, Michael S. Lewis-Beck, and Jean-Dominique Lafay. Ann Arbor: University of Michigan Press.

Becker, Gary S. 1976. *The Economic Approach to Human Behavior.* Chicago: University of Chicago Press.

Bem, Daryl J. 1978. "Self-Perception Theory." In *Cognitive Theories in Social Psychology,* ed. Leonard Berkowitz. New York: Academic Press.

Binmore, Ken. 1988. "Modeling Rational Players: Part II." *Economics and Philosophy* 4:9–55.

Binmore, Ken. 1993. "De-Bayesing Game Theory." In *Frontiers of Game Theory,* ed. Ken Binmore, Alan Kirman, and Piero Tani. Cambridge: MIT Press.

Blinder, Alan S. 1984. "Discussion." *American Economic Review* 74:417–19.

Boyd, Robert, and Peter Richerson. 1985. *Culture and the Evolutionary Process.* Chicago: University of Chicago Press.

Brennan, Timothy J. 1991. "The Trouble with Norms." In *Social Norms and Economic Institutions,* ed. Kenneth J. Koford and Jeffrey B. Miller. Ann Arbor: University of Michigan Press.

Broome, John. 1990. "Should a Rational Agent Maximize Expected Utility?" In *The Limits of Rationality,* ed. Karen Schweers Cook and Margaret Levi. Chicago: University of Chicago Press.

Broome, John. 1991a. *Weighing Goods.* Oxford: Basil Blackwell.

Broome, John. 1991b. "Rationality and the Sure Thing Principle." In *Thoughtful Economic Man,* ed. J. Gay Tulip Meeks. Cambridge: Cambridge University Press.

Buchanan, Allen. 1982. *Marx and Justice.* Totowa, NJ: Rowman and Littlefield.

Buchanan, James. 1979. *What Should Economists Do?* Indianapolis: Liberty Press.

Buiter, William H. 1984. "Granger Causality and Policy Effectiveness." *Economica* 51:151–62.

Burnham, Walter Dean. 1980. "The Appearance and Disappearance of the American Voter." In *Electoral Participation: A Comparative Analysis,* ed. Richard Rose. Beverly Hills: Sage.

Butler, David, and Donald Stokes. 1974. *Political Change in Britain.* New York: St. Martin's.

Campbell, Richmond, and Lanning Sowden, eds. 1985. *Paradoxes of Rationality and Cooperation.* Vancouver: University of British Columbia Press.

Cartwright, Nancy. 1989. *Nature's Capacities and their Measurement.* Oxford: Clarendon Press.

Chamberlain, Gary, and Michael Rothschild. 1981. "A Note on the Probability of Casting a Decisive Vote." *Journal of Economic Theory* 25:152–62.

Chappell, Henry W., Jr., and William R. Keech. 1985. "A New View of Political Accountability for Economic Performance." *American Political Science Review* 79:10–27.

Chow, Gregory C. 1975. *The Analysis and Control of Dynamic Economic Systems.* New York: Wiley.

Coleman, James S. 1990. *Foundations of Social Theory.* Cambridge: Harvard University Press.

Congleton, Roger D. 1991. "Ideological Conviction and Persuasion in the Rent-Seeking Society." *Journal of Public Economics* 44:65–86.

Conover, Pamela Johnston, and Stanley Feldman. 1981. "The Origins and Meaning of Liberal/Conservative Self-Identifications." *American Journal of Political Science* 25:617–45.

Conover, Pamela Johnston, and Stanley Feldman. 1989. "Candidate Perception in an Ambiguous World: Campaigns, Cues and Inference Processes." *American Journal of Political Science* 33:912–40.

Converse, Philip E. 1964. "The Nature of Belief Systems in Mass Publics." In *Ideology and Discontent,* ed. David Apter. Glencoe, IL: Free Press.

Converse, Philip E. 1966a. "Information Flow and the Stability of Partisan Attitudes." In *Elections and the Political Order,* ed. Angus Campbell, Philip E. Converse, Warren E. Miller, and Donald Stokes. New York: Wiley.

Converse, Philip E. 1966b. "The Problem of Party Distances in Models of Voting Change." In *The Electoral Process,* ed. M. Kent Jennings and L. Harmon Zeigler. Englewood Cliffs, NJ: Prentice-Hall.

Converse, Philip E. 1975. "Public Opinion and Voting Behavior." In *The Handbook of Political Science,* ed. Fred I. Greenstein and Nelson W. Polsby. Reading, MA: Addison-Wesley.

Converse, Philip E., and Gregory B. Markus. 1979. "Plus Ça Change . . . : The New CPS Election Study Panel." *American Political Science Review* 79:32–49.

Cooley, Thomas F. 1985. "*Individual Forecasting and Aggregate Outcomes:* A Review Essay." *Journal of Monetary Economics* 15:255–66.

Cooley, Thomas F., and Stephen F. LeRoy. 1985. "Atheoretical Macroeconometrics: A Critique." *Journal of Monetary Economics* 16:238–308.

Craine, Roger, and Gikas A. Hardouvelis. 1983. "Are Rational Expectations for Real?" *Greek Economic Review* 5:5–32.

Dalton, Russell J. 1988. *Citizen Politics in Western Democracies.* Chatham, NJ: Chatham House.

Davidson, Donald. 1980. *Essays on Actions and Events.* Oxford: Oxford University Press.

Davidson, Donald. 1984. *Truth and Interpretation.* Oxford: Oxford University Press.

Dawes, Robyn M. 1990. "The Potential Nonfalsity of the False Consensus Effect." In *Insight in Decision Making,* ed. Robin M. Hogarth. Chicago: University of Chicago Press.

Dawes, Robyn M., Alphons J. C. van de Kragt, and John M. Orbell. 1990. "Cooperation for the Benefit of Us—Not Me or My Conscience." In *Beyond Self-Interest,* ed. Jane J. Mansbridge. Chicago: University of Chicago Press.

Debreu, Gerard. 1952. "A Social Equilibrium Existence Theorem." *Proceedings of the National Academy of Sciences* 38:886–93.

DeGroot, Morris H. 1970. *Optimal Statistical Decisions.* New York: McGraw-Hill.

Dennett, Daniel C. 1984. *Elbow Room.* Cambridge: MIT Press.

Dennett, Daniel C. 1987. *The Intentional Stance.* Cambridge: MIT Press.

Dennett, Daniel C. 1988. "Précis of *The Intentional Stance.*" *Behavioral and the Brain Sciences* 11:495–505.

Diaconis, Persi, and Sandy L. Zabell. 1982. "Updating Subjective Probability." *Journal of the American Statistical Association* 77:822–30.

Diamond, Peter. 1967. "Cardinal Welfare, Individualistic Ethics, and Interpersonal Comparisons of Utility: Comment." *Journal of Political Economy* 75:765–66.

Dougan, William R., and Michael C. Munger. 1989. "The Rationality of Ideology." *Journal of Law and Economics* 32:119–42.

Downs, Anthony. 1957. *An Economic Theory of Democracy.* New York: Harper & Row.

Durr, Robert. 1993. "What Moves Policy Sentiment?" *American Political Science Review* 87:158–70.

Edel, Matthew. 1979. "A Note on Collective Action, Marxism, and the Prisoner's Dilemma." *Journal of Economic Issues* 13:751–61.

Eells, Ellery. 1982. *Rational Decision and Causality.* Cambridge: Cambridge University Press.

Eells, Ellery. 1985. "Levi's 'The Wrong Box'." *Journal of Philosophy* 82:91–104.

Elster, Jon. 1984. *Ulysses and the Sirens.* Cambridge: Cambridge University Press.

Elster, Jon. 1985a. *Making Sense of Marx.* Cambridge: Cambridge University Press.

Elster, Jon. 1985b. "Rationality, Morality, and Collective Action." *Ethics* 96:136–55.

Elster, Jon. 1985c. *Sour Grapes.* Cambridge: Cambridge University Press.

Elster, Jon. 1989a. *Solomonic Judgements.* Cambridge: Cambridge University Press.

Elster, Jon. 1989b. *The Cement of Society.* Cambridge: Cambridge University Press.

Elster, Jon. 1989c. "Social Norms and Economic Theory." *Journal of Economic Perspectives* 3:99–117.

Enelow, James M. 1992. "An Expanded Approach to Analyzing Policy-Minded Candidates." *Public Choice* 74:425–45.

Enelow, James M., and Melvin J. Hinich. 1984. *The Spatial Theory of Voting.* Cambridge: Cambridge University Press.

Enelow, James M., and Melvin J. Hinich. 1989. "A General Probabilistic Spatial Theory of Elections." *Public Choice* 61:101–13.

Engle, Robert F., David F. Hendry, and Jean-Francois Richard. 1983. "Exogeneity." *Econometrica* 51:277–304.

Erikson, Robert S., Norman R. Luttbeg, and Kent L. Tedin. 1988. *American Public Opinion: Its Origins and Impact.* New York: Macmillan.

Feldman, Stanley. 1988. "Structure and Consistency in Public Opinion: The Role of Core Beliefs and Values." *American Journal of Political Science* 32:416–40.

Ferejohn, John. 1986. "Incumbent Performance and Electoral Control." *Public Choice* 50:5–26.

Ferejohn, John A., and Morris P. Fiorina. 1974. "The Paradox of Not Voting: A Decision-Theoretic Analysis." *American Political Science Review* 68:525–36.

Festinger, Leon. 1957. *A Theory of Cognitive Dissonance.* Stanford: Stanford University Press.

Festinger, Leon, and James M. Carlsmith. 1959. "Cognitive Consequences of Forced Compliance." *Journal of Abnormal and Social Psychology* 58:203–10. Cited in Daryl J. Bem, "Self-Perception Theory," in *Cognitive Theories in Social Psychology,* ed. Leonard Berkowitz (New York: Academic Press, 1978); and in William Samuelson and Richard Zeckhauser, "Status Quo Bias in Decision Making," *Journal of Risk and Uncertainty* 1 (1988): 7–59.

Field, Hartry H. 1977. "Logic, Meaning, and Conceptual Role," *Journal of Philosophy* 84:379–409.

Field, Hartry H. 1986. "Critical Notice: Robert Stalnaker, *Inquiry.*" *Philosophy of Science* 53:425–48.

Finkel, Steven E., Edward N. Muller, and Karl-Dieter Opp. 1989. "Personal Influence, Collective Rationality, and Mass Political Action." *American Political Science Review* 83:885–903.

Fiorina, Morris P. 1981. *Retrospective Voting in American National Elections.* New Haven: Yale University Press.

Fishburn, Peter C. 1988. *Nonlinear Preference and Utility Theory.* Baltimore: Johns Hopkins University Press.

Fisher, R. A. 1959. *Smoking: The Cancer Controversy.* London: Oliver and Boyd.

Fiske, Susan T., and Shelley E. Taylor. 1984. *Social Cognition.* Reading, MA: Addison-Wesley.

Frank, Robert H. 1988. *Passions within Reason.* New York: Norton.

Frank, Robert H. 1989. "If *Homo Economicus* Could Choose His Own Utility Function, Would He Want One with a Conscience? Reply." *American Economic Review* 79:594–96.

Freeman, John R. 1983. "Granger Causality and the Time Series Analysis of Political Relationships." *American Journal of Political Science* 27:327–58.

Friedman, Milton, and Leonard J. Savage. 1948. "The Utility Analysis of Choices Involving Risk." *Journal of Political Economy* 56:279–305.

Gartner, Scott Sigmund, and Gary M. Segura. 1997. "Appearances Can Be Deceptive: Self-Selection, Social Group Identification, and Political Mobilization." *Rationality and Society* 9:131–61.

Geertz, Clifford. 1963. "The Integrative Revolution: Primordial Sentiments and Civil Politics in the New States." In *Old Societies and New States,* ed. Clifford Geertz. New York: Free Press.

Geertz, Clifford. 1964. "Ideology as a Cultural System." In *Ideology and Discontent,* ed. David Apter. Glencoe, IL: Free Press.

Gerber, Elisabeth R., and John E. Jackson. 1993. "Endogenous Preferences and the Study of Institutions." *American Political Science Review* 87:639–56.

Gibbard, Allan, and William L. Harper. 1978. "Counterfactuals and Two Kinds of Expected Utility." In *Foundations and Applications of Decision Theory,* ed. Clifford A. Hooker, James L. Leach, and Edward F. McClennen. Dordrecht, Holland: D. Reidel.

Glazer, Amihai. 1990. "The Strategy of Candidate Ambiguity." *American Political Science Review* 84:237–41.

Glymour, Clark, Richard Scheines, Peter Spirtes, and Kevin Kelly. 1987. *Discovering Causal Structure.* Orlando: Academic Press.

Godwin, Kenneth, and Robert Cameron Mitchell. 1982. "Rational Models, Collective Goods, and Nonelectoral Political Behavior." *Western Political Quarterly* 35:161–81.

Goodman, Nelson. 1983. *Fact, Fiction, and Forecast.* Cambridge: Harvard University Press.

Grafstein, Robert. 1991. "An Evidential Decision Theory of Turnout." *American Journal of Political Science* 35:989–1010.

Grafstein, Robert. 1992. *Institutional Realism: Social and Political Constraints on Rational Actors.* New Haven: Yale University Press.

Grafstein, Robert. 1995. "Group Identity, Rationality and Electoral Mobilization." *Journal of Theoretical Politics* 7:181–200.

Grafstein, Robert. 1997a. "Rationality in a Political-Economic Environment." *Economics and Politics* 9:151–72.

Grafstein, Robert. 1997b. "Comment." *Journal of Politics* 59:1040–47.

Gramsci, Antonio. 1971. *Selections from the Prison Notebooks.* New York: International Publishers.

Granato, Jim, and Renée M. Smith. 1994. "Exogeneity, Inference, and Granger Causality: Part 1, The Stationary Case." *Political Methodologist* 5:24–28.

Granger, C. W. J. 1969. "Investigating Causal Relations by Econometric Models and Cross-Spectral Methods." *Econometrica* 37:424–38.

Granger, C. W. J. 1980. "Testing for Causality: A Personal Viewpoint." *Journal of Economic Dynamics and Control* 2:329–352.

Granger, C. W. J. 1988. "Some Recent Developments in the Concept of Causality." *Journal of Econometrics* 39:199–211.

Grant, Simon. 1995. "Subjective Probability without Monotonicity: Or How Machina's Mom May Also Be Probabilistically Sophisticated." *Econometrica* 63:159–89.

Green, Donald P., and Ian Shapiro. 1994. *Pathologies of Rational Choice Theory.* New Haven: Yale University Press.

Grier, Kevin B. 1991. "Congressional Influence on U.S. Monetary Policy." *Journal of Monetary Economics* 28:201–20.

Hamilton, James D. 1994. *Time Series Analysis.* Princeton: Princeton University Press.

Hammond, Peter. 1988. "Consequentialist Foundations for Expected Utility." *Theory and Decision* 25:25–78.

Hampton, Jean. 1991. "Review of Jon Elster, *The Cement of Society.*" *Journal of Philosophy* 88:728–38.

Hampton, Jean. 1994. "The Failure of Expected Utility Theory as a Theory of Reason." *Economics and Philosophy* 10:195–242.

Hardin, Russell. 1982. *Collective Action.* Baltimore: Resources for the Future.

Hardin, Russell. 1995. *One for All.* Princeton: Princeton University Press.

Harless, David W., and Colin F. Camerer. 1994. "The Predictive Utility of Generalized Expected Utility Theory." *Econometrica* 62:1251–89.

Harper, William L. 1985. "Ratifiability and Causal Decision Theory." *PSA 1984* 2:213–28.

Harper, William L. 1993. "Causal and Evidential Expectations in Strategic Settings." *Philosophical Topics* 21:79–97.

Harrington, Joseph E., Jr. 1989. "If *Homo Economicus* Could Choose His Own Utility Function, Would He Want One with a Conscience? Comment." *American Economic Review* 79:588–93.

Hechter, Michael. 1975. *Internal Colonialism.* London: Routledge & Kegan Paul.

Hechter, Michael. 1978. "Group Formation and the Cultural Division of Labor." *American Journal of Sociology* 84:293–318.

Hechter, Michael. 1987. *Principles of Group Solidarity.* Berkeley: University of California Press.

Hechter, Michael. 1990. "On the Inadequacy of Game Theory for the Solution of Real-World Collective Action Problems." In *The Limits of Rationality,* ed. Karen Schweers Cook and Margaret Levi. Chicago: University of Chicago Press.

Heckathorn, Douglas D. 1989. "Collective Action and the Second-Order Free Rider Problem." *Rationality and Society* 1:78–100.

Herrnstein, Richard J. 1961. "Relative and Absolute Strengths of Response as a Function of Frequency of Reinforcement." *Journal of the Experimental Analysis of Behavior* 4:267–72.

Herrnstein, Richard J., and Dražen Prelec. 1991. "Melioration: A Theory of Distributed Choice." *Journal of Economic Perspectives* 5:137–56.

Herrnstein, Richard J., and Dražen Prelec. 1992. "Rational Addiction." In *Choice over Time,* ed. George Loewenstein and Jon Elster. New York: Russell Sage.

Hey, John D. 1993. "Rationality Is as Rationality Does." In *The Economics of Rationality,* ed. Bill Gerard. London: Routledge.

Hibbs, Douglas A., Jr. 1987. *The Political Economy of Industrial Democracies.* Cambridge: Harvard University Press.

Higgs, Robert. 1987. *Crisis and Leviathan.* New York: Oxford University Press.

Hinich, Melvin J. 1977. "Equilibrium in Spatial Voting: The Median Result Is an Artifact." *Journal of Economic Theory* 16:208–19.

Hinich, Melvin J., and Michael C. Munger. 1992. "A Spatial Theory of Ideology." *Journal of Theoretical Politics* 41:5–30.

Hinich, Melvin J., and Michael C. Munger. 1994. *Ideology and the Theory of Political Choice.* Ann Arbor: University of Michigan Press.

Hofstadter, Douglas R. 1983. "The Calculus of Cooperation Is Tested through a Lottery." *Scientific American* 248:14–28.

Holland, Paul W. 1986. "Rejoinder." *Journal of the American Statistical Association* 81:968–70.

Hoover, Kevin D. 1988. *The New Classical Macroeconomics.* Oxford: Basil Blackwell.

Hoover, Kevin D. 1990. "The Logic of Causal Inference." *Economics and Philosophy* 6:207–34.

Horowitz, Donald L. 1985. *Ethnic Groups in Conflict.* Berkeley and Los Angeles: University of California Press.

Iyengar, Shanto. 1991. *Is Anyone Responsible? How Television Frames Political Issues.* Chicago: University of Chicago Press.

Jacobi, N. 1993. "Newcomb's Paradox: A Realist Resolution." *Theory and Decision* 35:1–17.

Jacobs, Rodney L., Edward E. Leamer, and Michael P. Ward. 1979. "Difficulties with Testing for Causation." *Economic Inquiry* 17:401–13.

Jeffrey, Richard C. 1981. "The Logic of Decision Defended." *Synthese* 48:473–92.

Jeffrey, Richard C. 1983. *The Logic of Decision.* Chicago: University of Chicago Press.

Jeffrey, Richard C. 1988. "How to Probabilize a Newcomb Problem." In *Probability and Causality,* ed. James H. Fetzer. Dordrecht, Holland: D. Reidel.

Jeffrey, Richard C. 1992. *Probability and the Art of Judgment.* Cambridge: Cambridge University Press.

Jeffrey, Richard C. 1993. "Causality in the Logic of Decision." *Philosophical Topics* 21:139–51.

Jennings, M. Kent. 1992. "Ideological Thinking among Mass Publics and Political Elites." *Public Opinion Quarterly* 56:419–41.

Kadane, Joseph B. 1992. "Healthy Skepticism as an Expected-Utility Explanation of the Phenomena of Allais and Ellsberg." *Theory and Decision* 32:57–64.

Kadane, Joseph B., ed. 1984. *Robustness of Bayesian Analyses.* Amsterdam: North-Holland.

Kahneman, Daniel, Jack L. Knetsch, and Richard H. Thaler. 1987. "Fairness and the Assumptions of Economics." In *Rational Choice,* ed. Robin M. Hogarth and Melvin W. Reder. Chicago: University of Chicago Press.

Kahneman, Daniel, and Amos Tversky. 1979. "Prospect Theory: An Analysis of Decision under Risk." *Econometrica* 47:263–91.

Kalt, Joseph P., and Mark A. Zupan. 1984. "Capture and Ideology in the Economic Theory of Politics." *American Economic Review* 74:279–300.

Keech, William R. 1995. *Economic Politics.* Cambridge: Cambridge University Press.

Kiewiet, D. Roderick. 1983. *Macroeconomics and Micropolitics.* Chicago: University of Chicago Press.

Kinder, Donald R. 1983. "Diversity and Complexity in American Public Opinion." In *Political Science: The State of the Discipline,* ed. Ada Finifter. Washington, DC: American Political Science Association.

Klein, Richard. 1993. *Cigarettes Are Sublime.* Durham: Duke University Press.

Koford, Kenneth J. 1991. "Biological versus Cultural Indicators of Ability and Honesty." In *Social Norms and Economic Institutions,* ed. Kenneth J. Koford and Jeffrey B. Miller. Ann Arbor: University of Michigan Press.

Koford, Kenneth J., and Jeffrey B. Miller, eds. 1991. *Social Norms and Economic Institutions.* Ann Arbor: University of Michigan Press.

Kreps, David M. 1990. "Corporate Culture and Economic Theory." In *Perspectives on Positive Political Economy,* ed. James E. Alt and Kenneth A. Shepsle. Cambridge: Cambridge University Press.

Kreps, David M., and Robert Wilson. 1982. "Reputation and Imperfect Information." *Journal of Economic Theory* 27:253–79.

Kriegel, Annie. 1972. *The French Communists,* trans. Elaine P. Halperin. Chicago: University of Chicago Press.

Kripke, Saul A. 1982. *Wittgenstein on Rules and Private Language.* Cambridge: Harvard University Press.

Kyburg, Henry E., Jr. 1988. "Powers." In *Causation in Decision, Belief Change, and Statistics,* ed. William L. Harper and Bryan Skyrms. Dordrecht, Holland: Kluwer.

Laffont, Jean-Jacques. 1989. *The Economics of Uncertainty and Information.* Cambridge: MIT Press.

Lakoff, George. 1987. *Women, Fire, and Dangerous Things.* Chicago: University of Chicago Press.

Lancaster, Kelvin. 1973. "The Dynamic Inefficiency of Capitalism." *Journal of Political Economy* 81:1092–1109.

Lane, Robert E. 1962. *Political Ideology.* New York: Free Press.

Leamer, Edward E. 1985. "Vector Autoregressions for Causal Inference?" In *Understanding Monetary Regimes,* ed. Karl Brunner and Allan H. Meltzer. Amsterdam: North-Holland.

Ledyard, John O. 1984. "The Pure Theory of Large Two-Candidate Elections." *Public Choice* 44:7–41.

Leeper, Eric M., and Christopher A. Sims. 1994. "Toward a Modern Macroeconomic Model Useful for Policy Analysis." In *NBER Macroeconomics Annual 1994,* ed. Stanley Fischer and Julio J. Rotemberg. Cambridge: MIT Press.

Leifer, Eric M. 1981. "Competing Models of Political Mobilization: The Role of Ethnic Ties." *American Journal of Sociology* 87:23–47.

LeRoy, Stephen F. 1995. "On Policy Regimes." In *Macroeconometrics,* ed. Kevin D. Hoover. Boston: Kluwer.

Levi, Isaac. 1975. "Newcomb's Many Problems." *Theory and Decision* 6:161–75.

Levi, Isaac. 1982. "A Note on Newcombmania." *Journal of Philosophy* 79:337–42.

Levi, Isaac. 1983. "The Wrong Box." *Journal of Philosophy* 80:534–42.

Levi, Isaac. 1992. "Feasibility." In *Knowledge, Belief, and Strategic Interaction,* ed. Cristina Bicchieri and Maria Luisa Dalla Chiara. Cambridge: Cambridge University Press.

Lewis, David K. 1969. *Convention: A Philosophical Study.* Cambridge: Harvard University Press.

Lewis, David K. 1979. "Prisoners' Dilemma Is a Newcomb Problem." *Philosophy and Public Affairs* 88:235–40.

Lewis, David K. 1983. "Levi against U-Maximization." *Journal of Philosophy* 80:531–34.

Lichbach, Mark Irving. 1996. *The Cooperator's Dilemma.* Ann Arbor: University of Michigan Press.

Lippmann, Walter. 1965. *Public Opinion.* New York: Free Press.

Lipset, Seymour Martin. 1960. *Political Man.* Garden City, NY: Doubleday.

Loewenstein, George. 1992. "The Fall and Rise of Psychological Explanations in the Economics of Intertemporal Choice." In *Choice over Time,* ed. George Loewenstein and Jon Elster. New York: Russell Sage.

Loewenstein, George, and Dražen Prelec. 1992. "Anomalies in Intertemporal Choice: Evidence and Interpretation." In *Choice over Time,* ed. George Loewenstein and Jon Elster. New York: Russell Sage.

Lohmann, Suzanne. 1993. "A Signaling Model of Informative and Manipulative Political Action." *American Political Science Review* 87:319–33.

Lucas, Robert E., Jr. 1981. *Studies in Business-Cycle Theory.* Cambridge: MIT Press.

Lucas, Robert E., Jr. 1987. *Models of Business Cycles.* Oxford: Blackwell.

Luce, R. Duncan, and Howard Raiffa. 1957. *Games and Decisions.* New York: Wiley.

Lumsden, Charles, and E. O. Wilson. 1981. *Genes, Mind, and Culture.* Cambridge: Harvard University Press.

Machina, Mark J. 1987. "Choice under Uncertainty: Problems Solved and Unsolved." *Journal of Economic Perspectives* 1:121–54.

Machina, Mark J. 1989. "Dynamic Consistency and Non-Expected Utility Models of Choice under Uncertainty." *Journal of Economic Literature* 27:1622–68.

Mackie, J. L. 1980. *The Cement of the Universe.* Oxford: Clarendon Press.

Majeski, Stephen J. 1990. "An Alternative Approach to the Generation and Maintenance of Norms." In *The Limits of Rationality,* ed. Karen Schweers Cook and Margaret Levi. Chicago: University of Chicago Press.

Mankiw, N. Gregory. 1986. "Comment." In *NBER Macroeconomics Annual 1986,* ed. Stanley Fischer. Cambridge: MIT Press.

Manley, John F. 1983. "Neo-Pluralism: A Class Analysis of Pluralism I and Pluralism II." *American Political Science Review* 77:368–83.

Mansbridge, Jane J., ed. *Beyond Self-Interest.* Chicago: University of Chicago Press.

Margolis, Howard. 1984. *Selfishness, Altruism, and Rationality.* Chicago: University of Chicago Press.

Margolis, Michael, and Gary A. Mauser, eds. 1989. *Manipulating Public Opinion.* Pacific Grove, CA: Brooks/Cole.

Markowitz, Harry. 1952. "The Utility of Wealth." *Journal of Political Economy* 60:151–58.

Marx, Karl. 1967. *Capital.* Vol. 1. New York: International Publishers.

Marx, Karl, and Frederick Engels. 1968. *Selected Works.* New York: International Publishers.

Maynard Smith, John. 1982. *Evolution and the Theory of Games.* Cambridge: Cambridge University Press.

McClennen, Edward F. 1990. *Rationality and Dynamic Choice.* Cambridge: Cambridge University Press.

McKelvey, Richard D., and Thomas R. Palfrey. 1992. "An Experimental Study of the Centipede Game." *Econometrica* 60:803–36.

Mehrling, Perry G. 1986. "A Classical Model of Class Struggle: A Game Theoretic Approach." *Journal of Political Economy* 94:1280–1303.

Melson, Robert, and Howard Wolpe. 1970. "Modernization and the Politics of Communalism: A Theoretical Perspective." *American Political Science Review* 64:1112–30.

Milgrom, Paul, and Nancy Stokey. 1982. "Information, Trade and Common Knowledge." *Journal of Economic Theory* 26:177–227.

Miller, Arthur H., Patricia Gurin, Gerald Gurin, and Oksana Malanchuk. 1981. "Group Consciousness and Political Participation." *American Journal of Political Science* 25:494–511.

Miller, Nicholas R. 1996. "Majority Rule and Minority Interests." In *Nomos 38: Political Order,* ed. Ian Shapiro and Russell Hardin. New York: NYU Press.

Monroe, Kristen Renwick. 1996. *The Heart of Altruism.* Princeton: Princeton University Press.

Morton, Rebecca. 1987. "A Group Majority Voting Model of Public Good Provision." *Social Choice and Welfare* 4:117–31.

Morton, Rebecca. 1991. "Groups in Rational Turnout Models." *American Journal of Political Science* 35:758–76.

Munier, Bertrand R. 1988. "A Guide to Decision Making under Uncertainty." In *Risk, Decision and Rationality,* ed. Bertrand R. Munier. Dordrecht, Holland: D. Reidel.

Nadeau, Richard, Richard G. Niemi, and Timothy Amato. 1994. "Expectations and Preferences in British General Elections." *American Political Science Review* 88:371–83.

Nagel, Thomas. 1979. *Mortal Questions.* Cambridge: Cambridge University Press.

Nelson, Dale C. 1979. "Ethnicity and Socioeconomic Status as Sources of Participation: The Case for Ethnic Political Culture." *American Political Science Review* 73:1024–38.

Nie, Norman H., and Kristi Andersen. 1974. "Mass Belief Systems Revisited: Political Change and Attitude Structure." *Journal of Politics* 36:540–87.

Nie, Norman H., Sidney Verba, and John R. Petrocik. 1976. *The Changing American Voter.* Cambridge: Harvard University Press.

Nietzsche, Friedrich. 1954. *The Philosophy of Nietzsche,* trans. Thomas Common. New York: Random House.

Nisbett, Richard E., and Lee Ross. 1980. *Human Inference.* Englewood Cliffs, NJ: Prentice-Hall.

Nordhaus, William. 1975. "The Political Business Cycle." *Review of Economic Studies* 42:169–90.

North, Douglass C. 1990. *Institutions, Institutional Change and Economic Performance.* Cambridge: Cambridge University Press.

Nozick, Robert. 1969. "Newcomb's Problem and Two Principles of Choice." In *Essays in Honor of C. G. Hempel,* ed. Nicholas Rescher. Dordrecht, Holland: D. Reidel.

Nozick, Robert. 1974. *Anarchy, State, and Utopia.* New York: Basic Books.

Nozick, Robert. 1993. *The Nature of Rationality.* Princeton: Princeton University Press.

Offe, Claus. 1974. "Structural Problems of the Capitalist State." *German Political Studies* 1:31–57.

Offe, Claus. 1985. *Disorganized Capitalism.* Cambridge: MIT Press.

Offe, Claus, and Helmut Wiesenthal. 1985. "Two Logics of Collective Action." In *Disorganized Capitalism,* ed. Claus Offe. Cambridge: MIT Press.

O'Flaherty, Brendan, and Jagdish Bhagwati. 1997. "Will Free Trade with Political Science Put Normative Economists out of Work?" *Economics and Politics* 9:207–19.

Olson, Mancur, Jr. 1971. *The Logic of Collective Action.* Cambridge: Harvard University Press.

Orbell, John M., Alphons J. C. van de Kragt, and Robyn M. Dawes. 1991. "Covenants without the Sword: The Role of Promises in Social Dilemma Circumstances." In *Social Norms and Economic Institutions,* ed. Kenneth J. Koford and Jeffrey B. Miller. Ann Arbor: University of Michigan Press.

Ordeshook, Peter C. 1986. *Game Theory and Political Theory.* Cambridge: Cambridge University Press.

Ordeshook, Peter C. 1990. "The Emerging Discipline of Political Economy." In *Perspectives on Positive Political Economy,* ed. James E. Alt and Kenneth A. Shepsle. Cambridge: Cambridge University Press.

Ordeshook, Peter C. 1996. "Engineering or Science: What Is the Study of Politics?" In *The Rational Choice Controversy,* ed. Jeffrey Friedman. New Haven: Yale University Press.

Ostrom, Elinor. 1998. "A Behavioral Approach to the Rational Choice Theory of Collective Action." *American Political Science Review* 92:1–22.

Owen, Guillermo. 1982. *Game Theory.* Orlando: Academic Press.

Page, Benjamin I., and Robert Y. Shapiro. 1992. *The Rational Public.* Chicago: University of Chicago Press.

Palfrey, Thomas R., and Howard Rosenthal. 1983. "A Strategic Calculus of Voting." *Public Choice* 79:62–78.

Palfrey, Thomas R., and Howard Rosenthal. 1985. "Voter Participation and Strategic Uncertainty." *American Political Science Review* 79:62–78.

Parfit, Derek. 1984. *Reasons and Persons.* Oxford: Oxford University Press.

Parsons, Talcott. 1968. *The Structure of Social Action.* New York: Free Press.

Pears, David. 1984. *Motivated Irrationality.* Oxford: Clarendon.

Peffley, Mark, Stanley Feldman, and Lee Sigelman. 1987. "Economic Conditions and Party Competence: Processes of Belief Revision." *Journal of Politics* 49:100–121.

Penrose, Roger. 1989. *The Emperor's New Mind.* Oxford: Oxford University Press.

Persson, Torsten, and Guido Tabellini. 1990. *Macroeconomic Policy, Credibility and Politics.* Amsterdam: Harwood.

Pitkin, Hannah Fenichel. 1967. *The Concept of Representation.* Berkeley and Los Angeles: University of California Press.

Plott, Charles R. 1987. "Rational Choice in Experimental Markets." In *Rational Choice,* ed. Robin M. Hogarth and Melvin W. Reder. Chicago: University of Chicago Press.

Popkin, Samuel L. 1991. *The Reasoning Voter.* Chicago: University of Chicago Press.

Posner, Richard. 1995. *Aging and Old Age.* Chicago: University of Chicago Press.

Powell, G. Bingham, Jr. 1980. "Voting Turnout in Thirty Democracies: Partisan, Legal, and Socio-Economic Influences." In *Electoral Participation: A Comparative Analysis,* ed. Richard Rose. Beverly Hills: Sage.

Prelec, Dražen. 1982. "Matching, Maximizing, and the Hyperbolic Reinforcement Feedback Function." *Psychological Review* 89:189–230.

Prelec, Dražen. 1983. "The Empirical Claims of Maximization Theory: A Reply to Rachlin and to Kagel, Battalio, and Green." *Psychological Review* 90:385–89.

Prelec, Dražen, and Richard J. Herrnstein. 1991. "Preferences or Principles: Alternative Guidelines for Choice." In *Strategy and Choice,* ed. Richard Zeckhauser. Cambridge: MIT Press.

Price, Huw. 1986. "Against Causal Decision Theory." *Synthese* 67:195–212.

Price, Huw. 1991. "Agency and Probabilistic Causality." *British Journal for the Philosophy of Science* 42:157–76.

Przeworski, Adam. 1985a. *Capitalism and Social Democracy.* Cambridge: Cambridge University Press.

Przeworski, Adam. 1985b. "Marxism and Rational Choice." *Politics and Society* 14:379–409.

Przeworski, Adam, and Michael Wallerstein. 1982. "The Structure of Class Conflict in Democratic Capitalist Societies." *American Political Science Review* 76:215–38.

Quattrone, George A., and Amos Tversky. 1986. "Self-Deception and the Voters' Illusion." In *The Multiple Self,* ed. Jon Elster. Cambridge: Cambridge University Press.

Quattrone, George A., and Amos Tversky. 1988. "Contrasting Rational and Psychological Analyses of Political Choice." *American Political Science Review* 82:719–36.

Rabinowitz, George, and Elaine Stuart Macdonald. 1989. "A Directional Theory of Issue Voting." *American Political Science Review* 83:93–121.

Rabushka, Alvin, and Kenneth A. Shepsle. 1972. *Politics in Plural Societies.* Columbus, OH: Merrill.

Rachlin, Howard. 1983. "How to Decide between Matching and Maximizing: A Reply to Prelec." *Psychological Review* 90:376–79.

Rapoport, Anatol. 1966. *Two-Person Game Theory.* Ann Arbor: University of Michigan Press.

Riker, William H. 1986. *The Art of Political Manipulation.* New Haven: Yale University Press.

Riker, William H. 1990. "Heresthetic and Rhetoric in the Spatial Model." In *Advances in the Spatial Theory of Voting,* ed. James E. Enelow and Melvin J. Hinich. Cambridge: Cambridge University Press.

Riker, William H., and Peter C. Ordeshook. 1968. "A Theory of the Calculus of Voting." *American Political Science Review* 74:432–46.

Roberds, William T. 1995. "Commentary." In *Macroeconometrics,* ed. Kevin D. Hoover. Boston: Kluwer.

Roemer, John E. 1978. "Neoclassicism, Marxism, and Collective Action." *Journal of Economic Issues* 12:147–61.

Roemer, John E. 1979. "Divide and Conquer: Microfoundations of a Marxian Theory of Wage Discrimination." *Bell Journal of Economics* 10:695–705.

Roemer, John E. 1982. *A General Theory of Exploitation and Class.* Cambridge: Harvard University Press.

Roemer, John E. 1994. "The Strategic Role of Party Ideology when Voters Are Uncertain about How the Economy Works." *American Political Science Review* 88:327–35.

Rogoff, Kenneth. 1990. "Equilibrium Political Budget Cycles." *American Economic Review* 80:21–36.

Rogowski, Ronald. 1974. *Rational Legitimacy.* Princeton: Princeton University Press.

Rogowski, Ronald. 1985. "Conclusion." In *New Nationalisms of the Developed West,* ed. Edward A. Tiryakian and Ronald Rogowski. Boston: Allen & Unwin.

Rorty, Richard. 1989. *Contingency, Irony, and Solidarity.* Cambridge: Cambridge University Press.

Samuelson, Paul A. 1937. "A Note on Measurement of Utility." *Review of Economic Studies* 4:155–61.

Samuelson, Paul A. 1938. "A Note on the Pure Theory of Consumer's Behaviour." *Economica* 5:61–71.

Samuelson, Paul A. 1952. "Probability, Utility, and the Independence Axiom." *Econometrica* 20:670–78.

Samuelson, Paul A. 1993. "Altruism as a Problem Involving Group versus Individual in Economics and Biology." *American Economic Review* 83:143–48.

Samuelson, William, and Richard Zeckhauser. 1988. "Status Quo Bias in Decision Making." *Journal of Risk and Uncertainty* 1:7–59.

Sargent, Thomas J. 1981. "The Observational Equivalence of Natural and Unnatural Rate Theories of Macroeconomics." In *Rational Expectations and Econometric Practice,* ed. Robert E. Lucas, Jr., and Thomas J. Sargent. Minneapolis: University of Minnesota Press.

Sargent, Thomas J. 1984. "Autoregressions, Expectations, and Advice." *American Economic Review* 77:408–15.

Sargent, Thomas J. 1993. *Bounded Rationality in Macroeconomics.* Oxford: Clarendon Press.

Sargent, Thomas J., and Neil Wallace. 1981. "Rational Expectations and the Theory of Economic Policy." In *Rational Expectations and Econometric Practice,* ed. Robert E. Lucas, Jr., and Thomas J. Sargent. Minneapolis: University of Minnesota Press.

Sartori, Giovanni. 1969. "Politics, Ideology and Belief Systems." *American Political Science Review* 63:398–411.

Sartori, Giovanni. 1976. *Parties and Party Systems.* Vol. 1. Cambridge: Cambridge University Press.

Savage, Leonard J. 1962. *Foundations of Statistical Inference.* London: Methuen.

Savage, Leonard J. 1972. *The Foundations of Statistics.* New York: Dover.

Schotter, Andrew. 1981. *The Economic Theory of Institutions.* Cambridge: Cambridge University Press.

Schultz, Charles C. 1989. "Comment." *Brookings Papers on Economic Activity* 2:56–63.

Seidenfeld, Teddy. 1985. "Comments on Causal Decision Theory," *PSA 1984* 2:201–12.

Seidenfeld, Teddy. 1988. "Decision Theory without 'Independence' or without 'Ordering': What Is the Difference?" *Economics and Philosophy* 4:267–90.

Simon, Herbert A. 1957. *Models of Man.* New York: Wiley.

Simon, Herbert A. 1993. "Altruism and Economics." *American Economic Review* 83:156–61.

Sims, Christopher A. 1979. "A Comment on the Papers by Zellner and Schwert." In *Three Aspects of Policy and Policymaking,* ed. Karl Brunner and Allan H. Meltzer. Amsterdam: North-Holland.

Sims, Christopher A. 1981. "Money, Income and Causality." In *Rational Expectations and Econometric Practice,* ed. Robert E. Lucas, Jr., and Thomas J. Sargent. Minneapolis: University of Minnesota Press.

Sims, Christopher A. 1982. "Policy Analysis with Econometric Models." *Brookings Papers on Economic Activity* 1:107–52.

Sims, Christopher A. 1986. "Are Forecasting Models Usable for Policy Analysis?" *Federal Reserve Bank of Minneapolis Quarterly Review* 10:2–16.

Sims, Christopher A. 1987. "A Rational Expectations Framework for Short-Run Policy Advice." In *New Approaches to Monetary Economics,* ed. William A. Barnett and Kenneth J. Singleton. Cambridge: Cambridge University Press.

Skyrms, Brian. 1988. "Probability and Causation." *Journal of Econometrics* 39:53–68.

Skyrms, Brian. 1990. *The Dynamics of Rational Deliberation.* Cambridge: Harvard University Press.

Skyrms, Brian. 1996. *Evolution of the Social Contract.* Cambridge: Cambridge University Press.

Sniderman, Paul M., Richard A. Brody, and Philip E. Tetlock. 1991. *Reasoning and Choice.* Cambridge: Cambridge University Press.

Sowell, Thomas. 1983. *The Economics and Politics of Race.* New York: William Morrow.

Stalnaker, Robert C. 1984. *Inquiry.* Cambridge: MIT Press.

Stimson, James A. 1975. "Belief Systems: Constraint, Complexity, and the 1972 Election." *American Journal of Political Science* 19:393–417.

Stimson, James A. 1991. *Public Opinion in America.* Boulder: Westview.

Stimson, James A., Michael B. MacKuen, and Robert S. Erikson. 1995. "Dynamic Representation." *American Political Science Review* 89:543–65.

Strotz, Robert H., and Herman A. Wold. 1960. "Recursive Versus Nonrecursive Systems." *Econometrica* 28:417–27.

Sugden, Robert. 1986. *The Economics of Rights, Co-operation and Welfare.* Oxford: Basil Blackwell.

Sugden, Robert. 1989. "Spontaneous Order." *Journal of Economic Perspectives* 3:85–97.

Taylor, Michael. 1987. *The Possibility of Cooperation.* Cambridge: Cambridge University Press.

Taylor, Michael. 1988. "Rationality and Revolutionary Collective Action." In *Rationality and Revolution,* ed. Michael Taylor. Cambridge: Cambridge University Press.

Trivers, Robert. 1971. "The Evolution of Reciprocal Altruism." *Quarterly Review of Biology* 46:35–57.

Truman, David B. 1951. *The Governmental Process.* New York: Knopf.

Tsebelis, George. 1990. *Nested Games.* Berkeley and Los Angeles: University of California Press.

Tufte, Edward R. 1978. *Political Control of the Economy.* Princeton: Princeton University Press.

Turner, John C. 1982. "Towards a Cognitive Redefinition of the Social Group." In *Social Identity and Intergroup Relations,* ed. Henri Tajfel. Cambridge: Cambridge University Press.

Tversky, Amos, and Daniel Kahneman. 1987. "Rational Choice and the Framing of Decisions." In *Rational Choice,* ed. Robin M. Hogarth and Melvin W. Reder. Chicago: University of Chicago Press.

Uhlaner, Carole Jean. 1989a. "Rational Turnout: The Neglected Role of Groups." *American Journal of Political Science* 33:390–422.

Uhlaner, Carole Jean. 1989b. "'Relational Goods' and Participation: Incorporating Sociability into a Theory of Rational Action." *Public Choice* 62:253–85.

Ullman-Margalit, Edna. 1977. *The Emergence of Norms.* Oxford: Clarendon Press.

Verba, Sidney, and Norman H. Nie. 1972. *Participation in America.* New York: Harper & Row.

Viscusi, W. Kip. 1989. "Prospective Reference Theory: Toward an Explanation of the Paradoxes." *Journal of Risk and Uncertainty* 2:235–64.

von Neumann, John, and Oskar Morgenstern. 1953. *Theory of Games and Economic Behavior.* New York: Wiley.

Waters, Mary C. 1990. *Ethnic Options: Choosing Identities in America.* Berkeley: University of California Press.

Weber, Max. 1949. *On the Methodology of the Social Sciences.* Ed. and trans. Edward A. Shils and Henry A. Finch. Glencoe, IL: Free Press.

Williams, Bernard. 1985. *Ethics and the Limits of Philosophy.* Cambridge: Harvard University Press.

Wilson, James Q. 1993. *The Moral Sense.* New York: Free Press.

Wittman, Donald. 1983. "Candidate Motivation: A Synthesis of Two Theories." *American Political Science Review* 77:142–57.

Wittman, Donald. 1990. "Spatial Strategies when Candidates Have Policy Preferences." In *Advances in the Spatial Theory of Voting,* ed. James E. Enelow and Melvin J. Hinich. Cambridge: Cambridge University Press.

Wittman, Donald. 1991. "Contrasting Economic and Psychological Analyses of Political Choice." In *The Economic Approach to Politics,* ed. Kristen Renwick Monroe. New York: Harper-Collins.

Wlezien, Christopher. 1995. "The Public as Thermostat: Dynamics of Preferences for Spending." *American Journal of Political Science* 39:981–1000.

Yee, Albert S. 1997. "Thick Rationality and the Missing 'Brute Fact': The Limits of the Rationalist Incorporations of Norms and Ideas." *Journal of Politics* 59:1001–39.

Zaller, John R. 1992. *The Nature and Origins of Mass Opinion.* New York: Cambridge University Press.

Zaller, John R., and Stanley Feldman. 1992. "The Political Culture of Ambivalence: Ideological Responses to the Welfare State." *American Journal of Political Science* 36:268–307.

Zellner, Arnold. 1971. *An Introduction to Bayesian Inference in Econometrics.* New York: Wiley.

Zellner, Arnold. 1979. "Causality and Econometrics." In *Three Aspects of Policy and Policymaking,* ed. Karl Brunner and Allan H. Meltzer. Amsterdam: North-Holland.

Index